PENGUI

JOURNEY WITHOUT MAPS

GRAHAM GREENE, whose long life (1904–1991) nearly spanned the twentieth century, was one of its greatest novelists. Educated at Berkhamsted School and Balliol College, Oxford, he started his career as a subeditor of the London *Times.* He began to attract notice as a novelist with his fourth book, *Orient Express,* in 1932. In 1935, he trekked across northern Liberia, his first experience in Africa, told in *Journey Without Maps.* He converted to Catholicism in 1926 and reported on religious persecution in Mexico in 1938 in *The Lawless Roads,* which served as a background for his famous novel *The Power and the Glory,* one of his several "Catholic" novels (*Brighton Rock, The Heart of the Matter, The End of the Affair*). During the war he worked for the British secret service in Sierra Leone; afterward, he began wide-ranging travels as a journalist, reflected in novels such as *The Quiet American, Our Man in Havana, The Comedians, Travels with My Aunt, The Honorary Consul, The Human Factor, Monsignor Quixote,* and *The Captain and the Enemy.* As well as his many novels, Graham Greene wrote several collections of short stories, four travel books, six plays, two books of autobiography (*A Sort of Life* and *Ways of Escape*), two books of biography, and four books for children. He also contributed hundreds of essays and film and book reviews to *The Spectator* and other journals, many of which appear in the late collection *Reflections.* Most of his novels have been filmed, including *The Third Man,* which was first written as a film treatment. Graham Greene was named Companion of Honor and received the Order of Merit and many other awards.

PAUL THEROUX was born and educated in the United States. After graduating from university in 1963 he traveled to Italy and then Africa, where he worked as a teacher in Malawi and a lecturer at Makerere University in Uganda. He published his first novel, *Waldo,* while in Africa. His subsequent novels include *The Family Arsenal, Picture Palace, My Secret History,* and *Blinding Light.* His highly acclaimed travel books include *The Great Railway Bazaar* and *Dark Star Safari: Overland from Cairo to Cape*

Town. *The Mosquito Coast* and *Doctor Slaughter* have both been made into successful films. He is a frequent contributor to magazines, including *Granta* and *The New Yorker*. Theroux is a fellow of the Royal Society of Literature and the Royal Geographic Society in Britain. He divides his time between Cape Cod and the Hawaiian Islands, where he is a professional beekeeper.

GRAHAM GREENE

Journey Without Maps

Introduction by
PAUL THEROUX

PENGUIN BOOKS

PENGUIN BOOKS

Published by Penguin Group

Penguin Group (USA) Inc., 375 Hudson Street, New York, New York 10014, U.S.A.
Penguin Group (Canada), 90 Eglinton Avenue East, Suite 700, Toronto, Ontario,
Canada M4P 2Y3 (a division of Pearson Penguin Canada Inc.)
Penguin Books Ltd, 80 Strand, London WC2R 0RL, England
Penguin Ireland, 25 St Stephen's Green, Dublin 2, Ireland (a division of Penguin Books Ltd)
Penguin Group (Australia), 250 Camberwell Road, Camberwell,
Victoria 3124, Australia (a division of Pearson Australia Group Pty Ltd)
Penguin Books India Pvt Ltd, 11 Community Centre, Panchsheel Park,
New Delhi – 110 017, India
Penguin Group (NZ), 67 Apollo Drive, Rosedale, North Shore 0745, Auckland,
New Zealand (a division of Pearson New Zealand Ltd)
Penguin Books (South Africa) (Pty) Ltd, 24 Sturdee Avenue, Rosebank,
Johannesburg 2196, South Africa

Penguin Books Ltd, Registered Offices: 80 Strand, London WC2R 0RL, England

First published in Great Britain by William Heinemann Ltd 1936
First published in the United States of America by Doubleday, Doran & Company, Inc. 1936
Published in a Viking Compass edition 1961
Published in Penguin Books 1978
This edition with an introduction by Paul Theroux published in Great Britain
by Vintage, Random House 2005
Published in Penguin Books 2006

7 9 10 8

LIBRARY OF CONGRESS CATALOGING IN PUBLICATION DATA
Greene, Graham, 1904–
Journey without maps / Graham Greene ; introduction by Paul Theroux.
p. cm.
Includes bibliographical references.
ISBN 978-0-14-303972-3
1. Liberia—Description and travel. 2. Guinea—Description and travel.
3. Greene, Graham, 1904—Travel—Africa, West. I. Title.
DT626.G7 2006
916.604'3—dc22   2006041982

Printed in the United States of America

Contents

Introduction

Journey Without Maps is such an assured trip, so portentous in its Conradian shadings, you keep having to remind yourself that the book is a young man's balancing act. Come to think of it, Joseph Conrad's own inspirational trip, his piloting the *Roi des Belges* up the Congo River in August 1890, was also a balancing act: Conrad (still Captain Korzeniowski) was thirty-three, he needed money, he was thinking of ditching the sea forever, he was making tentative progress on his first novel, *Almayer's Folly*. African travel changed both men's careers by offering them epic subjects and jungly ambiguities. Long afterward, Graham Greene called the nervous journey he had taken at the age of thirty-one, "life altering." Conrad said something similar about his own hectic river trip: "Before the Congo I was a mere animal."

Greene's book is one of many on the travel shelf that suggests a mythical penetration of Africa to its essence, much like its predecessors, *Heart of Darkness,* Henry M. Stanley's *Through the Dark Continent* and *In Darkest Africa,* as well as its many successors, among them Laurens van der Post's *Venture to the Interior.* The quest-myth elaborated in these books has its parallel in a boy's adventure story—the ordeal that the white traveler must endure and overcome (with all the stereotypical obstacles of primitivism) in order to find life-changing revelation at the remote heart of Africa. This fanciful supposition of the heroic-romantic in a pith helmet, that *l'Afrique profonde* contains glittering mysteries, is one of the reasons our view of Africa has been so distorted. In Conrad's case the revelation was "The horror, the horror," in Greene's it was nuisance, homesickness. African porters wailing "Too far!" and psychoanalytic confirmation. But really, there is no mystery, only the obvious truth that difficult journeys, such as overland trips through Africa, tell us many things about ourselves—the limits of our strength, our wits, our spirit, our resourcefulness, even the limits of our love.

Greene's book is an ingeniously worked-up account of only four weeks in the Liberian bush by an absolute beginner in Africa. Greene admits this early on. "I had never been out of Europe before; I was a complete amateur at travel in Africa." Amazingly, he brings his young female cousin Barbara along for company. "You poor innocents!" a stranger cries at them in Freetown. He doesn't know the half of it.

Out of his element, Greene is gloomy, fidgety, nervous; and Barbara has no discernible skills. But the pitying man in Freetown can see from their helpless smiles and their lack of preparation that theirs is a leap in the dark. *Journey in the Dark* was one of the rejected titles for the book. How innocent was Greene? Here is an example. Just before arriving in Freetown, to start his trip, he confides, "I could never properly remember the points of the compass." Can a traveler be more innocent than that?

Greene and his cousin are not deterred by their incompetence. They seek guidance. They hire porters and a cook. They board the train for the Liberian frontier and start walking around the back of the country. They have twenty-six poorly paid African porters carrying their food and equipment. They have a pistol, they have a tent (never to be used), they have a table and a portable bath and a stash of whisky. They even have trinkets to hand out to natives—but the natives prefer gifts of money or jolts of whisky to trinkets. The trip is eventful: the travelers suffer fatigue, Greene falls ill with a serious fever, there are misunderstandings and wrong turns. There is a great deal of foot dragging on the part of the porters. A little more than a month after they set off, the Greenes are back on the coast, and in a matter of a week or so (the book skimps on dates) they are on a ship heading back to Britain.

It was 1935. Young, presentable, confident, well-educated, well-shod, and presumptuous Englishmen were showing up in remote corners of the world, boasting of their amateurishness,

wearing comic headgear (Greene sported a pith helmet), with
the assurance that all would be well. People would respect them
for their Englishness and would fall into line and be helpful;
and if they didn't fall into line, if the natives were cranky and
colorful and mangled their English idioms, the trip would be a
hoot. Back home the book would get written and talked about.
That was the case with the travels and writings of Greene's contemporaries, Evelyn Waugh, Robert Byron, Peter Fleming, and
others whose works over the past decades have been much
praised, even (to my mind) overpraised.

Journey Without Maps is seldom lumped with those books,
perhaps because it lacks humor, it is dark, it is broadly political. It is frankly appreciative of half-naked African women,
though. The book had an unlucky publishing life. Eighteen
months after it first appeared, it was withdrawn because of a
threatened libel action. That killed its chances at the beginning.
As for his being a tenderfoot, it seems to me that Greene's ner-
vousness and inexperience contributed to his memory of bat-
tling with the challenges of the trip, enlarging them perhaps,
making more of a drama, and his fears heightened his consciousness of every passing hour, making the trip seem something of a saga. It is Greene's first and best work of travel.

At some point in the early 1930s Greene conceived this idea
of walking through the African bush. He was a young man, six
years married and with a one-month-old baby girl. He had
never written about travel, which is not surprising—he had
hardly traveled. He had made jaunts out of England, but in a
hilarious, weekending way, and had never ventured beyond Europe. He knew nothing of Africa, had never camped or slept
rough or been on a long sea voyage or a long hike of any
consequence—certainly not a trek through the bush. Probably
influenced by the journeys his friends and contemporaries were
taking, he got it into his head to hike with porters and carriers
through an unmapped part of the Liberian hinterland; he did
not know exactly how many miles he would have to walk, or
how long it would take, or what his actual route would be.

Much odder than this vagueness—to me, at any rate: this
impulse, not to say batty notion, has never been seriously

questioned—was Greene's decision to take his young female cousin Barbara with him. She was twenty-three, she had never been anywhere, she'd had a privileged upbringing, she was not much of a walker. But Greene was lucky—though Barbara was a socialite, she was also a good sport; she learned how to hike and how to cope, and the trip hardened her to the rigors of travel. Though she was self-effacing in her role as part of the team—she hardly appears in Graham's book—Barbara was his equal on the trail, if not on the page. Her own account of the trip, first published in 1938 as *Land Benighted,* and reprinted (with my introduction) in 1982 as *Too Late to Turn Back,* is a modest but helpful gloss on Graham's allusive and at times ponderous book.

Why Greene took Barbara, why he did not go alone, why he did not choose an experienced man, are questions he does not answer in his book, nor are they seriously addressed in any biographies of the man. In an aside, Greene put the invitation down to his impulsiveness—too much champagne at a party. It is hard to imagine anyone so casual, not to say reckless, in choosing a partner for such a daunting journey. An inexperienced young traveler, lacking the ability to use a compass, and his much younger debby cousin in Africa, with (so she said) a volume of Saki's stories in her luggage, sounds like satire. Or was Greene infatuated? He could be impulsive where women were concerned. Barbara was lovely; Greene had been unfaithful to his wife Vivienne within months of his wedding. There have been whispers of his having an affair with Barbara. His largely excluding her from the narrative could be interpreted as a sheepish reflex, adulterer's remorse, a mood that afflicted the womanizing Greene for much of his life.

We don't know, and it probably doesn't matter, but our being aware that Greene was sharing his hardships with this young woman makes much of the mystique fall away. Imagine Kurtz with his Intended by his side at the Inner Station and he at once seems less of a loner, less of a leader, less of a problem-solver and mystery man—as Greene does with Barbara. Toward the end of the trip, Greene became feverish and took fewer notes and began to hurry. "I remember nothing of the trek to Zigi's Town and very little of the succeeding days. I was so exhausted that I couldn't write more than a few lines in my diary." For detail on that last part of the journey the reader has to turn to Barbara's narrative. She was not ill—on the contrary, she claimed in her book she became stronger on the journey, as Greene grew weaker.

A male companion might have challenged Greene; might have ridiculed his sketchy plans and all his improvisations. At the outset Greene did not have a clear idea of where he was going or how he could get there. He says he had only a hazy notion of his journey. "I intended to walk across the Republic [of Liberia], but I had no idea of what route to follow." Yet Greene saw it through to the end, with the help of his cousin. He penetrated the hinterland; he reached the coast. The reason his book is one of his best is perhaps that he was desperate the whole way through and in some important aspects the trip was the fulfillment of his childhood fantasies.

In later life, Greene often spoke of how he had been deeply influenced as a child by stories of adventure, of derring-do, of pirates and exiles, the colorful ordeals of travelers, of swordsmen and sinners. Most of us leave these books on the nursery shelf, but Greene never forsook them or their bright colors, their themes, their stark moralities, their preoccupation with heroes and villains, their exotic settings. Before he left for Africa he read a British government report about atrocities in Liberia, which caused him to remark, "The agony was piled on . . . with a real effect of grandeur." He is not shocked—he is excited; and the judgment is not a bad description of, say, *King Solomon's Mines*. In his essay "The Lost Childhood" Greene was to reflect on that book, saying it was his "incurable fascination of [the witch] Gagool with her bare yellow skull, the wrinkled scalp that moved and contracted like the hide of a cobra that led me [to Africa]."

Greene was a dreamy, at times brooding boy. He was feared to be suicidal. He so alarmed his parents with his dark withdrawals that he was psychoanalyzed while still in his teens, an early candidate for the then novel treatment of talk therapy and the interpretation of dreams. *Journey Without Maps* is crammed with evidence that it was written by someone who has spent time on a psychiatrist's couch. Speaking of his fear of rats and mice, moths and other flying creatures ("I shared my mother's terror of birds"), he explains, "But in Africa one couldn't avoid them any more than one could avoid the supernatural. The method of psychoanalysis is to bring the patient back to the idea which he is repressing: a long journey backwards without maps, catching a clue here and a clue there, as I caught the names of villages from this man and that, until one has to face the general idea, the pain or the memory." His African trip, he is saying, is therapeutic, a fresh-air confrontation with his fears.

His boyhood was a humdrum existence (but with a terror of birds and moths) in an unremarkable English market town noted for its boys' school and its furniture making. Greene was unwillingly conspicuous. A gawky failure-prone student at the school where his father was headmaster, he was too tall and too morose, a natural target of bullying and taunts, not only from other boys but also from his own rivalrous siblings. Greene fantasized escaping into the remoter and more vivid struggles of a hero out of H. Rider Haggard, Rudyard Kipling, Captain Marryat, Robert Louis Stevenson, or G. A. Henty. He yearned to be someone else and to be elsewhere—a writer's yearnings; but the fulfillment of them made Greene the writer we know.

He seems to have settled on Liberia because it was the sort of setting he had encountered in his early reading. Or at least that was what he imagined: jungle, mud huts, natives, witch doctors, talk of cannibals. He managed the trip in an old-fashioned way, leading a file of heavily laden porters down a foot-wide path. On his return to England in April 1935, he began writing the book. That same year, he also put his Liberian experience into one of his best short stories, "A Chance for Mr. Lever." In addition, he was working on a thriller, *A Gun for Sale*. He finished both books by the new year and they appeared in 1936.

In spite of mediocre sales and the threat of a libel action, the story of his Liberian trip secured Greene's reputation and became part of his personal myth, setting his life on course, fixing this melancholy and evasive soul in readers' imaginations as a stoical adventurer. Never mind that he could not read a map or use a compass or drive a car, or that he was afraid of moths. People still read the book in order to understand his cast of mind, in which none of those deficits figure. Greene found a setting and a way of writing about travel that was quite different from his literary contemporaries. Greene's book is self-consciously strewn with literary allusions, with many tags and quotations from Conrad, Richard Burton, A. E. Housman, Henry James, Louis-Ferdinand Céline, Charles Baudelaire, Ronald Firbank, George Santayana, Franz Kafka, Siegfried Sassoon, Saki, John Milton, Thomas Paine, Samuel Butler, Sir Walter Raleigh, and the Bible. On the subject of travel he compares the relative merits of two of his near contemporaries in travel, Somerset Maugham and Beverly Nichols.

In the book he dismisses Soviet junkets and (an odd assertion for Greene) Soviet-inspired hypocrisy. And he opts for the disorderly West African coast rather than the more orderly farming towns of British East Africa. Though a questionable claim, it seems like praise for him when he writes that in Liberia, "Civilization ends fifty miles from the coast." He would have correctly guessed that in East Africa, hundreds of miles from the coast, there were towns with coffee growers, cattle raisers, polo players, tea plantations, and gymkhana clubs. And Liberia had been in the news. Not long before, in 1926, the Firestone rubber company leased—for a pittance—a million acres of the republic for its production of latex. In 1931, the League of Nations accused Firestone, and the Liberian government, of unfair labor practices and exploitation, forced labor and slavery—the precise abuses Conrad had denounced in King Leopold's Congo in 1890. These facts got Greene's attention.

Greene claimed that the maps of Liberia were largely blank, with the tantalizing white spaces that Marlow speaks of early on in *Heart of Darkness*. Writing fifty years later Greene seems to be promoting the notion (as he does throughout the book) that much of Liberia is terra incognita. But Liberia had been an independent republic since 1847. Until 1919, the country was beset by continual border disputes from the neighboring French colonies, of French Guinea and the Ivory Coast. Greene's blank map claim seems extraordinary, since to meet such territorial challenges, accurate mapping would have been essential.

Greene also maintained that the American maps he examined were designated in certain places *Cannibals*. Fanciful claims of this sort appear on eighteenth-century maps of Africa, but are improbable in the twentieth, for the very good reason that cannibalism was not practiced except in the minds of timid fantasists whom one does not normally lump with modern cartographers. Still, you can see what Greene is driving at. The country is blank, the bush is trackless, it is filled with magic and devil dancers and anthropophagous tribes; it is *l'Afrique profonde*. Because he is so scared, he is emphatic about dangers. Even in his own book he alludes now and then to cannibalism. This is a libel on his hosts, of course, but it puts him firmly in the company of Conrad, who made cannibalism one of the insistently whispered motifs in his own richly ambiguous narrative of the Congo.

But even though he later lived for a year—a miserable year, so he said—as a British spy in Freetown, Greene was essentially a visitor to Africa. He dropped in, he did some journalism, he wrote pieces; he romanced Africa and like many another ardent suitor was uncritical. Africa rewarded him by showing him her drama, her ambiguities, but seldom her ordinariness or her true virtues—flourishing family life and self-sufficiency come to mind. Greene loved Africa in the way only a visitor can— never a long-term expatriate, the long-suffering alien, the belittled missionary, the overworked doctor, the despised schoolteacher.

Greene would have found it hard as a resident writer in the African bush, had he chosen to live there for any length of time. He was unable to drive a car. He did not know how to use a typewriter. His exasperation with details of bush life shows in his book. Halfway through the trip—that is, a mere fourteen days into it—he is sick and impatient for the thing to end. "Now all I wanted was medicine, a bath, iced drinks, and something other than this bush lavatory of trees and dead leaves. . . ." A few days later, "I was happy with the sense that every step was towards home." On the seventeenth day: "I felt irritated with everyone and everything. . . ." Soon after that, "I felt crazy to be here in the middle of Liberia. . . . It was like a bad dream. I couldn't remember why I had come." In his diary at Bassa Town, he referred to "This silly trip," but this—and his more serious apprehensions—he kept out of his published book. Less than a week later he is at the coast and the whole thing is a memory.

In retrospect, rationalized on the page, the journey was both breezier and more profound, with suspenseful highlights and shaped to seem as though it was plotted; an unexpected ordeal for this unprepared traveler. Yet his struggle elevated it in Greene's mind. He realized that what he had accomplished was unique and difficult—and of course it was: the amateur had broken through and acquired experience. "I wanted to laugh and shout and cry; it was the end, the end of the worst boredom I had ever experienced, the worst fear and the worst exhaustion." His instinct had been right: this was a trip he needed to take.

Claims are made that Greene was a superior sort of traveler, that his trips were monumental, even ground breaking. I don't see this at all. He was a fortunate traveler. His life had been sheltered, he was rather fearful, and manic-depressive, as he himself confided in his autobiography. He always had a taxi waiting. His achievement was that such a nervy soul was able to succeed in such challenges, for he was essentially an urbane man who boasted of disliking exercise and valuing his privacy and his comforts.

His fears made Africa vivid—for himself, for the reader. The uneasy traveler, the dilettante, which Greene was (always looking up contacts, always dependent on being shown the way), tends to invent the landscape he is traversing. Out of muddle he imagines it as much wilder than it is. There are robust assertions of cannibalism in *Journey Without Maps*. But there are no cannibals in Liberia. He mentions at one point "a tribe, about a week ahead . . . still supposed to practise cannibalism" and traveling "in the land of the Manos, where ritual cannibalism practiced on strangers has never been entirely wiped out" and in Ganta: "Human sacrifice had once been offered at the falls." Equally unlikely, in a country that a few years earlier had made the important deal with Firestone for rubber plantations (and the eagerness of Firestone to possess the country), are "the places where I and my cousin were the first white people to be seen in living memory." But these are the endearing self-deceptions of a man inventing a landscape he first imagined as a child in England scaring himself rigid with images of the witch Gagool.

Greene's Africa is worth studying, because so much of it is in his head. He sees the bush as hostile—not neutral. If the ants and the rats and the cockroaches fail to nibble you to death, then answering a call of nature at the latrine you are likely (so he says) to be bitten by a poisonous snake. Yet the snakes can be decorous: "Once a beautiful little green snake moved across the path, upright, without hurry, bearing her bust proudly forward into the grasses like a hostess painted by Sargent, poisonous with gentility, a Fabergé jewel."

Greene's Africa is a place for an outsider to go to pieces, a dramatic backdrop, not always as specific as a landscape but often an atmosphere—heat and dust, insects and birdcalls; it represents romance and the possibility of reinvention. There is no big game in Greene's Africa but there are predatory people—whites usually—and there is illness, there is betrayal, there is adultery and lost love. Politics hardly figure at all, and except for Deo Gratias in *A Burnt-Out Case* and a couple of the carriers in *Journey Without Maps,* few Africans are delineated or have personal histories.

Returning to Freetown in 1941 to do wartime intelligence work, Greene got better acquainted with Sierra Leone. Even so, he stuck to the city. The novel that came out of his experience, *The Heart of the Matter,* is largely theological in its theme, set in the coastal capital, with excursions to Pende in the bush. Africa is not the subject but the shadowy backdrop for this essentially inward-looking novel that questions the elements of belief and damnation, heaven and hell.

A Burnt-Out Case (1961) was an even more deliberate book, the result of an African trip, which Greene described in the short nonfiction account he entitled *In Search of a Character*. Many parts of the novel are direct transcriptions from his notebook, and portraits of people he met on his stay at a leprosarium in the Belgian Congo. By the time this novel appeared, Greene was well established as a describer of tropical decay and disorder, of drunken expatriates, and whose prose was never lacking in an uneasy awareness of the judgmental presence of the omniscient Christian God, the Deity peeping especially into the humid bedrooms of Greene's wayward characters. Africa looms large in these two novels, but Christian faith looms much larger. Africa is the stage on which adulterers wonder if they have spoiled their chances for salvation. Africa suits Greene because it is unformed, suggestive of risk and danger and disease; something like a war zone without the shooting. Such is Africa's power to bewitch the credulous visitor.

When Greene finally found a true rebellion in Africa, reporting the events of the Mau-Mau uprising in colonial Kenya in 1953, he was less inclined to sympathize with the rebels than with the British farmers in the so-called White Highlands. He did not stay long enough to understand the exploitation, the political unfairness and fundamental racism of British Kenya, yet by inclination he was fair-minded himself and a well-wisher in the cause of African independence. Greene's Africa, unlike the more particular landscapes of London, Brighton, Saigon, and Port-au-Prince, is a landscape of the mind, a set of vivid, sometimes stereotypical, images which, precisely because they match our own stereotypes in their oversimplification, could account for the success of his vision of Africa as seedy. "The deep appeal of the seedy" is adumbrated in his Liberian journey, but it seems to me that "seedy" describes little more than the down-at-heel coastal communities of expatriates, a far cry from the sense of the verdant everlastingness of the bush, which is the true heart of Africa.

Greene was an admitted sentimentalist where Africa is concerned. This sentimentality occurs very early in his work; indeed it first surfaces in *Journey Without Maps*. One of his memories of England is of sitting in a bar where a young woman is crying. Drinking and watching her, "I thought for some reason even then of Africa, not a particular place, but a shape, a strangeness, a wanting to know. The unconscious mind is often sentimental; I have written 'a shape,' and the shape, of course, is roughly that of a human heart."

This thought is unlikely to occur to the long-term expatriate in an African country, who would never think of a map of the whole continent. Such a person, unsentimental for reasons of survival, would think of Africa as the small town or clearing he is working in. Any maps he thinks of would be maps of his district, or at the very most, his province.

Greene's reaction to Africa is literary and somewhat abstract, derived from Conrad, who though he had strong views on Belgian colonialism, hardly knew Africa at all beyond the banks of the river. Yet, in his typically virile and spontaneous way, and perhaps as a side effect of his anxiety in the bush, Greene is highly responsive to Africa. In this respect he was ahead of his time, unprejudiced, and true to the spirit of his boyhood adventure stories. In a word, for Greene, Africa is naked. Some of the women greatly entrance him. The book is a compendium of brown breasts. The unforced and I should say unconscious way Greene notices the pretty women is like a grace note in the book. Only Sir Richard Burton—in East Africa— demonstrated an equal connoisseurship of brown breasts.

Though he could be contradictory, for *Journey Without Maps* is a moody book in which he changes his mind about Africa a number of times, in general Greene regards Africa as representing life and hope and vitality. Greene's shipboard observations of the green continent contrast with Marlow's in *Heart of Darkness* as his ship approaches the Congo, for while the vantage point is the same, the conclusions are different. Marlow saw a continent beset, possessed, fired upon and spooky; Greene sees on the lush coast a happier place, "a sense of warm and sleepy beauty" that reminds him of Baudelaire at his most sensual.

For Greene, Africa also represents visceral excitement, freedom, "the life one was born to live." At this early joyous point in the book he has glimpsed his first African women in a market, with "lovely features . . . young and old, lovely less from sexual attractiveness than from a sharp differentiated pictorial quality." In a bright memory farther down the coast he refers to "the neat tarts of Dakar." His gaze lingers in Freetown, when a young woman approaches the car he is riding in: "her bare breasts were small and firm and pointed; she had the neat rounded thighs of a cat." A few days later, peering from the train as he travels up country, he sees "the women pressed up along the line, their great black nipples like the centre point of a target." Arrived at the border of Liberia and French Guinea, he fastens onto a figure as the very embodiment of the place, "something lovely, happy and unenslaved, something like the girl who came up the hill that morning, a piece of bright cloth twisted above her hips, the sunlight falling between the palms on her dark hanging breasts."

He had gone to some trouble to arrange a meeting with Liberia's President Barclay, but on the day Greene is less impressed by this powerful man than by a woman who is present, looking "more Chinese than African . . . She was the loveliest thing I saw in Liberia; I couldn't keep my eyes off her." In a bush settlement Greene calls "The Horrible Village," he measures the village by its women and concludes, "Only a few of the women broke the monotonous ugliness of the place . . . there was one small girl in a turban with slanting Oriental eyes and small neat breasts who did appeal to European sexual tastes even in her dirt." Detouring through French Guinea he approves of the women who "lived up to the standard of a country which provides the handsomest whores and the most elegant brothels," and he goes on to provide a minutely detailed description of their coiffures and their distinctive makeup.

Greene's response to the nakedness of African women is clearly an aspect of his relief of being liberated as well as tantalized. At these times Africa seems Eden-like. Farther on in the French colony Greene is entertained by a chief, whose daughter is present and is slightly drunk. Greene eyes the girl: "her thigh under the tight cloth about her waist was like the soft furry rump of a kitten; she had lovely breasts; she was quite clean, much cleaner than we were. Then chief wanted us to stay the night, and I began to wonder how far his hospitality might go."

Even at the end of his tether, sick and impatient, and staggering near the conclusion of his journey in Bassa Town, noticing hardly anything in his feverishness, he is aware of women watching him. To his now practiced eye, he sees one woman as representing an advanced culture, "a sign that we were meeting the edge of civilization pushing up from the Coast. A young girl hung around all day posturing with her thighs and hips, suggestively, like a tart. Naked to the waist, she was conscious of her nakedness; she knew her breasts had a significance to the white man they didn't have to the native."

The "tart" is an exception to Greene's equating African nakedness with innocence. As a spectator at a village dance that sounds like a ghastly rigadoon ("emaciated old women slapping their pitted buttocks") he is happy: "the freedom of Africa began to touch us at last." In the next paragraph he presses this point about the attraction of a country—and he quotes—"that hath yet her maidenhead, never sacked, turned, nor wrought . . . the mines not broken with sledges, nor their images pulled down out of their temples." This quotation is unattributed—I had to ask a scholarly friend to identify it, which he readily did: Sir Walter Raleigh—but the message could not be clearer. It is still early enough in his journey (about ten days) for Greene to be fascinated by the notion of Africa as undefiled. He believes he has gone deep. His notion is that he is in virgin territory and "There is not so much virginity in the world that one can afford not to love it when one finds it."

This was not a final judgment. Later, muddled and ill, he confessed that Liberia was hellish and that he could hardly wait for the trip to end. He hated the last two weeks and was glad when it was all over. So the book is contradictory, but the contradictions are truthful reflections of Greene's traveling moods. Greene is scrupulous in dramatizing all the stages of his emotional journey, from anxiety to fear to bewitchment to romance to disillusionment and back again (reflecting in tranquility) to fascination.

Now, seventy years later, Liberia is more dangerous than it was when Greene walked through with his cousin, depending on the kindness of strangers—and receiving hospitality. For decades, not much changed in Liberia's political system characterized by patronage, corruption, nepotism, homburg hats, and three-piece suits. President William Tubman ruled much in the Barclay mode, with United States backing, and after twenty-seven years he was overthrown by a young upstart soldier, Samuel Doe, who presided over a reign of terror. In his turn, Doe was overthrown, captured, his ears cut off and was brutally killed. After a few years his murderer (and successor) was forced to flee to exile in Nigeria.

The country was plagued by armed gangs, child soldiers, and self-appointed leaders. In 2005 Liberia had an interim government, a free election, and in 2006 its first woman president, but the country was (as in Greene's time) one of the poorest in Africa. There are roads (though bumpy ones) where in Greene's time there had been bush tracks. You can trace his route on a modern map. Peace Corps volunteers staff the schools in some of the very settlements Greene mentions—for example, Tapeta (Tapee-Ta), where he and his cousin spent "a Victorian Sunday" and met Col Elwood Davis ("Dictator of Grand Bassa"). Even in its distress, Liberia remains a stronghold of the Firestone rubber empire and a continuing source of illegal diamonds.

Greene never returned to Liberia. His trip—like many difficult trips—remained glamorous in retrospect. Yet it turned him into a more ambitious traveler. Within a few years he was in Mexico, riding on a mule for *The Lawless Roads* (1938). He began to explore more of Africa, and other equatorial places, in South East Asia, the Caribbean, and Latin America; he developed an instinct for troubled countries with dramatic landscapes, where the women (whom he never stopped scrutinizing) were lovely. In his seventies, on an anniversary of the trip, he wrote to Barbara, "To me that trip has been very important—it started a love of Africa which has never quite left me . . . Altogether a trip which altered life."

Suggestions for Further Reading

Norman Sherry's *Life of Graham Greene* is now available complete in three volumes: the first, which appeared in 1989, covers Greene's life from 1904 to 1939; the second (1995) covers the period from 1939 to 1955; and the third (2004) takes the story from 1955 until the writer's death in 1991. There is a competing, and prosecutorial, one-volume life by Michael Shelden, *Graham Greene: The Enemy Within* (London: Heinemann, 1994). Two of Greene's own books provide useful context for his fiction. His comments on other novelists invariably supply a commentary on his practice, and he was also an acute critic of his own work. See the *Collected Essays* (New York: Viking, 1969) and *Ways of Escape* (New York: Simon and Schuster, 1980). The essential critical volume remains the collection edited by Samuel Hynes, *Graham Greene: A Collection of Critical Essays* (Englewood Cliffs, NJ: Prentice-Hall, 1973). It reprints seminal essays by Morton Dauwen Zabel, R. W. B. Lewis, and Richard Hoggart; reviews by Evelyn Waugh and George Orwell; a fine essay on the theology of *The End of the Affair* by Ian Gregor; and an overview of Greene's career by Frank Kermode. Interested readers may also find the following of use:

Adamson, Judith. *Graham Greene and Cinema*. Norman, OK: Pilgrim Books, 1984.
———. *Graham Greene: The Dangerous Edge*. New York: St. Martin's, 1990.

Baldridge, Cates. *Graham Greene's Fictions: The Virtues of Extremity*. Columbia and London: University of Missouri Press, 2000.

Lodge, David. *Graham Greene*. New York and London: Columbia University Press, 1966.

Mudford, Peter. *Graham Greene*. Plymouth, England: Northcote House in association with the British Council, 1996.

Sharrock, Roger. *Saints, Sinners and Comedians: The Novels of Graham Greene*. Notre Dame, IN: Notre Dame Press, 1984.

Smith, Grahame. *The Achievement of Graham Greene*. Sussex: The Harvester Press, 1986.

Spurling, John. *Graham Greene*. London and New York: Methuen, 1983.

Journey Without Maps

Preface to Second Edition

Six years after this book was written I found myself living in Sierra Leone—a writer should be careful where he goes for pleasure in peacetime, for in wartime he is only too likely to return there to work. It was odd flying up from Lagos, following from the sky the line of surf along the Liberian coast, seeing the huddle of tiny shacks which called itself Grand Bassa, where I had dismissed my carriers, passing over the small white isolated building which was the British Consulate at Monrovia. It was odd too retracing my steps from Freetown to Kailahun, traveling in the same tiny lamp-lit train, staying in the same rest-houses.

I can look back now with a certain regret at the hard words I used about Freetown, for Freetown is now one of the homes I have lived and worked in through all the seasons. I have been able to recognize in myself after a year's sojourn the inertia which as a tourist I condemned so harshly in other people. But if there are fallacies into which the passing visitor falls, there are fallacies too which come from a close acquaintance. After a little while there is so much one ceases to notice, and if I were writing of Freetown now, how unnaturally rosy would my picture be, for I begin to remember mainly the sunsets when all the laterite paths turned suddenly for a few minutes the colour of a rose, the old slavers' fort with the cannon lying in the grass, the abandoned railway track with the chickens pecking in and out of the little empty rotting station, the taste of the first pink gin at six o'clock. I have begun to forget what the visitor noticed so clearly—the squalor and the unhappiness and the involuntary injustices of tired men. But as that picture is true too, I let it stand.

London, November 1946

'O do you imagine,' said fearer to farer,
'That dusk will delay on your path to the pass,
Your diligent looking discover the lacking
Your footsteps feel from granite to grass?'

W. H. Auden

The life of an individual is in many respects like a child's dissected map. If I could live a hundred years, keeping my intelligence to the last, I feel as if I could put the pieces together until they made a properly connected whole. As it is, I, like all others, find a certain number of connected fragments, and a larger number of disjounted pieces, which I might in time place in their natural connection. Many of these pieces seem fragmentary, but would in time show themselves as essential parts of the whole. What strikes me very forcibly is the arbitrary and as it were accidental ways in which the lines of junction appear to run irregularly among the fragments. With every decade I find some new pieces coming into place. Blanks which have been left in former years find their complement among the undisturbed framents. If I could look back on the whole, as we look at the child's map when it is put together, I feel that I should have my whole life intelligently laid out before me . . .

Oliver Wendell Holmes

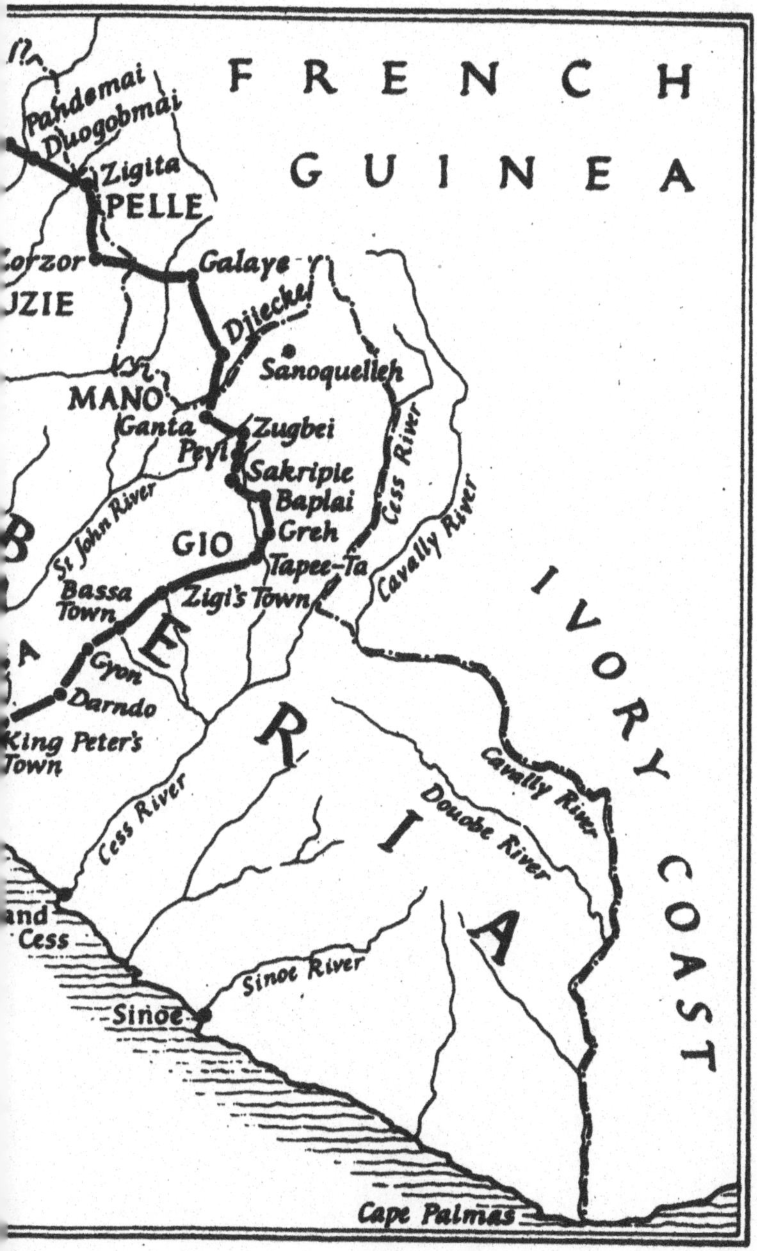

FRENCH
GUINEA
Pandemai
Duogobmai
Zigita
PELLE
Galaye
Djiecke
Sanoquelleh
MANO
Ganta
Zugbei
Peyi
Sakripie
Baplai
Greh
GIO
Tapee-Ta
St John River
Cess River
Cavally River
Bassa Town
Zigi's Town
Gyon
Darndo
King Peter's Town
IVORY COAST
Cavally River
Douobe River
Cess River
Sinoe River
Sinoe
Cape Palmas

PART ONE

The Way to Africa

HARVEST FESTIVAL

The tall black door in the narrow city street remained closed. I rang and knocked and rang again. I could not hear the bell ringing; to ring it again and again was simply an act of faith or despair, and later sitting before a hut in French Guinea, where I never meant to find myself, I remembered this first going astray, the buses passing at the corner and the pale autumn sun.

An errand boy came to my help, asking me whether I wanted the Consul, and when I said yes, that was what I wanted, the boy led me straight to the entrance of St Dunstan's Church and up the steps and into the vestry. It wasn't the sort of beginning I'd expected when I was accumulating the tent I never used, the hypodermic syringe I left behind, the automatic pistol which remained hidden underneath boots and shoes and bags of silver in the money-box. They were preparing for the harvest festival; the vestry was crowded with large dressy yellow blooms and litters of vegetable marrow; I couldn't see the Consul anywhere. The errand boy peered among the flowers in the dim light and at last pointed to a little intent woman bent above the blooms. 'There she is,' he said, 'that's her. She'll tell you.'

I felt very self-conscious, picking my way among the vegetables in St Dunstan's asking: 'Could you by any chance tell me? Is the Liberian Consul—?' But she knew and I left that street for another.

It was three o'clock and lunch at the Consulate was just over. Three men, I could not distinguish their nationality, overcrowded the tiny room which was deeply buried in the huge new glittering office block. The window-sill was lined with old telephone directories, school textbooks of chemistry. One man was washing up lunch in a basin stuck in the top of a waste-paper bas-ket. Unidentifiable yellow threads like bast floated in the greasy water. The man poured a kettle of boiling water from a gas jet over a plate which he held above the basket; then he wiped the plate with a cloth. The table was littered with bursting parcels of what looked like stones, and the lift porter kept on putting his head in at the door and flinging down more parcels on the floor. The room was like a shabby caravan held up for a moment in a smart bright street. One doubted whether, returning in a few hours' time to the gleaming mechanized block, one would still find it there; it would almost certainly have moved on.

But everyone was very kind. It all came down to a question of paying money; no one asked me why I wanted to go, al-though I had been told by many authorities on Africa that the Republic of Liberia resented intruders. In the Consulate they had little guttural family jokes among themselves. 'Before the war,' a large man said, 'you didn't need passports. Such a fuss. Only to the Argentine,' and he looked across at the man who was making out my papers. 'If you wanted to get to the Argen-tine you even had to give your fingerprints a month ahead, so that Scotland Yard and Buenos Aires could get together. All the scoundrels in the world went to the Argentine.'

I examined the usual blank map upon the wall, a few towns along the coast, a few villages along the border. 'Have you been to Liberia?' I asked.

'No, no,' the large man said. 'We let them come to us.'

The other man stuck a round red seal on my passport; it bore the National Mark, a three-masted ship, a palm tree, a dove flying overhead, and the legend 'The love of liberty brought us here'. Above the same red seal I had to sign the 'Declaration of an Alien about to depart for the Republic of Liberia'.

I have informed myself of the provisions under the Immigra-tion Law, and am convinced that I am eligible for admission into the Republic thereunder.

I realize that if I am one of a class prohibited by law from ad-mission, I will be deported or detained in confinement.

I solemnly swear that the above statements are true to the best
of my knowledge and that I fully intend when in the Republic to
obey and support the laws and constituted authorities thereof.

The only thing which I knew of the law was that it forbade a
white man to enter the country except through the recognized
ports unless he had paid a large sum for an explorer's licence. I
intended to enter the country from the British border and make
my way through the forest of the interior to the coast. I am a
Catholic with an intellectual if not an emotional belief in Catholic
dogma; I find that intellectually I can accept the fact that to
miss a Mass on Sunday is to be guilty of mortal sin. And yet 'I
solemnly swear' . . . these contradictions in human psychology
I find of peculiar interest.

BLUE BOOK

I had read in a British Government Blue Book that May:

The rat population may fairly be described as swarming, the
wooden and corrugated iron houses lend themselves to rat har-
bourage . . .

The absence of any attempt by the Government, not only to
take effective steps to control yellow fever or plague, but even to
arrange for the notification of yellow fever, as well as the complete lack of medical supervision of ships touching the Liberian
coast . . .

The great majority of all mosquitoes caught in Monrovia are
of a species known to carry yellow fever . . .

Altogether forty-one villages have been burnt and sixty-nine
men, forty-five women and twenty-seven children, making a to-
tal of one hundred and forty-one, killed . . .

A case was also reported to me from several sources of a man
who had been wounded close to Sasstown and wished to surrender. Although unarmed and pleading for mercy he was shot down
in cold blood by soldiers in the presence of Captain Cole.

The soldiers crept into the banana plantations, which surround
all native villages, and poured volleys into the huts. One woman

who had that day been delivered of twins was shot in her bed, and the infants perished in the flames when the village was fired by the troops . . .

In one village the charred remains of six children were found after the departure of the troops . . .

In this connection it may be mentioned that a man who had been a political prisoner at New Sasstown stated that he had heard soldiers boasting of having cut children down with cutlasses and thrown them into burning huts . . .

And when I learnt that Colonel Davis had fought with Tiempoh, who are my children and make farm for me, and had caught Payetaye men and women and ill-treated them, I and all my people were afraid . . .

As far as is known, the principal diseases in the interior include elephantiasis, leprosy, yaws, malaria, hookworm, schistosomiasis, dysentery, smallpox and nutritional conditions. In the whole country there are only: two doctors in Monrovia, both foreign and both engaged in private practice, a medical officer on the Firestone Plantations, and three or four missionary doctors working in the interior . . .

In Monrovia itself malaria is practically universal . . .

In other places the producer sets the prices for his goods, but in this country the buyer enforces the price to suit his convenience . . .

The Government can kill all the people of Sasstown and all the tribes of the Kru Coast before we surrender to the Government. We will not return to the coast or surrender until we hear from the British Consul in Monrovia that there will be no more war. Then we will return to Old Sasstown . . .

There was something satisfyingly complete about this picture. It really seemed as though you couldn't go deeper than that; the agony was piled on in the British Government Blue Book with a real effect of grandeur; the little injustices of Kenya became shoddy and suburban beside it.

And it was saved from melodrama by its irony, by the fact that the Republic was founded as an example to all Africa of a Christian and self-governing state. An American philanthropic society at the beginning of the nineteenth century (many of its directors, it is said, were slave-owners who found it convenient thus to get rid of their illegitimate children) began to ship released slaves to the Grain Coast of Africa. Land was bought from the native rulers and a settlement established at Monrovia. 'The love of liberty brought us here,' but one can hardly blame these first half-caste settlers when they found that love of their own liberty was not consistent with the liberty of the native tribes. The history of the Republic was very little different from the history of neighbouring white colonies: it included the same broken contracts, the same resort to arms, the same gradual encroachment, even the same heroism among the early settlers, the peculiarly Protestant characteristic of combining martyrdom with absurdity. There were, for example, the black Quakers from Pennsylvania, teetotallers and pacifists, who when they were attacked by Spanish slavers depended on prayer and were massacred. Only a hundred and twenty escaped and settled in Grand Bassa.

From the first these American half-caste slaves were idealists in the American manner. Their Declaration of Independence, when the Republic was declared, had the glossy white marble effect of the American. The year was 1847, but the phrases were eighteenth century; they belonged to Washington; they had the rhetoric of an expensive tomb. The inalienable rights of life and liberty gravely led off the scroll; but then one passed to 'the right to acquire, possess, enjoy, and defend property'. Today the 'ideals' are still American, something a little like the American of Tammany Hall; the descendants of the slaves have taken to politics with the enthusiasm of practised crap players.

'If you desire the prosperity of your people, the independence of your Government, a place of honour for the Lone Star among the flags of all nations, you will support the reelection of President Barclay in this campaign . . .'

This too attracted me. There seemed to be a seediness about the place you couldn't get to the same extent elsewhere, and seediness has a very deep appeal: even the seediness of civilization, of the sky-signs in Leicester Square, the tarts in Bond

Street, the smell of cooking greens off Tottenham Court Road, the motor salesman in Great Portland Street. It seems to satisfy, temporarily, the sense of nostalgia for something lost; it seems to represent a stage further back.

> Streets that follow like a tedious argument of insidious intent
> To lead you to an overwhelming question . . .

But there are times of impatience, when one is less content to rest at the urban stage, when one is willing to suffer some discomfort for the chance of finding—there are a thousand names for it, King Solomon's Mines, the 'heart of darkness' if one is romantically inclined, or more simply, as Herr Heuser puts it in his African novel, *The Inner Journey,* one's place in time, based on a knowledge not only of one's present but of the past from which one has emerged. There are others, of course, who prefer to look a stage ahead, for whom Intourist provides cheap tickets into a plausible future, but my journey represented a distrust of any future based on what we are.

The motive of a journey deserves a little attention. It is not the fully conscious mind which chooses West Africa in preference to Switzerland. The psychoanalyst, who takes the images of a dream one by one—'You dreamed you were asleep in a forest. What is your first association to forest?'—finds that some images have immediate associations; to others the patient can bring out nothing at all; his brain is like a cinema in which the warning 'Fire' has been cried; the exits are jammed with too many people trying to escape, and when I say that to me Africa has always seemed an important image, I suppose that is what I mean, that it has represented more than I could say. 'You dreamed you were in Africa. Of what do you think first when I say the word Africa?' and a crowd of words and images, witches and death, unhappiness and the Gare St Lazare, the huge smoky viaduct over a Paris slum, crowd together and block the way to full consciousness.

But to the words 'South Africa' my reaction, I find, is immediate: Rhodes and the British Empire and an ugly building in Oxford and Trafalgar Square. After 'Kenya' there is no hesitation: 'gentleman farmers, aristocracy in exile and the gossip columns'. 'Rhodesia' produces: 'failure, Empire Tobacco', and 'failure' again.

It is not then *any* part of Africa which acts so strongly on this unconscious mind; certainly no part where the white settler has been most successful in reproducing the conditions of his country, its morals and its popular art. A quality of darkness is needed, of the inexplicable. This Africa may take the form of an unexplained brutality as when Conrad noted in his Congo diary: 'Thursday, 3rd July . . . Met an off^{er} of the State inspecting. A few minutes afterwards saw at a camp place the dead body of a Backongo. Shot? Horrid smell'; or a sense of despair as when M. Céline writes: 'Hidden away in all this flowering forest of twisted vegetation, a few decimated tribes of natives squatted among fleas and flies, crushed by taboos and eating nothing all the time but rotten tapioca.' The old man whom I saw beaten with a club outside the poky little prison at Tapee-Ta, the naked widows at Tailahun covered with yellow clay squatting in a hole, the wooden-toothed devil swaying his raffia skirts between the huts seem like the images in a dream to stand for something of importance to myself.

Today our world seems peculiarly susceptible to brutality. There is a touch of nostalgia in the pleasure we take in gangster novels, in characters who have so agreeably simplified their emotions that they have begun living again at a level below the cerebral. We, like Wordsworth, are living after a war and a revolution, and these half-castes fighting with bombs between the cliffs of skyscrapers seem more likely than we to be aware of Proteus rising from the sea. It is not, of course, that one wishes to stay for ever at that level, but when one sees to what unhappiness, to what peril of extinction centuries of cerebration have brought us, one sometimes has a curiosity to discover if one can from what we have come, to recall at which point we went astray.

VIA LIVERPOOL

But none the less I was a little scared at the prospect of going back by way of Africa alone; I feel very grateful to my cousin Barbara, who was willing to accompany me, to share the

journey, for which no maps were to be bought, from its start in
the restaurant car of the 6.5 from Euston, as we sat before the
little pieces of damp white fish. A headline told me that there
was another clue in a trunk murder case; a man on the dole had
killed himself; while along the line the smaller stations were
dashed out like so many torches plunged in water.

The huge Liverpool hotel had been designed without aesthetic taste but with the right ideas about comfort and a genuine idea of magnificence. It could probably house as many
passengers as an Atlantic liner; passengers, because no one goes
to Liverpool for pleasure, to the little cramped square and the
low sky-signs which can almost be touched with the hand,
where all the bars and the cinemas close at ten. But there was a
character hidden in this hotel; it wasn't chic, it wasn't bright,
it wasn't international; there remained somewhere hidden,
among its long muffled corridors, beneath the huge cliff-like
fall of its walls, the idea of an English inn; one didn't mind asking for muffins or a pint of bitter, while the boats hooted in the
Mersey and the luggage littered the hall; there was quite probably a Boots. Anyway enough remained for me to understand
the surprise of Henry James when he landed in England, 'that
England should be as English as, for my entertainment, she
took the trouble to be'.

The natural native seediness had not been lost in the glitter
of chromium plate; the muffin had been overwhelmingly, perhaps rather nauseatingly, enlarged. If the hotel were silly, it was
only because magnificence is almost always a little silly. The
magnificent gesture seldom quite comes off. When on rare oc-
casions beauty and magnificence do coincide, one gets a sense
of the theatre or the films, it is 'too good to be true'. I find myself always torn between two beliefs: the belief that life should
be better than it is and the belief that when it appears better it
is really worse. But in the huge lounge at Liverpool, like the
lounge of a country inn fifty times magnified, one was at home
on the vast expanse of deep dark carpet, only one business man
asleep with his mouth open; at home as one would certainly
not have been if the Hollywood imagination had run riot. One
was protectively coloured, one was seedy too.

Next morning, in the public house near the Prince's Stage, four middle-aged women sat drinking with an old dirty man of eighty-four. Three had the dustbin look; they carried about them the air of tenements, of lean cats and shared wash-houses; the fourth had risen a little way in the world, she was the old man's daughter over from America for Christmas. 'Have another drink, Father?' He was seeing her off. Their relationship was intimate and merry; the whole party had an air of slightly disreputable revelry. To one the party didn't really matter; she had caught the American accent. To the other women, who must return to the dustbin, it was perilous, precarious, breathtaking; they were happy and aghast when the old man drew out a pound note and stood a round himself, 'Well, why shouldn't he?' the daughter asked them, asked Jackie boy, the bartender, the beer advertisements, the smutty air, the man who came in selling safety-razor blades, half a dozen for threepence, 'it's better than spending it on a crowd of strange dames.'

The Liverpool waterside at least had not changed since James's day: 'The black steamers knocking about in the yellow Mersey, under a sky so low that they seemed to touch it with their funnels, and in the thickest, windiest light';—even the colour was the same, 'the grey mildness, shading away into black at every pretext'.

The cargo ship lay right outside the Mersey in the Irish Sea; a cold January wind blew across the tender; people sat crammed together below deck saying good-bye, bored, embarrassed and bonhomous, like parents at a railway station the first day of term, while England slipped away from the port-hole, a stone stage, a tarred side, a slap of grey water against the glass.

2
The Cargo Ship

MADEIRA

My cousin and I had five fellow passengers in the cargo ship: two shipping agents, a traveller for an engineering firm, a doctor on his way to the Coast with anti-yellow-fever serum, and a woman joining her husband at Bathurst. All except the woman and the traveller knew the Coast; they knew the same people; they had a common technique of living enforced by common conditions. The daily dose of quinine, mosquito-netting over all the port-holes: these to them were as natural as the table-cloth at meals.

It is a condition favourable to the growth of legend. Legend belongs naturally to primitive communities where minds are so little differentiated, by work or play or education, that a story can move quickly from brain to brain uncriticized. But some-times these conditions arise artificially. A common danger, pur-pose or way of life can very nearly destroy differences of intellect and class; then you get the angels of Mons and the miracles at a shrine.

'Yes,' they were saying in the smoking-room, 'you won't find a tougher man than Captain W.' They all knew of him because they all belonged to the Coast: the captain, the doctor, the shipper.

'If he ran into a broken bottle,' the doctor said, 'his face wouldn't look any different.'

'He'd take a tug round the world as soon as look at you.'

'He doesn't insure his cargo. He bears the risk himself. That's why his freight-rates are so cheap.'

'Will people take the risk?'

'His word's as good as an insurance company's.'

'But when he loses a cargo?'

'He hasn't lost one yet.'

In the wireless room on a Saturday night the young agent waited hour after hour for the League results. He and the wire-less officer shared an esoteric gossip of the sea: how this or that man had quarrelled with the Old Man and joined another line. The bulbs flickered overhead; tubes hummed in the little cabin with its rows of discs and bulbs, as mechanized as was the engine-room below, a great black polished cliff, pipes tied up at the joints in blue, yellow or scarlet bags like hot-water bottles, a solitary Negro with a polishing rag in all the glittering desert of brass and iron.

Coming in from the bulbs and gossip and the dusk I overheard the Captain talking to the doctor in the smoking-room. 'Four hundred and sixteen people at Dakar,' he was saying. The subject came up again at breakfast: plague at Dakar, yellow fever at Bathurst, outbreaks hushed up on the French coast, never reported on the Liberian: one was seldom allowed to escape the subject of fever. One could begin a conversation with religion, politics, books; it always ended with malaria, plague, yellow fever. As long as one was at sea it was a joke, like somebody else's vicious wife; when one was on land it was like a grim story intended to make the flesh creep, but one became conscious then of people who wouldn't play, who preferred something comforting.

Something like *A Village in a Valley* by Mr Beverley Nichols, which was in the small library. One reads strange books in a ship, books one would never dream of reading at home: like Lady Eleanor Smith's *Tzigane,* and the novels of Warwick Deeping and W. B. Maxwell: a lot of books, written without truth, without compulsion, one dull word following another, books to read while you wait for the bus, while you strap-hang, in between the Boss's dictations, while you eat your A. B. C. lunch; a whole industry founded on a want of leisure and a want of happiness.

At Madeira it was raining. The touts were out at ten in the morning in the shabby notorious town. One drank sweet wine at the Golden Gates, and the rain dripped off the curious phallic hats hanging outside the shops. The touts wore straw hats with Cambridge ribbons; they kept at one's elbow all the way round Funchal; they weren't a bit discouraged because it was raining, because it was only just after breakfast. 'Luxe,' they kept on saying, and 'Sex' and something about dancing girls. Their industry, like Mr Beverley Nichols's, was founded on a want of leisure and a want of happiness. Quick, quick, you are only on shore for half an hour, you are only vigorous for a few more years, have another girl before it's too late, you aren't happy with the one you've got, try another. The women sold violets and lilies and roses in the rain, the phallic hats dripped, the touts couldn't understand that one didn't want a girl just after breakfast on a wet day. There were other ways of filling up time, one could drink sweet wine at the Golden Gates, one could go back on board and read Lady Eleanor Smith or Mr Beverley Nichols.

A young German artist and his wife came on board at Funchal as deck passengers and were given the little hospital to sleep in. He was a thick spotty man in a velvet jacket; he had known D. H. Lawrence at Taos and Mabel Dodge Luhan. It hadn't made any difference, he wasn't going to write a book about it. In the little hospital he put out his canvases, crude realistic landscapes and the baked faces of Mexican Indians; it grew dark; and everyone drank bad Madeira out of the bottle and he talked about Art and Sport and the Body Beautiful, and his wife, small and curved and lovely and complaisant, was quiet and seasick. He believed in Hitler and Nationalism and swimming and love, he liked the pictures of Orpen and de Laszlo, but Munch's pictures left him dissatisfied. They left out the Soul, he said, they were materialist; not that he disbelieved in the Body, the Body Beautiful and in physical Love. He agreed to come to Africa too, and illustrate this book; an artist was at home anywhere—but after dinner he changed his mind; and his sweet complaisant nubile wife said, Yes, she wouldn't mind coming to Africa, and after dinner she changed her mind too. He was a bad artist, but he wasn't a bogus one. He lived on almost nothing; he believed in himself and in his hazy Teutonic ideas; and there was a sensual beauty in their relationship. The two lived in a kind of continuous intimacy, she had no ideas but his, no vitality but his; he supplied all the life for both of them and she supplied a warm friendly sensual death; they shared the universe between them. All the time, in the cabin, at dinner, at a café table, they gave the impression of having only just risen from bed.

By dinner-time everyone was drunk on bad Madeira and the pink gin they called Coasters. The shipping agent sang *The Old Homeland* and *The Floral Dance* and *I Shot an Arrow into the Air* and the fat traveller called Younger said, 'Pass me some more eau de cow,' spilling his coffee. The aliens went to their cabin, picking their way across the lower deck and up the iron stairs into the stern; she was seasick, but it only made her quieter; it didn't alter her beautiful sensuous receptivity. The agent sang *The Old Homeland* again—'Far across the sea, I wonder will they pray for me'—and everyone felt English and exiled and wistful, everyone except Younger, who climbed carefully up the stairs, clinging to the banister: 'I'm going home by rail.' He was more English than any of them; the north country was in his heart; he was firmly local and unsentimental and bawdy and honest. He drank because he needed a holiday, because he had heavy work before him on the Coast, because he loved his wife and had desperate anxieties. He had more cause to drink than anyone. The boom years were in his heavy flesh and his three chins; one couldn't at first sight tell how the depression lay like lead in his stomach. If one were to paint his portrait in the old style of tiny landscapes and Tuscan towns, one would have given him as background an abandoned blast-furnace or the girders of a great bridge left a perch for birds.

Even when drunk, even when bawdy, he had an admirable sanity. 'Eighteen months on the Coast. Tell me, doctor, what do people do about it?'

'Insoluble,' the doctor said.

'But what do they do about it?'

'Even the Governor has asked me that. There's no answer.'

He was the last to go to bed, he would reel for ten minutes up and down the corridor, there was something common and royal about him which called for devotion, nothing he did could offend. 'Kipper,' he would shout outside the captain's door, 'Kipper,' and obediently the Captain would emerge. He had the way of Falstaff with a woman, an absurd innocence that was quite content with a slap and a tickle. 'You saucy little sausage,' and even the young shy inhibited married woman who had never left Liverpool, who wouldn't drink and wouldn't smoke and wouldn't look at the moon, slapped him back. There was a ballad quality about his bawdry. His words had the merit of children's art; they were vivid, unselfconscious, uncorrupted.

BALLYHOO

The cinema in Tenerife was showing a film which had been adapted from one of my own novels. It had been an instructive and rather painful experience to see it shown. The direction was incompetent, the photography undistinguished, the story sentimental. If there was any truth in the original it had been carefully altered, if anything was left unchanged it was because it was untrue. By what was unchanged I could judge and condemn my own novel: I could see clearly what was cheap and banal enough to fit the cheap banal film.

There remained a connection between it and me. One had never taken the book seriously; it had been written hurriedly because of the desperate need one had for the money. But even into a book of that kind had gone a certain amount of experience, nine months of one's life, it was tied up in the mind with a particular countryside, particular anxieties; one couldn't disconnect oneself entirely, and it was curious, rather pleasing, to find it there in the hot bright flowery town. There are places where one is ready to welcome any kind of acquaintance with memories in common: he may be cheap but he knew Annette; he may be dishonest but he once lodged with George; even if the acquaintance is very dim indeed and takes a lot of recognizing.

Two Youthful Hearts in the Grip of Intrigue. Fleeing from Life. Cheated? Crashing Across Europe. Wheels of Fate.

Never before had I seen American ballyhoo at work on something I intimately knew. It was magnificent in its disregard of the article for which it had paid. Its psychological insight was either cynically wrong or devastatingly right.

The real Orient Express runs across Europe from Belgium to Constantinople. Therefore, you will go wrong if you interpret the word 'Orient' to indicate something of a Chinese or Japanese nature. There is enough material of other kinds to arrange a lively colourful ballyhoo, as you will see as soon as you turn to the exploitation pages in this press book.

Date Tie-Up. In the exhibitor's set of stills available at the exchange are three stills which show Norman Foster explaining the sex life of a date to Heather Angel, passing dates to Heather Angel and Heather Angel buying dates from the car window. The dialogue is quite enlightening on the date subject at one point in the picture. Every city has high-class food shops which feature fancy packages of dates. Tie-in with one of these for window displays, and for a lobby display, using adequate copy and the three stills.

Another angle would be to have a demonstration of date products, the many uses of dates, etc. This would be quite possible in the much larger cities. And in cases where working with large concerns, patrons may be permitted to taste samples. These tie-ups must be worked out locally despite the fact that we are contacting importers of important brands.

Don't underestimate the value of a real smart window fixed up with date products, baskets of delicious fruits and dates, and the three stills shown here with adequate copy for your picture. 'Buy a package of delicious dates, and take 'The Orient Express' for Constantinople, a most thrilling and satisfying evening's entertainment, at the Rialto Theatre.'

Do You Know That: Heather Angel's pet kitten Penang had to have its claws clipped because it insisted on sharpening them on the legs of the expensive tables;

That the pet economy of Heather Angel is buying washable gloves and laundering them herself;

That Una O'Connor permits only a very few of her intimate friends to call her Tiny?

The blast of ballyhoo had not sold the film; to my relief, because by contract my name had to appear on every poster, it had kept to the smaller shabbier cinemas, until now it was washed up in Tenerife, in a shaded side street behind an old carved door like a monastery's. This was what made it an agreeable acquaintance; it hadn't the shamelessness of success; it might be vulgar, but it wasn't successfully vulgar. There was something quite un-Hollywood in its failure.

The Canaries were half-way to Africa; the Fox film and the pale cactus spears stuck in the hillside, a Victorian Gothic hotel smothered in bougainvillaea, parrots and a monkey on a string, innumerable themes were stated like the false starts and indecisions of a lifetime: the Chinese job from which one had resigned, the appointment in Bangkok never taken up, the newspaper in Nottingham. I can remember now only the gaudy poster, the taste of the sweet yellow wine, flat roofs and flowers and an arbour full of empty bottles, and in the small dark cathedral a Christmas crib (castles and little villages and women with baskets of carrots, a donkey and a motor-car and a comic man in a top-hat, little caves where hermits or gipsies sat asleep on mass-covered rocks, a man on an old-fashioned bicycle, and somewhere right up in a corner, dwarfed by the world, the flesh, those bright spring carrots, and the devil, the man in a top-hat, sat the Mother of God with an old-young child, wrinkled and careworn and cross-eyed, while Herod leant over a wall with his crown tilted).

LAS PALMAS

Of Las Palmas I can remember little more: a man selling women's pyjamas from a rowing boat after midnight, the women in the '33' with black theatrical eyes and heavy figures. It was half-past one in the morning before we got ashore and found a taxi. Nobody could speak a word of anything but Spanish; the drink was bad and dear, but Younger didn't mind. His inevitable expression, 'You saucy little sausage,' could be heard through all the rooms, his progress was one long slap and tickle and free drink. The manager followed him round with bills he wouldn't pay and Phil brought up the rear, the young shipping agent who was afraid there would be trouble, who had the unrequited devotion of a page in an Elizabethan play. Every now and again to keep the manager quiet Phil paid a bill and the manager tore it up and dropped it on the floor and wrote another. Then Younger stole the woman belonging to a man with a guitar and the man kissed him and had a drink; the manager wrote a bill, and Phil plucked at Younger's sleeve and said, 'Go steady, old man. Go steady.' A madman came up and threatened Younger, but Younger didn't understand, didn't care anyway, didn't even hear perhaps. He sat on a chair playing pat-paw with his stout black bitch; sometimes he made a pass at her mouth, but she avoided that, nudging with her elbow, pushing forward her empty glass while the manager wrote out another bill. Then it began all over again, the refusal to pay, the arguments, Phil's 'Go steady, old man, go steady,' another drink all round, pat-paw, 'You saucy little sausage,' another bill. On the way to the waterside he passed out altogether, had to be carried, fourteen stone of him, into the rowing boat in the dark, dragged up the rocking companion, undressed and put to bed. But no one grudged it him, he could do these things, next day he was as well as ever, bathed in a costume which wouldn't meet across him, called 'Kipper, Kipper' in the passage, was drunk by lunch-time, explained it was his last drink before the Coast: he was going to work now. No one believed him, but we were wrong.

He had the stamina of a bull; he could stop drinking when he chose. The islands were past, next port of call was on the Coast, he had work to do. Nobody knew how far afield his work was taking him and of its importance; he was fat and boisterous, one couldn't tell from his manner the anxiety of his journey. He was taking a big risk; he had to get orders; and yellow fever was not going to stop him. There was an epidemic at one of the points on his route; he didn't know of it when he came on board; everyone laughed at him about the fever, and one could tell that he was a little scared; but one could tell too that it was not going to make any difference. He was like an old fighter who is forced back into the ring because he needs the purse; he may be out of condition, may be afraid of getting hurt, but he cannot afford to lose, even if the effort kills him. Younger talked about his wife; he had never before been to a place where he couldn't ring her up at nine o'clock of an evening; he'd always done it when he was in Brussels, in Berlin, in Warsaw.

GRAVEYARD

The day after Las Palmas, passengers in West Coast boats wake to a completely new air. It lasts for a day and a day only. My sheets were damp with a kind of dew; there was a warm wet

wind and a haze over the sea. The air smelt as salt and fishy as
the air on Brighton front. The sodden damp to a traveller back
from the Coast with malarial infection in his blood is said to be
dangerous, and among sailors this part of the Atlantic is known
as the Elder Dempster Graveyard. But the tradition is older
than the Line. Burton wrote of it in his *Anatomy*: 'Such a complaint I read of those islands of Cape Verde, fourteen degrees
from the Equator, they do *male audire*; one calls them the un-
healthiest clime of the world, for fluxes, fevers, frenzies, calen-
tures, which commonly seize on seafaring men that touch at
them, and all by reason of a hot distemperature of the air. The
hardiest men are offended with the heat, and stiffest clowns
cannot resist it.'

It made Younger think of yellow fever at Kano. In the
smoking-room that night, the first night of his new sobriety, he
said that he thought death was a great adventure. But life, Phil
said, was a great adventure too. Science was making great
strides these days; you never knew; though of course Wells and
Jules Verne had foreseen it all; what wonderful prophets they
were. He said, 'I thought Hannen Swaffer was a prophet too
once, but he let me down.'

'Isn't Hannen Swaffer a woman?' Younger asked.

'No, he's a man.'

'Are you sure?' Younger said. But Phil was sure. He'd seen
him. He had even spoken to him one night when he came up to
address their literary club. It was a change from bridge, that
club; they got really famous writers to talk to them. Chesterton
had been and Cecil Roberts. Then he went out to look at the
moon, leaning over the side, waiting in vain for my cousin or
the other woman on board to join him. If one did, he put his
arm round her and talked about Wallasey or his wife or League
results. He was only formally romantic; he had a great respect
for women. He was really far more at home with Younger,
looked after Younger when he was drunk, protected him, undressed him if necessary; when Younger became sober he was
rather lost, looked at the moon more often, padding round the
deck earnestly romantic, irritable because no one would play at
tropic nights with him, disappearing at last into the little wire-

less room to talk about football to 'Sparks'. One night his vitality which had no outlet overcame him and he began to throw glasses overboard.

DAKAR

It must have been two days later that I woke to the grating of iron against stone, and there was the Coast. The world was already over-familiar. People said, 'Eldridge. Of course, he's an old Coaster,' and Eldridge, the middle-aged shipping agent, at the beginning of every meal would say, 'Chop, as we call it on the Coast,' or handing a plate of onions, 'Violets, we say on the Coast.' One's pink gin was called a Coaster. There was no other Coast but the West Coast and this was it.

On the quay the Senegalese strolled up and down, long white and blue robes sweeping up the dust blown from the ridge of monkey-nuts twenty-five feet high. The men walked hand-in-hand, laughing sleepily together under the blinding vertical glare. Sometimes they put their arms round each other's necks; they seemed to like to touch each other, as if it made them feel good to know the other man was there. It wasn't love; it didn't mean anything we could understand. Two of them went about all day without loosing hold; they were there when the boat slid in beside the monkey-nuts; they were there in the evening when the loading was finished and the labourers washed their hands and faces in the hot water flowing from the ship's side; they hadn't done a stroke of work themselves, only walked up and down touching hands and laughing at their own jokes; but it wasn't love; it wasn't anything we could understand. They gave to the blinding day, to the first sight of Africa, a sense of warm and sleepy beauty, of enjoyment divorced from activity and the weariness of willing.

> Là, tout n'est qu'ordre et beauté,
> Luxe, calme et volupté.

One found it hard to believe at Dakar that Baudelaire had never been to Africa, that the nearest he had come to it was the body of Jeanne Duval, the mulatto tart from Le Théâtre du

Panthéon, for Dakar was the Baudelaire of *L'Invitation au Voyage*, when it was not the René Clair of *Le Million*.

It was René Clair in its happy lyrical absurdity; the two stately Mohammedans asleep on the gravel path in the public gardens beside a black iron kettle; the tiny Syrian children going to school in white topees; the men's sewing parties on the pavements; the old pock-marked driver who stopped his horses and disappeared into the bushes to tell his beads; the men laden with sacks moving rhythmically up and down a ladder of sacks, building higher the monkey-nut hill, like the tin toy figures sold in Holborn at Christmas-time; in the lovely features of the women in the market, young and old, lovely less from sexual attractiveness than from a sharp differentiated pictorial quality. In the restaurant, a little drunk on iced Sauterne, one didn't trouble about the Dakar one had heard about, the Dakar of endemic plague and an unwieldy bureaucracy, the most unhealthy town on the Coast. Mr Gorer in his *Africa Dances* tells how in Dakar the young negroes simply die, not of tuberculosis, plague, yellow fever, but of inanition, of hopelessness. He stayed too long, I suppose, and saw too much; that sudden sense of happiness which came to one in Dakar doesn't last, which came to one in *Le Million*, a happiness that tingles behind the eyes, beautiful and insecure, a wish fulfilment.

> Do not expect again a phoenix hour,
> The triple-towered sky, the dove complaining,
> Sudden the rain of gold and heart's first ease . . .

Undoubtedly the other Dakar (the Dakar of the four hundred and sixteen dead, of the despair and injustice) was there, but something else was momentarily shining through, something which was always stubbornly exciting. So in an early René Clair film one could believe that this was the life one was born to live, breaking through life as one had been made to live it, breaking through anxiety and irritation and financial depression and a lust which had gone on too long, these voices in the air, this chase of a lottery ticket among the flying opera-hats, this tuneful miniature love behind cardboard scenery: nothing

was really serious, nothing lasted, you didn't have to think
about tomorrow's food or tomorrow's girl; you stuck up your
leg in derision sewing pants on the pavement, you fell asleep
among the flowers with your black kettle, you touched hands
and felt good and didn't care a damn.

One soon enough discovered, of course, that this impression
was not the Coast. The hawks flapping heavily over Bathurst, a
long low backcloth of houses and trees along a sandy beach;
a swarm of figures in the native quarter like flies on a piece of
meat; the not being allowed to land because of yellow fever; the
sense of isolation that the woman had as she went off to join
her husband in the quarantined town; this was more really the
Coast—the seedy Pole in a singlet and a pair of dirty white
trousers who came on board at Conakry, couldn't speak any
English or French and wanted to learn the name of the suits in
bridge. The Captain took his gun and shot a hawk which sat in
the rigging, the gulls scattered, twisting in the glittering air, and
the dusty body plunged through them on to the deck, like a reminder of darkness.

THE SHAPE OF AFRICA

A reminder of darkness: the girl in the Queen's Bar. I met her
weeping across Leicester Square when the leaves had dropped
and made the pavements slippery; she went into the vestibule
of the Empire Cinema and veered violently away again (that
wouldn't do), settled at last on a high chair in the Queen's Bar,
made up her face, had a gin and tonic; I hadn't the nerve to say
anything and find out the details. Besides, it's always happen-
ing all the time everywhere. You don't weep unless you've been
happy first; tears always mean something enviable.

The aeroplane rocked over Hanover, the last of the storm
scattering behind it, dipped suddenly down five hundred feet
towards the small air station, and soared again eastwards. Behind the plane the sun set along the clouds; we were above the
sunset; looking back it lay below, long pale ridges of stained
clouds. The air was grey above the lakes; they were sunk in the
ground, like pieces of lead; the lights of villages in between. It
was quite dark long before Berlin, and the city came to meet

the plane through the darkness as a gorse fire does, links of
flame through the heavy green night. A sky-sign was the size of
a postage stamp; one could see the whole plan of the city, like
a lit map in the Underground when you press a button to find
the route. The great rectangle of the Tempelhof was marked
in scarlet and yellow lights; the plane swerved away over the
breadth of Berlin, turned back and down; the lights in the cabin
went out and one could see the headlamps sweeping the asphalt
drive, the sparks streaming out behind the grey Lufthansa wing,
as the wheels touched and rebounded and took the ground
and held. That was happiness, the quick impression; but on the
ground, among the swastikas, one saw pain at every yard.

Arrived about nine o'clock at the Gare St Lazare, Easter,
1924, went to an hotel, then on to the Casino to see Mist-
inguette, the thin insured distinguished legs, the sharp 'catchy'
features like the paper face of an Ugly-Wugly in *The Enchanted
Castle* (' "Walk on your toes, dear," the bonneted Ugly-Wugly
whispered to the one with the wreath; and even at that thrilling
crisis Gerald wondered how she could, since the toes of one
foot were but the end of a golf club and of the other the end of
a hockey stick'). The next night the Communists met in the
slums at the end of a cul-de-sac. They kept on reading out
telegrams from the platform and everyone sang the *Interna-
tionale;* then they'd speak a little and then another telegram arrived. They were poor and pinched and noisy; one wondered
why it was that they had so much good news coming to them
which didn't make any difference at all. All the good news and
the singing were at the end of an alley in a wide cold hall; they
couldn't get out; in the little square the soldiers stood in tin
helmets beside their stacked rifles. That night from the window
of a hotel I saw a man and woman copulating; they stood against
each other under a street lamp, like two people who are supporting and comforting each other in the pain of some sickness.
The next day I read in the paper how the Reds had tried to get
out, but the soldiers had stopped them; a few people were hurt,
a few went to prison.

The first thing I can remember at all was a dead dog at the
bottom of my pram; it had been run over at a country cross-

roads, where later I saw a Jack-in-the-Green, and the nurse put it at the bottom of the pram and pushed me home. There was no emotion attached to the sight. It was just a fact. At that period of life one has an admirable objectivity. Another fact was the man who rushed out of a cottage near the canal bridge and into the next house; he had a knife in his hand; people ran after him shouting; he wanted to kill himself.

Like a revelation, when I was fourteen, I realized the pleasure of cruelty; I wasn't interested any longer in walks on commons, in playing cricket on the beach. There was a girl lodging close by I wanted to do things to; I loitered outside the door hoping to see her. I didn't do anything about it, I wasn't old enough, but I was happy; I could think about pain as something desirable and not as something dreaded. It was as if I had discovered that the way to enjoy life was to appreciate pain.

I watched from the other end of the bar; she wept and didn't care a damn; she embarrassed everybody; they cleared a space as if a fight was on and she sat there drinking gin and tonic and crying with empty chairs on either side; the barman kept on serving drinks at the other end. I thought for some reason even then of Africa, not a particular place, but a shape, a strangeness, a wanting to know. The unconscious mind is often sentimental; I have written 'a shape', and the shape, of course, is roughly that of the human heart.

3
The Home from Home

FREETOWN

Freetown, the capital of Sierra Leone, at first was just an impression of heat and damp; the mist streamed along the lower streets and lay over the roofs like smoke. Nature, conventionally grand, rising in tree-covered hills above the sea and the town, a dull uninteresting green, was powerless to carry off the shabby town. One could see the Anglican cathedral, laterite bricks and tin with a square tower, a Norman church built in the nineteenth century, sticking up out of the early morning fog.

There was no doubt at all that one was back in home waters. Among the swarm of Kru boats round the ship the *Princess Marina* with its freshly painted name was prominent. '*Princess Marina,*' the half-naked owner kept on calling. 'Sweetest boat on the Coast.'

Tin roofs and peeling posters and broken windows in the public library and wooden stores, Freetown had a Bret Harte air without the excitement, the saloons, the revolver shots or the horses. There was only one horse in the whole city, and it was pointed out to me by the proprietor of the Grand Hotel, a thin piebald beast pulled down the main street like a mule. There had been other horses from time to time, but they had all died. Where there wasn't a tin shed there were huge hoardings covered with last year's Poppy Day posters (the date was January the fifteenth). On the roofs the vultures sat nuzzling under their wings with horrible tiny undeveloped heads; they squatted in the gardens like turkeys; I could count seven out of my bedroom window. When they moved from one perch to another they gave no sensation of anything so aerial as flight; they seemed to hop across the street, borne up just high enough by the flap-flap of their dusty wings.

This was an English capital city; England had planted this town, the tin shacks and the Remembrance Day posters, and had then withdrawn up the hillside to smart bungalows, with wide windows and electric fans and perfect service. Every call one paid on a white man cost ten shillings in taxi fares, for the railway to Hill Station no longer ran. They had planted their seedy civilization and then escaped from it as far as they could. Everything ugly in Freetown was European: the stores, the churches, the Government offices, the two hotels; if there was anything beautiful in the place it was native: the little stalls of the fruit-sellers which went up after dark at the street corners, lit by candles; the native women rolling home magnificently from church on a Sunday morning, the cheap European cottons, the deep coral or green flounces, the wide straw hats, dignified by the native bearing, the lovely roll of the thighs, the swing of the great shoulders. They were dressed for a garden party and they carried off cheap bright grandeur in the small back-yards among the vultures as nature couldn't carry off Freetown.

The men were less assured; they had been educated to understand how they had been swindled, how they had been given the worst of two worlds, and they had enough power to express themselves in a soured officious way; they had died, in so far as they had once been men, inside their European clothes. They didn't complain, they hinted; they didn't fight for what they wanted, they sourly prevaricated. 'From what I garnered here and there,' suggested the Creole gossip-writer in the Sierra Leone *Daily Mail*, 'it is not the intention of the Governor and his wife to make Governor's Lodge, Hill Station, the official residence of the representative of His Majesty the King; those who maintain the view that the environments at Hill Station may influence them to the prejudice of the interest of the people are quite mistaken. In fact, it is considered improbable to entertain such an opinion, and I believe His Excellency will burst into peals of laughter if he were to hear such a thing. I leave it at that.'

That was the nearest they could get to a Petition of Right. They wore uniforms, occupied official positions, went to parties at Government House, had the vote, but they knew all the time they were funny (oh, those peals of laughter!), funny to the heartless prefect eye of the white man. If they had been slaves they would have had more dignity; there is no shame in being ruled by a stranger, but these men had been given their tin shacks, their cathedral, their votes and city councils, their shadow of self-government; they were expected to play the part like white men and the more they copied white men, the more funny it was to the prefects. They were withered by laughter; the more desperately they tried to regain their dignity the funnier they became.

FASHIONABLE WEDDING AT ST GEORGE'S CATHEDRAL

St George's Cathedral was the scene of the first fashionable wedding to take place there this year, on Wednesday, the 11th instant.

The contracting parties were Miss Agatha Fidelia Araromi

Shorunkeh-Sawyerr, fourth daughter of the late Mr J. C. Shorunkeh-Sawyerr, Barrister-at-law, and Mrs Frances M. Shorunkeh-Sawyerr of 'Bells Ebuts', King Tom's Peninsula, and Mr John Buxton Ogunyorbu Logan of the Survey Dept, son of Mr S. D. Logan, Retired Civil Service Officer.

The bride entered the church at 1.15 p.m. leaning on the arm of her only brother, Mr J. C. I. Shorunkeh-Sawyerr, who subsequently gave her away.

She wore a frock of white lace lined with white satin, and of full length. Its full court train was of white lace lined with rose-pink satin and it fell from the shoulders. She had on a short veil held in place on her head by a coronet of orange blossoms. She carried a bouquet of natural flowers.

She was followed by five bridesmaids, the Misses Molaké Shorunkeh-Sawyerr (bride's sister) and Annie Macaulay, being the chief. They wore salmon-pink lace frocks with georgette coatees of the same colour with white straw hats with pink bands. The others were the Misses Fitzjohn, Olivette Stuart, and Eileen Williams. These wore pink georgette frocks and pink hats. The hymn *Gracious Spirit, Holy Ghost,* was sung as the bridal procession moved slowly up the nave. The full choir of the cathedral, of which the bridegroom's father is the Dux, was present, and Mr A. H. Stuart, F G C O, the organist, presided at his organ.

Immediately after the ceremony, the guests repaired to the Crown Bottling Restaurant for Cake and Wine. This function was presided over by Mr A. E. Tuboku-Metzger, M A, J P, an old friend of the bride's late father.

Here six toasts were proposed and responded to. After this the company broke up, some going to the bridegroom's parents in Waterloo Street, and others to the bride's at King Tom's for more solid refreshments.

About 6 p.m. Mr and Mrs John B. Logan left for their honeymoon somewhere on the Wilkinson Road.

Before leaving them there, we wish them connubial bliss, and the best of luck.

Sometimes it was almost Firbank, it recalled the Mouth family forcing their way into the highest social circles of the city of

Cuna-Cuna, but alas! the smell of the fish laid fourteen deep in the roadway, the flowers withered and everlasting in the small public gardens, the low-church hymns did not belong to Cuna—'Cuna, full of charming roses, full of violet shadows, full of music, full of love, Cuna . . . !' Wilkinson and Waterloo streets and the Crown Bottling Restaurant were a poor exchange for Carmen Street, the Avenue Messalina, the Grand Savannah Hotel.

Freetown's excitements are very English, as Dakar's are very French; the Governor-General's garden party, where white and black, keeping sedulously apart on either side the beds, inspected the vegetables to the sound of a military band: 'Look, he's really managed to grow tomatoes. Darling, let's go and see the cabbages. Are those really lettuces?'; the Methodist Synod: 'Notices of motions fall thick and fast. We pass over some questions in the agenda meanwhile. We sit intently waiting to hear the Missionary Committee's letter, everyone is attentive, we listen, the air is still, we can hear the dropping of a pin'; literature from the Freetown Ededroko Store which advertised, 'Novels, Works of Hall Caine, Marie Corelli, R. L. Stevenson, Bertha Clay, etc., e.g., by Corelli: Wormwood, Sorrows of Satan, Barabbas, Vendetta, Thelma, Innocent; by Caine, The Deemster, A Son of Hagar, The Woman Thou Gavest Me; by Stevenson: Treasure Island, The Black Arrow; by Clay: A Woman's Temptation, Married for her Beauty, Beyond Pardon.'

The contributions of Dorothy Violetta Mallatson to the local daily Press vividly summarize the evangelical fun of Freetown: 'Looking behind us, Christmas is just round the corner and out of sight. Outspreading away into the distance there is sunshine, sports, and all the outdoor joys we love so well. For the school girl or boy there are school sports to take away the dullness and flatness of the schoolroom life. Then there is the Prize Distribution and Thanksgiving Service. For older people there is the All-Comers Tennis Competition and there is coming up shortly many dances and concerts. For instance, there is the Danvers Dance on the 8th of February, and the Play and Dance of the Ladies of the National Congress of British West Africa which comes on the 15th proximo.'

It would be so much more amusing if it was all untrue, a fictitious skit on English methods of colonization. But one cannot continue long to find the Creole's painful attempt at playing the white man funny; it is rather like the chimpanzee's tea-party, the joke is all on one side. Sometimes, of course, the buffoonery is conscious, and then the degradation is more complete. A few Creoles make money out of their prefects, by deliberately playing the inferior, the lower boy: R. Lumpkin alias Bungie is the most famous example. He has become a character. Tourists are taken to see his shop. You are advised by every white man you meet, in the long bar at the Grand, in the small bar at the City, on board ship: 'You must go to Bungie's.' He is the proprietor of the British-African Workmen Store and he styles himself 'Builder for the Dead, Repairer for the Living'. This is one of his advertisements:

Fear God Honour Your King, be just to mankind—Says Bungie.

*

Easy System
British-African Workmen Store undertake to supply Coffin with Hearse, Men, Grave, etc., by special arrangements for easy payment by installment.

*

Contracts taken up for Carpentry, Masonry, Painting, etc., at moderate charges.

*

Ready-made Plain and Polished Coffin supplied with Hearse and Uniformed men at any moment. Corpse washed and dressed.

*

Come! I'll bury the dead by easy system only be true to your sympathetic friend.
                        That's Bungie.

*

Do not live like a fool and die like a big fool. Eat and drink good stuff, save small, be praying for a happy death, then a decent funeral. Bungie will do the rest.

*

I'll bury the Dead.
   (Book of Tobias)
I'll bury the dead and feed the living.
   THAT'S BUNGIE ALL OVER

THE CITY BAR

I wanted to do a pub crawl. But one can't crawl very far in Freetown. All one can do is to have a drink at the Grand and then go and have a drink at the City. The City is usually more crowded and noisy because there's a billiard table; people are rather more dashing, get a little drunk and tell indecent stories; but not if there's a woman present. I had never found myself in a place which was more protective to women; it might have been inhabited by rowing Blues with Buchman consciences and secret troubles. Everyone either had a wife at Hill Station and drank a bit and bought chocolates at the weekend and showed photographs of their children at home:

   ('I'm afraid I don't care much for children.'
   'O, you'd like mine.')

or else they had wives in England, had only two drinks, because they'd promised their wives to be temperate, and played Kuhn-Kan for very small stakes. They played golf and bathed at Lumley Beach. There wasn't a cinema that a white man could go to, and books of course rotted in the damp or developed worms. You developed worms too yourself, after you'd been out a little time; it was inevitable; nobody seemed to mind. Freetown, they told you, was the healthiest place on the Coast. The day I left a young man in the educational department died of yellow fever.

Worms and malaria, even without yellow fever, are enough to cloud life in 'the healthiest place along the Coast'. These men in the City bar, prospectors, shipping agents, merchants, engineers, had to reproduce English conditions if they were to be happy at all. They weren't the real rulers; they were simply out to make money; and there was no hypocrisy in their attitude towards 'the bloody blacks'. The real rulers came out for a few years, had a long leave every eighteen months, gave garden parties, were supposed to be there for the good of the ruled. It was these men who had so much to answer for: the wages, for example, of the platelayers on the little narrow-gauge line which runs up to Pendembu near the French and Liberian borders. These men were paid sixpence a day and had to buy their own food, and yet in the days of the depression they were docked one day's pay a month. This was perhaps the meanest economy among the many mean economies which assisted Sierra Leone through the depression, a depression caused by the fall in price of palm oil and palm kernels, the preference Levers at that time were showing for whale oil. The economies were nearly all at the expense of the coloured man; government staffs were reduced by a clerk here and a messenger there. Until the visit of Lord Plymouth, the Under-Secretary of State, who arrived in Freetown on the day that I did, there had been only one sanitary inspector for the whole colony and protectorate. Badgered by the central authority, constantly moved from a district which he was attempting to clean up, he would apply in vain for assistants. Forced labour is illegal in a British Colony, but the sanitary inspector without a staff had to choose between breaking the law or leaving villages as dirty as he found them.

One could exonerate the men in the bar; they were not guilty of these meannesses; they were only guilty of the shabbiness of Freetown, the tin roofs and the Poppy Day posters. Santayana, with the romanticism of a foreign Anglophile, has written that 'what governs the Englishman is his inner atmosphere, the weather in his soul'. The inner atmosphere, he explains, 'when compelled to condense into words may precipitate some curt maxim or over-simple theory as a sort of war-cry; but its puerile language does it injustice, because it broods at a much deeper level than language or even thought. It is a mass of dumb instincts and allegiances, the love of a certain quality of life,' and in a finely chosen if romantic metaphor, he describes how 'it fights under its trivial fluttering opinions, like a smoking battleship under its flags and signals'. So to be fair to these men one must recognize a certain fidelity, a kind of patriotism in the dust and anglicanism and the closing hours; this is their 'corner of a foreign field', just as much as the flowers and cafés and the neat tarts of Dakar are the Frenchman's corner. If you are English, they would argue, you will feel at home here: if you don't like it you are not English. If one must condemn, one should condemn not the outposts but the headquarters of Empire, the country which has given them only this: a feeling of respectability and a sense of fairness withering in the heat.

NO SCREWS UNTURNED

When I came on shore I was met by an elderly Kruman carrying an umbrella. He said reproachfully, 'I've been waiting for some hours.' He held a cable in his hand from London; it asked him to get in touch with Greene, who was leaving for the Republic. 'My name,' the Kruman said, 'is Mr D.' He knew the Republic well, he could be of use.

An even more august authority was giving me unwanted help. Before I left the boat I had been handed a letter from His Majesty's Chargé d'Affaires in Monrovia, the capital of the Republic, saying that he had announced my visit to the Secretary of the Interior, and the Secretary had informed all the District Commissioners in the Western Province. 'Any courtesies shown these persons by the Commissioners and Chiefs with whom they contact will be very highly appreciated, and it is incumbent that you leave no screws unturned to make their trip a pleasant one.' The phrase about the screws had a slightly sinister ring, but this fairylike activity had been no part of my plan. If there was anything to hide in the Republic I wanted to surprise it. Luckily the Secretary of the Interior had suggested a route for me to follow, and it would be quite easy for me to avoid it, to avoid indeed the Western Province, after a few days, altogether.

It would have been easier if I had been able to obtain maps. But the Republic is almost entirely covered by forest, and has never been properly mapped, mapped that is to say even to the rough extent of the French colonies which lie on two sides of it.

I could find only two large-scale maps for sale. One, issued by the British General Staff, quite openly confesses ignorance; there is a large white space covering the greater part of the Republic, with a few dotted lines indicating the conjectured course of rivers (incorrectly, I usually found) and a fringe of names along the boundary. These names have been curiously chosen: most of them are quite unknown to anyone in the Republic; they must have belonged to obscure villages now abandoned. The other map is issued by the United States War Department. There is a dashing quality about it; it shows a vigorous imagination. Where the English map is content to leave a blank space, the American in large letters fills it with the word 'Cannibals'. It has no use for dotted lines and confessions of ignorance; it is so inaccurate that it would be useless, perhaps even dangerous, to follow it, though there is something Elizabethan in its imagination. 'Dense Forest'; 'Cannibals'; rivers which don't exist, at any rate anywhere near where they are put; one expects to find Eldorado, two-headed men and fabulous beasts represented in little pictures in the Gola Forest.

But this was where Mr D, the elderly Kruman, could help; he knew the Republic.

Mr D lived in Krutown. Krutown is one of the few parts of Freetown with any beauty; the Krus, the great sailors of the coast, whose boast it is that they have never been slaves and have never dealt in slaves, have escaped Anglicanization. The native huts still stand among the palm trees on the way to Lumley Beach, the women sitting outside with their long hanging breasts uncovered. Mr D's house was in the only Europeanized street. A bare wooden stair led into a room with wooden walls on which were hung a few religious pictures in Oxford frames. There were four rickety chairs and an occasional table with a potted plant on it. Crudely painted Mothers of God bore the agony of seven swords with indifference, Christ just above his head exposed a heart the colour of raw liver. Insects hopped about on the wooden floor and Mr D gently instructed me how to reach the frontier. A little way over the border there was an American mission, the Order of the Holy Cross at Bolahun; it would be as well to stay there a few days and try to get carriers to go through with me to Monrovia. He examined the route suggested by the Secretary of the Interior; that had got to be avoided as far as possible; though I should have to follow it to Zigita. On the blank spaces of the English map, Mr D made his pencilled suggestions; he couldn't be really sure to a matter of ten miles where to put the places he mentioned; the English map confused him with its inaccuracies. At last he gave it up altogether, and I simply wrote the names down in my notebook, spelling them as best I might: Mosambolahun, Gondolahun, Jenne, Lombola, Gbeyanlahun, Goryendi, Bellivela, Banya. But it is unnecessary to give them all here, for as it turned out I did not follow this route at all, didn't even aim at Monrovia, which had been my object when I sailed. Circumstances in a country where the only way to travel is to know the next town or village ahead and repeat it as you go, like the Syrian woman in *Little Arthur's History* who said 'Gilbert, London' across England, were to alter my plans again and again until my small book was filled with lists of probably mis-spelt names in smudged pencil of places I never succeeded in finding. Examining it now I discover this cryptic entry: 'Steamer calling C. Palmas and Sinoe. Keep S. dark. Get off at S. Take the beach to Setta Kru, Nana Kru. At N K, Dr V, Am. missionary. To Wesserpor or Dio. Tell people to take me to Nimley. On to New Sasstown and CP.'

This is the record of another plan which came to nothing through lack of money and exhaustion. I had brought with me from England a letter of introduction to Paramount Chief Nimley of the Sasstown Tribe of Krus, the leader of the rebellion on the coast in 1932. It was in the fight against Nimley that the Frontier Force under the command of Colonel Elwood Davis, the President's special agent, a North American black, had, according to the British Consul's report, killed women and children, destroyed villages, tortured prisoners. Peace had been patched up but not with Nimley, who with the remains of his tribe was hidden in the bush vainly hoping for white intervention. No white man, Mr D said, would be allowed to travel to the Kru coast, but it would be allowed by booking a passage on a coasting steamer from Monrovia to Cape Palmas to change one's mind on board and land unexpectedly at Sinoe. From Sinoe one would travel along the beach to Nana Kru, and from there it would be necessary to get guides who knew the way to Nimley's hiding-place.

I only mentioned these plans which came to nothing, these routes which were not followed, because they may give some idea of the vagueness of my ideas when I landed at Freetown. I had never been out of Europe before; I was a complete amateur at travel in Africa. I intended to walk across the Republic, but I had no idea of what route to follow or the conditions we would meet. Looking at the unreliable map I had thought vaguely that we would go up to the Sierra Leone railway terminus at Pendembu, then go across the frontier the nearest way and strike diagonally down to the capital. There seemed to be a lot of rivers to cross, but I supposed there would be bridges of some kind; there was the forest, of course, but that was everywhere. One apparently reliable book I had read on Sierra Leone mentioned a number of prospectors who had crossed the border into what was supposed to be an uninhabited part of the forest looking for gold and had never returned; but that was a little lower down (the Republic was on the bulge of Africa's coastline, and I could never properly remember the points of the compass).

Mr D discouraged me. It wasn't possible, he said, that way. It was evident that he was particularly anxious for me to travel down by Bellivela. Bellivela was the headquarters of the Frontier Force and was being used as a concentration camp for political prisoners, those who had given evidence before the League of Nations Commission of Inquiry into slavery in the Republic. 'They'll have to invite you inside the camp for the night,' Mr D said, 'and then you can poke around and see things.'

That night I dreamed of Mr D and the Customs at the border, a muddled irritating dream. I was always forgetting something; I had arrived at the Customs with all my bags and boxes and Mr D tied up in a bale, but I'd forgotten to get any carriers and I had no boys. I was afraid all the time that the Customs inspector would discover Mr D, that I would be fined for smuggling, and have to pay a heavy duty.

THE THREE COMPANIONS

We arrived in Freetown on a Saturday and the train for Pendembu left on the following Wednesday; I had hoped to find servants engaged for me when I arrived; but Jimmie Daker, to whom I had an introduction, who had promised months before to do his best, had forgotten all about it. He was vague, charming, lost, and a little drunk. He sat in the Grand bar drinking whisky and bitters and talking about the Nazis and the war; he began as a pacifist but after his third drink he was ready to serve again at any moment; his face was scarred from the last war. He hadn't any idea of how to get boys for the journey, though he agreed that it wouldn't be wise to take any of those who stood all day at the entrance to the hotel offering their services. He didn't know anybody who knew anything at all about the Republic. No one in Sierra Leone had ever crossed the border.

'Oh, Jimmie,' they all said in Freetown, 'poor dear Jimmie,' when I said that Jimmie was finding me boys. 'Jimmie doesn't know a thing.'

In the end I got the best boys in Freetown. My head boy, Amedoo, was famous all the way up the line, and Amedoo chose the second boy, Laminah, and the old Mohammedan cook, Souri. And Jimmie Daker was, in a way, responsible. If I had not been to Jimmie's for a sun-downer, I wouldn't have met Daddy, who had been twenty-five years in Freetown and knew every native in the place. He was quite drunk. He drove rapidly up and down the hills choosing the worst roads, he nearly got arrested for taking off a black policeman's hat, the atmosphere was rather like Boat Race night in Piccadilly. 'Everyone knows Daddy,' he said, trying to drive into Government House at two in the morning (but the gates were closed), reversing rapidly to the edge of a ditch, plunging uphill again while the sentries stood at attention and watched the car disappear with impassive faces, roaring past the barracks (the guardroom emptied at sight of a car on to the grass and everyone stood to attention in the green underwater light), up a muddy track off the road, coming to a halt against a bank. 'You poor innocents,' he said. We were stranded like criminals in a small lit cage above

Freetown. 'Have you ever been in Africa before? Have you ever
been on trek? What on earth made you choose to go There?'
'There,' it appeared, was quite unspeakable, though, of course,
he knew it only from hearsay; *he* would never dream . . . Had
we any idea of what we were up against? Had we any reliable
maps? No, I said. There weren't any to be got. Had we any boys?
No. Had we let the DCs up the line know of our coming and engaged rest-houses? No, I hadn't known it was necessary. When we
crossed the border, how were we going to sleep? In native huts.

'You poor innocents,' he said. He nearly wept over the wheel.
Had we ever considered what a native hut meant? The rats, the
lice, the bugs. What would happen if we got malaria, dysentery? 'Something's got to be done,' he said, reversing, driving
rapidly backwards downhill. His mind switched over to the al-
ternate theme: 'Everyone here knows Daddy.' He stopped the
car in Krutown beside a policeman and thrust his head out of
the window. 'Who am I?' The policeman approached nervously
and shook his head: 'No. Come here. Come close. Tell me; Who
am I? The policeman shook his head and tried to smile; he was
scared; he supposed it was a game, but he didn't know how to
play. 'Who am I, you black varmint?' A young girl tried to slip
through the zone of headlight back into the dark: she had no
business out at that hour, but Daddy saw her. 'Hi,' he said,
sticking his head out from the other side of the car, 'come here.'
She came up to the car; she was far too pretty to be scared; her
bare breasts were small and firm and pointed; she had the neat
rounded thighs of a cat. 'Tell him,' Daddy said, 'who am I?' She
grinned at him. She wasn't scared by any game a man could
play. 'You know who I am?' Daddy said. She leant right into
the car and grinned and nodded. 'Daddy,' she said. He slapped
her face in a friendly way and drove off. He seemed to think
he'd proved something. 'Have you thought of the leeches?' he
said. 'They'll drop on you from the trees.' We stopped outside
our hotel; the wooden floors, the stairs, were alive with ants.
Daddy said, 'I've got to do something for you, I can't just let
you go like this,' drooping over the wheel with sleep.

At dawn a madman began to go groaning down the street; I
had heard him at intervals all day; I slipped out from under my

mosquito net—to watch him trail his rags through the grey early morning; he moved his head from side to side, groaning inhumanly like a man without a tongue. There were no vultures to be seen so early, the tin roofs were bare; do vultures nest? and the bats had gone, the fruit bats which streamed out across the town at seven o'clock.

Strange to say, Daddy remembered next morning that he had promised something. He turned up early at the hotel and said he had the boys outside waiting. I didn't know what to say to them; they stared back at me from the bottom of the hotel steps waiting for orders: Amedoo, grey-faced and expressionless, holding his fez to his chest, a man of about thirty-five; Souri, the cook, a very old toothless man, in a long white robe; Laminah, the second boy, very young, in shorts and a little white jacket like those barbers wear, with a knitted woollen cap on his head crowned by a scarlet bobble. It was several days before I learnt their names, and I could never fully understand what they said to me. I told them to come back next day, but they haunted the hotel from that moment, the two older men appearing suddenly in the passage, standing silently in front of me with lowered head and fez pressed to their chests. I never knew what they wanted; they always waited for me to speak. It was only later that I realized Amedoo was as shy as myself. I couldn't have imagined then the affection I would come to feel for them.

Our relationship was to be almost as intimate as a love-affair; they were to suffer from the same worn nerves; to be irritated by the same delays; but our life together, because it had been more perfectly rounded, seemed afterwards less real. For there is so much left over after a love-affair; letters and mutual friends, a cigarette case, a piece of jewellery, a few gramophone records, all the usual places one has seen each other in. But I had nothing left but a few photographs to show that I had ever known these three men; I would never again see the towns we had passed through together and never run into them in familiar places.*

---

*Six years later when the fortune of war brought me back to Freetown, I met Laminah and asked after Amedoo. He broke into peals of laughter, 'Old cook,' he said, 'he all right, but Amedoo he under ground.' (1946)

UP TO RAILHEAD

Everything was strange from the moment we pressed our way into Water Street Station through the crowd which always watched the twice-weekly train depart, and waved good-bye to Younger, beyond the black barrier of faces. I felt more at one then with the Kuhn-Kan players; I could appreciate the need in a strange place of some point of support, of one or two things scattered round which are familiar and understandable even if they are only Sydney Horler's novels, a gin and tonic. For even the railway journey was strange. It is a small-gauge line, and the train noses its way up-country with incredible slowness (it took two days to go two hundred and fifty miles). There are three first-class compartments. The experienced traveller (there was one on the train) engages the middle compartment, which is quite empty, and puts up his own deck-chair; in the other two compartments the company provides wicker armchairs.

One was 'off', and one was horribly afraid of doing the wrong thing; the etiquette of travel in wild places is as exacting as the etiquette of a new club. Nobody in England had warned me of the centre compartment, although I now understood that as a white man I should have made some effort to engage it. I began to fear, too, my first meeting with a chief; I had been told that I would be 'dashed', probably a chicken or some eggs or rice, and I would have to 'dash' back money in return; I must shake hands and be friendly but aloof (it was a relief to enter the Republic and no longer feel that I was a member of the ruling race).

This question of dashes was a complicated one; in the course of the journey we found ourselves dashed not merely the usual chicken (value 6d. or 9d. according to quality; return dash, which should always slightly exceed the true value, 1s. or 1s. 3d.), eggs (return dash 1d. each), oranges and bananas (value about forty for 3d.; return dash 6d.), but a goat, a dancing monkey, a bundle of knives, a leather pouch, and innumerable gourds of palm wine. It was not always easy to calculate the value, and it was a long time before I overcame my reluctance to press a shilling into a chief's hand.

I had been told by Mr D that I might meet three chiefs before we left Sierra Leone, Chief Coomba and Chief Fomba at Pendembu, the end of the line, and Chief Momno Kpanyan at Kailahun, our last stopping place before the frontier. Chief Momno Kpanyan was a very rich man, and the thought of having to dash him a few shillings clouded the whole of the journey.

I had never been so hot and so damp; if we pulled down the blinds in the small dusty compartment we shut out all the air; if we raised them, the sun scorched the wicker, the wooden floor, drenched hands and knees in sweat. Outside, the dusty Sierra Leone countryside unrolled, like a piece of drab cloth along a draper's counter, grey and dull green and burnt up by the dry season which was now approaching its end. The train rattled and reeled forward at fifteen miles an hour, burrowing intimately through the native villages almost within hand's reach of the huts, the babies rolling in the dust, the men lounging in torn hammocks hung under the thatch. The bush was as ragged and uninteresting as a back garden which has been allowed to run wild and in which the aspidistras from the parlour have seeded and flourished among the brown-scorched grasses and the tall wrinkled greenery.

All the way along the line the price of oranges went down, from six a penny at Freetown to fifteen a penny the other side of Bo. The train stopped at every station, and the women pressed up along the line, their great black nipples like the centre point of a target. I was not yet tired of the sight of naked bodies (later I began to feel as if I had lived for years with nothing but cows), or else these women were prettier and more finely-built than most of those I saw in the Republic. It was curious how quickly one abandoned the white standard. These long breasts falling in flat bronze folds soon seemed more beautiful than the small rounded immature European breasts. The children took their milk standing; they ran to the breasts in pairs like lambs, pulling at the teats. But though the region of modesty had shrunk, it was still there. The train crossed the Mano river; far down below the bridge, a hundred yards away, natives were bathing; they covered their private parts with their hands as the train went by.

The railway journey began before eight and finished some time after five; the first stage of the journey ended at Bo; here the train and passengers stayed the night. At some point during the day one had emerged from the Colony into the Protectorate. The change was more than a matter of geography or administration, it was a change of manner. The Englishmen here didn't talk about the 'bloody blacks' nor did they patronize or laugh at them; they had to deal with the real natives and not the Creole, and the real native was someone to love and admire. One didn't have to condescend; one knew more about some things, but they knew more about others. And on the whole the things they knew were more important. One couldn't make lightning like they could, one's gun was only an improvement on their poisoned spear, and unless one was a doctor, one had less chance of curing a snake-bite than they. The Englishmen here were of a finer, subtler type than on the Coast; they were patriots in the sense that they cared for something in their country other than its externals; they couldn't build their English corner with a few tin roofs and peeling posters and drinks at the bar.

It might be thought that these men were more fortunate, that their 'corner', just because it was less material, demanded less effort to construct. But one cannot carry a country's art in one's head, and in the climate of West Africa books rot, pianos go out of tune, and even a gramophone record buckles.

Beside the line Sergeant Penny Carlyle, DC's messenger, swagger-stick under arm, waited for us. Bare-legged and bare-footed, with a cap like a Victorian messenger boy's perched on one side, a row of medals on his tunic, he had the smartness and efficiency of an NCO in the Guards. He marshalled his carriers, led the way to the rest-house, squashed a beetle under his toes, clicked his bare heels and dismissed. There were egrets everywhere, like thin snow-white ducks with yellow beaks. They provided, in their slender Oriental beauty, the final contrast to Freetown; there wasn't a vulture to be seen, and suddenly, inexplicably, I felt happy in the rest-house, the square squat bungalow built on cement piles to keep out the white ants, as the hurricane lamps were lit and the remains of the tough, dry, tasteless coast chicken were laid out. There was a cockroach larger than a black beetle in the bathroom, there were no mosquito rods with the camp beds, my medical outfit, which had cost me four pounds ten at Burroughs Wellcome, had been left behind, a native stood outside the rest-house all the evening complaining of something with folded hands, but I was happy; it was as if I had left something I distrusted behind.

On the lawn outside the headmaster's house, beside a tree covered with wax blossoms like magnolia, we sat and drank gin and lime-juice; it was warm and quiet; they talked of the Republic. I carried an introduction to C, a young Dutchman who was said to be somewhere in the Republic looking for diamonds. The traffic superintendent had heard of him; C had slipped over the frontier somewhere near Pendembu, and rumours had come back that he had found the stones. He was alone, working for some small Dutch company outside the Great Trust. But the Trust, so the story went, had been frightened by the rumours; if diamonds were mined on a large scale in the Republic, the Trust could no longer control the price.

They had sent spies over to trace C, slipped them across from Sierra Leone, from French Guinea and from the Ivory Coast; they had to discover the truth; the price of diamonds and their own existence depended on it. It was a good story to hear there in the dark, near the borders of a country of which no one in Sierra Leone had been able to tell me anything. It was a good story because it didn't go too far and tell too much, because it had not merely a plot but a subject; it cast a light in so many directions, the satiric, the social, the psychological; one only had to wait for one's own experience to add colour and facts, though I was almost afraid to find C, lest the vivid outline should be marred by detail.

It was useless in Sierra Leone to ask for information about the Republic. No one had been across; any traffic there was came from the other side. President King, who had been forced to resign soon afterwards by the disclosures of the League of Nations Commission of Inquiry, had visited Sierra Leone a few years back. He was received with royal honours; there were banquets and receptions, guns were fired the royal number of rounds. What the President never knew was that he had been used as a dummy for the Prince of Wales, who visited the Colony soon afterwards; the salutes had been rehearsed, the committees had tried out their arrangements on him. Later he came up to Bo on his way home. He had planned to go back by land from the boundary, escorted by his troops; it wasn't safe for a President to make his way through the tribes he ruled without two hundred soldiers to guard him. There was a dinner in his honour; it went well to the end; there were the usual toasts; but when the President rose there was an interruption. The Colonel Commandant of the Republic's Frontier Force was having a good time. 'Sit down, Mr President,' he said, 'I want some more brandies and sodas.'

A few days later his host got tired of the President and had him escorted with proper ceremony to the border, but at the wrong place. The Frontier Force had marched to meet him at Foya and here he was at Kabawana. The Presidential party sat on the ground and waited and hoped; they were very frightened; the British platoon marched off and left them there.

BORDER TOWN

As it turned out I had no cause to fear a meeting with the diamond prospector. The story was left vague, unverified, suggestive. Six months in the Republic had been too much for C's health; he had gone home. This I learnt the next afternoon at Pendembu, at the small German store where I had been told to inquire for him. The train left Bo soon after nine and arrived in the late afternoon. All my food was still in bond, but I bought tinned food at the PZ store in Bo. One could buy everything there, drinks and tinned foods and clothes and ironware and cures for gonorrhoea. (PZ have branches all down the coast, even in the Republic; they are a Manchester firm, a kind of West African Selfridge, and in towns where there is no accommodation for white men, the PZ store can always be depended on for hospitality.)

At Pendembu another court messenger was waiting for us, and a lorry to take us to Kailahun, to the Government rest-house, but I called first at the Deutsche Kamerun Gesellschaft to inquire for C. 'You'll find his partner, Mr Van Gogh,' the

German manager said, 'somewhere near Bolahun.' Mr Van Gogh was looking for gold as well as for diamonds. He had been out there for nine months. He would be at Bolahun or somewhere in the forest. They couldn't say more. The Paramount Chief was waiting by the lorry; he was a small man in a robe of native cloth with a cocky little woollen cap; we had nothing to say to each other, we shook hands and smiled, and then the lorry drove away.

The old engine boiled, and the metal of the footboard burnt through my shoes; the driver was bare-footed. We drove wildly up- and down-hill for an hour on a road like a farm track, but the impression of reckless speed was deceptive, formed by the bumps, the reeling landscape, the smell of petrol and the heat; the lorry couldn't have gone more than twenty miles an hour. Cars are still rare in that corner of Sierra Leone, men scrambled up the banks, women fled into the bush or crouched against the bank with their faces hidden, as civilization went terrifyingly by them in a fume of evil smoke.

In Kailahun at the time when we arrived there were only two white men, the District Commissioner and a Scottish engineer who was building a bridge, but a third man, a stranger, drifted in during the evening in a singlet and dirty ducks, with a little black beard and shaven monkish head. The Commissioner had arrived by the same train; he had been down the line to Segbwana to investigate a Gorilla Society murder. A child had been carried off and killed, and a woman had sworn she had seen the gorilla and that he wore trousers. A man confessed, but none of the Commissioners believed that he was the real murderer. He had in his possession a gorilla knife with curved prongs to make the rough clawing wounds, and possession of the knife was alone sufficient to earn him fourteen years' imprisonment. The Commissioner was small, dark, lively, subtle and sensitive; he was new to the place; something had happened to three of his predecessors. There had been a boundary dispute in the district for years between two chiefs, a suspicion of 'medicine' in the food, and in a month's time he would be alone again (the engineer gone). Books came out to him from the Times Book Club, he read them and then they rotted on the shelves.

The engineer sat and smoked in silence. He didn't read books; he had no conversation; he was white-haired, rocky, slow; he might have been sixty and it was a shock to hear that he was in his early forties. He didn't mind the loneliness, he said, he was happier here than in England, it suited him. But he had more nerves than he cared to admit.

'There's a Liberian messenger waiting here for you,' the DC said. It was what I had feared, that the authorities would send a guide to keep us to the route they had suggested. The DC sent a man into the village to find him, and soon afterwards the stranger turned up in his dirty trousers and singlet. Everyone took him to be the Liberian messenger, nobody got up or offered him a drink; he was the Enemy with his shaven head and his curious black tuft of beard. He had nothing to say for himself, standing there patiently while he was told what he had to do. 'You are going to show this gentleman the way to Bolahun. He will start the day after tomorrow. You know the way to the Holy Cross Mission?'

Yes, he said, he had come from there.

It was a long while before anyone thought of asking whether he was the Liberian messenger. He wasn't, the messenger had disappeared from Kailahun, the stranger was a German. He wanted a bed; he had dropped in to Kailahun as casually as if it were a German village where he would be sure to find an inn. He had a bland secretive innocence; he had come from the Republic and he was going back to the Republic; he gave no indication of why he had come or why he was going or what he was doing in Africa at all.

I took him for a prospector, but it turned out later that he was concerned with nothing so material as gold or diamonds. He was just learning. He sat back in his chair, seeming to pay no attention to anyone; when he was asked a question, he gave a tiny laugh (you thought: I have asked something very foolish, very superficial), and gave no answer until later, when you had forgotten the question. He was young in spite of his beard; he had an aristocratic air in spite of his beachcomber's dress, and he was wiser than any of us. He was the only one who knew exactly what it was he wished to learn, who knew the exact extent of his ignorance. He could speak Mende; he was picking up Buzie; and he had a few words of Pelle: it took time. He had been only two years in West Africa.

I discovered this very gradually; it took longer than the breakfast to which he came next day, more aristocratic than ever in a clean shirt and a pair of fawn trousers, with an ivory-headed stick, a round white topee, a long cigarette-holder in the corner of his mouth. It was a formal courtesy, but he wasn't interested in anyone; he was only interested in learning what he wanted to know, and he could tell at once that from us he could learn nothing at all. We asked him questions and he retired more than ever into his reserve of secrecy. Had he ever been to Africa before he came out to the Republic two years ago? No, never. Hadn't he found things difficult? No, he said with a tiny smile, it had all been very simple. Would one have trouble with the Customs at the frontier? Well, of course, it was possible; he himself had no trouble, but they knew him. Should one bribe them? That was one of the questions he didn't answer, putting it aside, smiling gently, tipping the ash off his cigarette on to the beaten earth of the floor. The cockchafers buzzed in and out and he sat with lowered head, smoking. No, he wouldn't have another biscuit. Only after a time he exerted himself to give one piece of information; teaching tired him as much as learning invigorated him. It would be as well, he said, while we were at the Holy Cross to visit the Liberian Commissioner at Kolahun. The Commissioner was a scoundrel; he could make things very unpleasant; besides, it was necessary to take out a permit of residence before one had been in the Republic a week. Then he walked briskly away, twirling his ivory-headed stick, his topee sloped at a smart angle, looking around, learning things. One day (it took a week to discover so much) he was going to write a thesis for Berlin University (he came from Hamburg, but Dr Westermann was at Berlin and he hoped to win the approval of that great Africa scholar). The thesis was an end, but the collection of material for the thesis had no end. The thesis was as evasive as the Castle in Kafka's religious parable.

We met him again in the long flat village. The chief's new house stood up above the huts, an absurd concrete skyscraper with row on row of stained-glass windows not made to open; in one corner, tucked away, an unpainted door and a flight of splintery steps. This was the house of Momno Kpanyan, one of the richest chiefs in the Protectorate. In the market we got small change; the penny was too large a sum for marketing, and the currency most in use was irons. Their price varied; one could speculate in irons: the rate that day was twenty for fourpence. They were flat strips of iron about fourteen inches long, like blunt arrows; the points must be undamaged and the tails unchipped (this was as good a way as a milled edge to ensure that the currency was not debased); men were coming in to the market with bundles of several hundred irons on their heads.

Kailahun, in memory, has become a clean village, one of the cleanest we stayed in, but what impressed me at the time was the dirt and disease, the children with protuberant navels re-lieving themselves in the dust among the goats and chickens, the pock-marked women smeared about the face and legs and breasts with some white ointment they squeezed from a plant in the bush and used for beauty and for medicine. They used it for smallpox, for fever, for toothache, for indigestion; for every ailment under their bleak sun; when they were young it soothed their headaches; when they were older they smeared it on their big bellies to bring them ease in their confinement; when they were dying it lay like a sediment of salt on their dried-up breasts and in their pitted thighs. Here you could measure what civi-lization was worth; looking back later to Kailahun from the villages of the Republic, where civilization stopped within fifty miles of the Coast, I could see no great difference.

'Workers of the World Unite': I thought of the wide shallow slogans of political parties, as the thin bodies, every rib show-ing with dangling swollen elbows or pock-marked skin, went by me to the market; why should we pretend to talk in terms of the world when we mean only Europe or the white races? Nei-ther ILP nor Communist Party urges a strike in England be-cause the platelayers in Sierra Leone are paid sixpence a day without their food. Civilization here remained exploitation; we had hardly, it seemed to me, improved the natives' lot at all, they were as worn out with fever as before the white man

came, we had introduced new diseases and weakened their re-
sistance to the old, they still drank from polluted water and
suffered from the same worms, they were still at the mercy of
their chiefs, for what could a District Commissioner really
know, shifted from district to district, picking up only a few
words of the language, dependent on an interpreter? Civilization so far as Sierra Leone was concerned was the railway to
Pendembu, the increased export of palm-nuts; civilization, too,
was Lever Brothers and the price they controlled; civilization
was the long bar in the Grand, the sixpenny wages. It was not
civilization as we think of it, a civilization of Suffolk churches
and Cotswold manors, of Crome and Vaughan. The District
Commissioner's work was to a great extent the protection of
the native from the civilization he represented. The 'noble savage' no longer exists; perhaps he never existed, though in the
very young (among the few who are not disfigured by navel
hernia) you seem to see behind the present to something lovely,
happy and unenslaved, something like the girl who came up the
hill that morning, a piece of bright cloth twisted above her
hips, the sunlight falling between the palms on her dark hanging breasts, her great silver anklets, the yellow pot she carried
on her head.

FREEDOM TO TRAVEL

Kailahun is on the border of French Guinea; that presumably is
why the District Commissioner's office was transferred there
from Pendembu at the railhead. At Kailahun there is no railway and no telegraph: to communicate with Freetown the Commissioner must send a messenger the eighteen miles to
Pendembu. It is difficult to understand what control he has
over the border; natives pass freely to and fro; indeed with a little care it would be possible to travel all down West Africa
without showing papers from the moment of landing. There is
something very attractive in this great patch of 'freedom to
travel'; absconding financiers might do worse than take to the
African bush. They could be buried there for a lifetime, and
they could carry all the money they needed with them in a country where oranges are fifteen a penny, chickens sixpence each,

and wages, if you go deep enough, three shillings a week; where you can feed thirty men, as I found, on thirty shillings a week.

That afternoon we went for a walk into French Guinea with the engineer. The border is the Moa River, about twice the width of the Thames at Westminster. We crossed in a dug-out canoe, standing and balancing with the roll. It was quite easy, only a little frightening because there were alligators in the Moa. The curious thing about these boundaries, a line of river in a waste of bush, no passports, no Customs, no barriers to wandering tribesmen, is that they are as distinct as a European boundary; stepping out of the canoe one was in a different country. Even nature had changed; instead of forest and a rough winding road down which a car could, with some difficulty, go, a narrow path ran straight forward for mile after mile through tall treeless elephant grass. Along the hot wrinkled surface lay the skins of snakes. Natives came stooping up the path, bowed under green hammocks of palm-nuts; they looked like grasshoppers in a Silly Symphony. We walked for an hour and a half without coming to a village and at last turned back to Sierra Leone: The engineer said the path went straight down to the Coast by Conakry, and again one felt the happy sense of being free; one had only to follow a path far enough and one could cross a continent. Sweating in the hot dry day and growing cool again, one found it hard to believe that this part of Africa should have so unhealthy a reputation; one forgot C's sickness and the diseased villagers. I had not so much as heard a mosquito and the daily five grains of quinine seemed a waste of medicine.

But that was during the day; when it was dark, sitting in the engineer's bare bungalow and drinking warm beer, I wasn't so sure about the place. The man looked sixty; one had to explain somehow the fifteen years of white hair and lines he hadn't really lived. He said again how happy he was; he hadn't been able to settle in England, his wife was nervy, she had never been out with him, West Africa wouldn't suit her, she was afraid of moths, and as he spoke, the moths flocked in through the paneless windows to shrivel against the hurricane lamp, the cockchafers and the beetles detonated against the walls and ceiling and fell on our hair. He didn't mind insects himself, he said, leaping from his chair, hitting at the moths with his hand, squashing the beetles underfoot. (He couldn't keep still for a moment.) The only thing he feared, he said, was elephants. He had been watching a shoot once beside his motor-cycle when an elephant charged him; it was a hundred yards away and he couldn't start his cycle. When it was ten yards away he got his cycle started, and after a quarter of a mile at twenty miles an hour he looked back and saw that the elephant hadn't lost a yard. He got up from his chair again and made for a beetle, but it was too quick for him, driving up against the ceiling. He said he wasn't lonely, he didn't know what nerves were—bringing his hand against the wall—he always believed in having one hobby; the last tour it had been the wireless, another tour butterflies, this tour it was his car.

'Those things are so noisy,' he complained. 'They keep one awake at night.'

'Surely it's only the light that brings them in,' I said.

'Oh,' he said. 'I always leave a light burning at night,' and his eyes followed the beetles up and down the bare room. Somebody was playing something; the sound came all the way from the village: a kind of harp playing without melody, an endless repetition of notes.

He said, 'I'm sorry you are off tomorrow.' He said it so often that one couldn't doubt him, even though in the next breath he would explain that he wasn't lonely, that he liked the life.

I had sent off a messenger that morning with a letter to the Father Superior at the mission at Bolahun. The act of sending a letter by messenger a day's journey ahead into another country was pleasantly medieval. One paid the messenger nothing when he left; he met one somewhere on the road on his return journey, the road a foot-wide path through thick forest, crossed and recrossed by other paths. But the messengers never went astray; they were as reliable as the English Post Office. Once, when the message was urgent, I sent a man by night, giving him a fill of paraffin for his lamp, and with a dagger hanging over his shoulder he ran out into the dark bush, the letter stuck in a cleft stick.

It was January the twenty-sixth when we left for the Republic (snow in London, yellow fever in Freetown, mist over the burnt grasses at Kailahun). There was a road for another fifteen miles towards the border; I had ordered two lorries to call for myself and the German, who had brought carriers with him from the Republic, at seven o'clock. It was a twenty-mile march from the end of the road to the mission on the other side of the frontier and I was anxious to be there before dark. Nor had I any idea how long we might be held up at the Customs. Only one lorry turned up and it was an hour and a quarter late. The German doubted whether my cousin and I would reach Bolahun before night, for we had only one hammock and his aristocratic mind recoiled from the idea of walking with the men, from the stumbling and scrambling in the dust, and the tiredness. He himself had a chair slung on poles so that he could sit upright above the carriers. But I had to think of money; one couldn't have less than six carriers for a four-man hammock and by walking from Biedu I was saving seven and sixpence. We packed ourselves on the one small lorry; three whites, three boys, eleven carriers, and thirty loads, and drove unsteadily down the rough road through the thin morning mist. Great flattened thimbles of perpendicular rock rose above the dripping palms; we drove between.

I was vexed by the delay at Kailahun. I had not yet got accustomed to the idea that time, as a measured and recorded period, had been left behind on the coast. In the interior there was no such thing as time; the best watches couldn't stand the climate. Sooner or later they stopped. My own watch and my cousin's were the first to go, and afterwards, one by one, I used up the six cheap watches I had brought with me for 'dashes' from Marks and Spencer's. Only one reached the coast and it had long ceased to record the 'real' time; when it got dark I simply put the hands at six-thirty. If I wanted to get up earlier in the morning I put the hands on. Perhaps this was what Stanley had in mind when he heard Big Ben strike as he lay dying and exclaimed at the strangeness, 'So that is Time!'

But on the lorry from Kailahun I still believed that I could plan my journey by time-table. I thought that we were going to

Monrovia, the capital, straight from Bolahun and that we would be there within a fortnight; I would not have admitted the possibility that in four weeks we should be in a place I had never heard of, in the middle of the Republic, watching an old skinny woman who had made lightning in her village carry water back on her head to her fellow-prisoners in the horrible little gaol at Tapee-Ta.

For one thing I hadn't the money for so extended a journey. I had cashed the last of my credit at Freetown and carried with me about twenty-five pounds in shillings, sixpences and threepenny-bits. In a steel money-box with a padlock it made about half a man's load. It was no good taking anything but silver into the Republic, and I was to find curious objections here and there to the silver money I *had* brought. One tribe wouldn't look at money with Queen Victoria's head on it; the news of her death had penetrated to the most unlikely places, to places where I and my cousin were the first white people to be seen in living memory, and the value of the coins, they believed, had died with her. When we approached the coast, among the Bassa tribe, we found that nobody would accept the ordinary English silver stamped with a crown or acorns; they would only take the British West African coinage stamped with a palm tree. But this trouble was for the future; I was concerned only at the moment with time, with the need to get to Bolahun before dark. It was an unpractised traveller's anxiety; it led to unnecessary strain and my carriers' mistrust. Later I got used to not caring a damn, just to walking and staying put when I had walked far enough, at some village of which I didn't know the name, to letting myself drift with Africa.

TO THE FRONTIER

At Biedu the chief was waiting in the village with the carriers and an interpreter. I knocked the price down from one and sixpence a man to one and threepence, conscious of the faint cynical amusement of the German, who never paid more than sixpence. The loads were spread out down the centre of the village and for the first time I could see the full extent of the luggage we had brought with us: the six boxes of food, the two beds and chairs and mosquito-nets, three suitcases, a tent we were never to use, two boxes of miscellaneous things, a bath, a bundle of blankets, a folding table, a money-box, a hammock; I couldn't help being a little shamed by my servants, who each brought with them a small flat suitcase.

Later I tried to calculate how lightly a man could travel with safety for any length of time in the West African bush. I had spent more than fifty pounds on equipment and my invoices read like the list of goods supplied to an Everest expedition, but I do not think I could have cut down the loads by more than four with safety, for in West Africa there are strict limits to the lightness of travel, as the story of Dr D, a German botanist, suggests.

A week after I crossed the frontier Dr D died at Ganta in the Central Province, a town which I reached on February the fourteenth. His pathetic and dignified death, which was obviously deliberate, brought the world of Hitler, of Dachau and the concentration camps and Nazi self-righteousness even into this corner of Africa. Dr D had had forty years' experience of West Africa. Before the war he was German Consul in Monrovia and an agent for the Woermann Line, but he was already known at Hamburg University as a botanist. After the war he was the first German to reopen business in the Republic, but he failed, he left debts behind him, and the new Hitler's Germany to which he returned was not sympathetic to failure. He was seventy years old and a ruined man, and after forty years on the Coast he cannot have been at home among the swastika banners of Berlin, the Sunday processions with drums and bugles and bayonets under the Brandenburg Gate, the demonstrations at Tempelhof. He was interested in tropical flowers, he wasn't interested in who fired the Reichstag. Harvard University gave him a little money to return to the Republic and make a collection of botanical specimens in the interior. He found Hitler's Germany well established in Monrovia; the two enthusiastic Nazis there disapproved of Dr D. Hearing a rumour that he would be staying at the German Legation, they called on the Consul-General to protest, so that in those last days he was forced to find hospitality at an English store. There is no evidence of Dr D's intention, but it seems obvious that he had no wish to return to Europe and that he preferred to die in Africa. It is the only satisfactory explanation of his recklessness. For he went up from Monrovia through Bassa country to Sanoquelleh, ten days' trek, without a hammock, without provisions, without even a bed or a mosquito-net; he can hardly have travelled lighter when his body was brought down from Ganta for burial in the Lutheran Mission at Mühlenberg. He slept on native beds, ate the native food, and died of dysentery.

There are limits, then, to travelling light. A District Commissioner in Sierra Leone seldom travels with less than twenty-five carriers for himself alone, and for much shorter treks than ours proved to be, while at one time, after we had lost two men from sickness, we were travelling with twenty-three. At Biedu, with a four-man hammock for my cousin, I had to take twenty-five carriers. A journey of about twenty miles therefore cost a little more than thirty shillings. Travel in Africa, if carriers have to be hired by the day, is expensive. This was the experience in the Republic of Sir Alfred Sharpe, whose route I followed at the start. He was forced to take carriers from village to village, sometimes paying two sets of carriers in twenty-four hours at the fixed rate of a shilling a day. At most villages there would be delay in finding new carriers; all the men might be working on the farms; and often it was impossible to travel more than eight miles in a day. I learned from his experience and waited at Bolahun a week until I had engaged carriers willing to come with us all the way, and apart from the saving in wages I was able to average more than twelve miles a day over a period of four weeks.

The chief at Biedu gave me a chicken, I gave the chief a shilling. Souri, the cook, tied the chicken's legs together, Amedoo went down the line of loads testing the weights, the German sat down on his hammock chair, and 'Off!' I said. I felt like a subaltern facing my platoon for the first time. I couldn't really believe that when I said 'Off!' the twenty-five carriers would be set in motion. I stood back and watched them with an odd feeling of pleasure, an absurd sense of pride, when like a long mechanical toy they were set in motion and wavered and

straightened and strode out through the village on to a wide
track which narrowed soon into a path through the elephant
grass, into a tree-trunk over a stream, which wound into woods
and clearings and woods again, and at last after two hours
broadened out into a wide plateau which was the frontier; three
or four huts, a few riflemen in scarlet fezes with a gold device,
the Liberian flag (a star and stripes), and a little man with a
black moustache and a yellow skin and a worn topee who came
out into the clearing and greeted me with a shifty nervous jubi-
lant air as much as to say: we've got you here, 'leave no screws
unturned', plenty of tin for yours truly. He said, oh yes, he was
expecting me; he had been warned.

One couldn't help having, however unjustifiably, a sense of
the dramatic; the way forward through the clearing was as
broad as the primrose way, as open as a trap; the way back was
narrow, hidden, difficult, to the English scene.

THE WAY BACK

Rather more than two thousand miles away Major Grant was
probably buttonholing another friend. 'It's just how you look
at it,' he would say: 'the fellows are always bragging about
Paris, but I say England's good enough for me.' He used to visit
a brothel in Savile Row; there were scenes of luxurious aban-
donment in close proximity to the select tailors. He would ring
up on the phone and make an appointment, 'Three this afternoon,' then explain rather guardedly what he wanted, guardedly because you never knew when the police might listen in
and to procure a woman was a criminal offence. 'Young,' he
would say, 'mind it's young'; 'Fair or dark?' the maid would
say at the other end and sometimes Major Grant replied 'fair'
and sometimes 'dark', according as his passion urged him at
the moment towards his fair or dark angel. Then it was as well
to add a few details, 'Something rather lean,' and in another
mood, 'Curved but not too curved.' He didn't, he told me, find
the place very satisfactory; stop-girls and nursery-maids adding
a little to their wages on the slant were pitiably lacking in fi-
nesse. I think it was the theatre rather than the play which ex-
ercised its fascination over Major Grant; he liked the idea of

ordering a woman, as one might order a joint of meat, according to size and cut and price. There was a wealth of dissatisfaction in his indulgence; he knew the world, and all the time he took his revenge for the poor opinion he had of it. Presently he shifted his custom to an address in Hanover Street, and faded out of my knowledge, though occasionally the old voice came to me insinuatingly across the Corner House tables. 'Like a pig in a poke. That's what I enjoy. Never know what you are going to get.' 'And if they were not quite up to mark?' 'I take what comes,' the voice would say, 'I always accept 'em.'

'Having to construct something upon which to rejoice.'

Miss Kilvane lived in the Cotswolds in a strange high house like a Noah's ark with a monkey-puzzle tree and a step-ladder of terraces. The rooms were all tiny and of the same shape, like the rows of rooms in an advertising exhibition or in the brothel quarter of an eastern city. The rooms were packed with china ornaments, like Staffordshire and Woolworth pieces and Gross presents from Bournemouth. She was a follower of the Regency prophetess, Joanna Southcott, had a manuscript collection of her prophecies, two counterpanes the prophetess had made, seals and locks of hair and a Communion glass engraved with little ludicrous symbolical figures. She was old and innocent and terribly sure of herself; she took down Joanna's life from the ghost's lips. At tea a mouse ran backwards and forwards in a cupboard behind Miss Kilvane's back; I could see it moving through a crack, between the tins of rather dry biscuits. The old lady, with clear pale-blue eyes, wore an old-fashioned dress of faded mauve and horn-rimmed glasses; in the drawing-room there was a portrait of Joanna, china ornaments, antimacassars on horsehair chairs, a wireless set and a *Radio Times*. She spoke with complete confidence of the millennium which would come in the next fifty years; she described it in mundane detail. 'I have always wanted to see Jerusalem.' She showed me her volumes of manuscript, prophecies taken down by Joanna's servant, sometimes in doggerel verse. 'Impostors can copy the prose,' she said, 'but not the poetry. People go away and think they can write like that too. Gentlemen send me the strangest sensual verses.' She spent a long time looking for someone to publish her life of Joanna. She made her way down Paternoster Row and saw a publisher's office called Sion House; it really looked, she said, as if inspiration had brought her to the right place. She told a man behind a counter that she had brought the manuscript of Joanna's life and he went away and never came back. 'It's the worst snub I've ever received,' she said, but nothing could deter her. She was so innocent and in a way she was so worldly; she printed the life at her own expense; she founded a press to do it. Maori followers of Joanna sent her a motor-car, but she couldn't learn to drive it; it lay in a garage in the village. A pity; it would have been useful, for since the Lindbergh Baby Case (she kept her old clear horn-rimmed eyes sharply on the world) she had made the discovery that even babies could be 'sealed' for Joanna. Her companion was in the north at the time sealing babies. 'Isn't it beautiful?' she said, turning over the *Radio Times*. Before I left she sold me a pound of tea 'from my plantations'; she meant she had some shares in the company; she thought I would like it; the blend was very soothing. It was hot in the small shut rooms and the mice were restless. I climbed down the terraces to the road, past the monkey-puzzle tree, and she watched me go, perched up beside the Noah's ark with the lonely convictions she shared with the Maoris. She had been made to pay two hundred pounds for her relics; the printing press had passed out of her hands; but she had an immense conviction of success. 'They tell me the movement is making great progress in the Oxford colleges.'

Mr Charles Seitz was the son of a doctor. He was born in Bombay two years before the Mutiny and he died in 1933 frozen to death in a cottage on a bed of straw. He was the kind of figure that attracts legends. Even his real name was lost in common speech, so that he was known among the Campden villagers as Charlie Sykes, as he padded down the High Street bent double under a weight of incredible rags, clutching a tall stick, his bearded Apostle face bent to the pavement, his eyes flickering sideways, aware of everyone who passed. He was suspiciously like a stage madman; he played up to strangers, bellowing and shaking his stick, so that they edged away, a little daunted. Sometimes in summer he went berserk in the market-place, shouting and shaking all alone in a desert of indifference; no one took him seriously, least of all himself. He earned money from Americans with Kodaks, snapped picturesquely in front of the ancient butter market.

There were two rival stories of how his madness started. One was romantic, an unhappy love-affair. The other was probably the true one, that his brain gave way from overwork for a medical degree. Once an inhabitant of Campden spoke in his hearing of an operation; Charlie Sykes, beating his chest, described the operation in detail. That was how he would speak, gruffly and disconsolately, beating his chest. He had a grudge against God. 'There He is,' he said to me, 'up there. We think a lot about Him, but He doesn't think about us. He thinks about Himself. But we'll be up there one day and we won't let Him stay.'

He had an extraordinary vitality. There was a time when five men could not hold him, and once when two policemen tried to arrest him at Evesham for begging, he flung them both over a hedge. He walked several times a week into Evesham; it was eight miles each way by road, but he didn't go by road. He knew every gap in every hedge for miles around, and once two men camping in a field above Broadway woke up to see his face in the tent-opening. 'Naughty,' he said and disappeared.

He had banked several hundred pounds which he never touched. The only work he ever did, after his reason went, was cattle-droving. He begged, if that word can be applied to his friendly demands, 'Now, what about potatoes? Or a cabbage? Well then, turnips? What have you done with all that dough you had yesterday?' I never saw him in a shop, but on Friday mornings he toured the dustbins in the long High Street, turning over their contents in a critical unembarrassed way like a lady handling silk remnants on a bargain counter.

His cottage in Broad Campden had two rooms with one broken chair and a pile of straw in the corner and sixteen pairs of old shoes. He stopped a sweep in the village once and asked him to clean his chimney, repeating the one word, 'Shilling—shilling.' The sweep began to clean, but he couldn't finish, in the airless room and the appalling stench. But the stench didn't keep out the cold of a hard winter, and when a policeman broke in because no smoke had been seen from the chimney, he found Mr Charles Seitz frozen to death on his straw in the upper room. They didn't care to undress him; he was so verminous that the fleas jumped on them from his wrists; they put round his shoulders the web with which coffins are lowered into the grave, and dragged him head first down the stairs. Then they crammed him quickly into his coffin, rags and all, and nailed him down. It was terrible weather for grave-diggers, the ground hard enough for an electric drill six inches down.

Major Grant said with relish that the shabbiest adventure he had ever had was in a flat off the Strand with two bawds. They wouldn't give him change for his note or give him his note back; it was only a question of ten shillings, but he suddenly grew tired of being cheated; he had made a bargain and he'd stick to it. He sat on the bed and wouldn't leave the flat; they threatened him and badgered him, but he wouldn't move; through a crack in the blind he could see the flame and flicker of the Strand reflected in the windows of a winehouse. They gave in and he went home.

Buckland digging in the garden turned up a she-mandrake. He said that it was good for cows and pigs to keep them in con-dition; he put some snails on one side to take home for his sup-per. Buckland was a didicoi, which was the name they gave in Gloucestershire to gipsies. He had run away from home when he was a boy and walked for two days without food; then he stole a loaf from a baker's van and ate it behind a hedge. The next day he got a job at a dairy farm. The farmer asked him whether he could milk a cow; he said yes, and the other men milked his cow for him, until he'd learnt to do it for himself, and the farmer never knew.

On either side of the Ridge Way the fields were being har-rowed, the horses disappeared over the swell of the down, the men singing in the pale autumn sunlight. Once when one of them came parallel with the other, he called out: 'Old Molly George has a night out tonight.' A flock of crows was picking at the turf beside the White Horse. A man was ploughing in a cup of land so far below that he was the size of a grain of oats; the brown-turned earth grew in size, the olive-coloured unturned earth diminished until there was only a thin lozenge in the middle of the field. The crows were flat below, wheeling in mid-air at the height of a cathedral spire. The man sang as he ploughed, his voice as loud as a gramophone in the next room, but I could only catch one word—'angels'. When the lozenge disappeared, I could see him lead his horse to the hedge and a thin fume of smoke came up but dispersed long before it reached me. He was burning weeds.

It was winter now, snow in London, the fierce noon sun on the clearing, yellow fever in Freetown, behind on the way to the Coast the mist was rising from the forest, drifting slowly upwards, like the smoke of burning weeds below the Ridge Way. We turned away from Major Grant and Miss Kilvane, from the peace under the down and the flat off the Strand, from the holy and the depraved individualists to the old, the unfamiliar, the communal life beyond the clearing.

PART TWO

Western Liberia

THE FOREST EDGE

It was midday. We followed the Customs man into a thatched shelter, sat on high uncomfortable drawing-room chairs and smoked: the little yellow man sat opposite us in a hammock and smoked too, swinging back and forth. I smiled at him and he smiled back; they were surface smiles; there was no friendliness anywhere. The man was thinking how much he could exact. I with how little loss I could escape. A woman brought in a child to see the white people and it screamed and screamed uncontrollably. The men of the Frontier Force lounged and spat in the vertical sunrays, and one could almost see the brown earth cracking. I began a second cigarette.

Then Laminah burst in, a small detonating bomb of fury in the stillness, the doing nothing. He was like a Pekinese who has been insulted by an Alsatian. Somebody had told him he must pay duty on his white barber's jacket which had a rubber lining. The Customs officer surrendered the point with courtesy, but it seemed to be the signal for the fun to start. I produced my invoices, the German opened a small suitcase and paid half a crown; the officer was in a hurry to get on to bigger game, and the German passed out of the frontier station bobbing above the heads of his carriers. The officer settled to work on the invoices and the soldiers spat and grinned and passed remarks and I wiped off the sweat.

'This will take all day,' the Customs man said. 'Everything here except the tin of Epsom salts, the quinine and the iodine has got to pay duty.' He explained that he would let me go through to Bolahun if I left a deposit; any change would be sent after me; he calculated that four pounds ten would be sufficient guarantee. I extracted a bag of sixpenny-bits from the money-box without disclosing the automatic. But it wasn't quite the end. I had to pay two cents each for the eight forms on which my dutiable goods were to be set down in detail. I had to pay for two Revenue stamps, and I had to sign my name at the bottom of the eight blank sheets saying that the items listed above were correct. I was completely in their power; they could fill up anything they liked on the forms. The alternative was to stay where I was for the night and have all my bags and bales opened.

As it was I didn't escape so easily. The next day he sent a soldier over to Bolahun demanding another six pounds ten, and when the soldier went back empty-handed, he came himself, borne in a hammock on the long rough path from Foya with four carriers and a couple of soldiers, a dirty white topee on his head and a ragged cigarette in the corner of his mouth. He swaggered across the verandah, a little sour, mean, avaricious figure, grinning and friendly and furious and determined. He got his money, drank two glasses of whisky, smoked two cigarettes; there was nothing one could do about it; it was impossible to bribe an official who probably took a lion's share anyway of what he exacted.

I enjoyed the first day's trek into the Republic because everything was new: the sense of racing the dark, even the taste of warm boiled water, the smell of the carriers; it wasn't an unpleasant smell, sweet or sour; it was bitter, and reminded me of a breakfast food I had as a child after pleurisy, something vigorous and body-building which I disliked. This bitter taint was mixed with the rich plummy smell of the kola nuts the carriers picked from the ground and chewed, with an occasional flower scent one couldn't trace in the thick untidy greenery. All the smells were drawn out, as the heat increased, like vapour from moist ground. The carriers walked naked except for loin-cloths, the sweat leaving marks like snails on their black polished skins. They didn't look strong, they hadn't the ugly muscular development of a boxer; their legs were as thin as a woman's, but they ended in typical carrier's feet, flat like enormous empty gloves, spreading on the earth pancake-wise as if the weights they carried had pressed them out in a *peine forte et dure*. Even their arms were childishly thin, and when they raised the fifty-pound cases a few inches to ease their skulls, the muscles hardly swelled, were no thicker than whipcord.

We were on the edge of the immense forest which covers the Republic to within a few miles of the coast; we climbed steeply from the frontier post at Foya and from the first village we came to we could see the bush below the huts, falling away, a ragged cascade, towards the sea, lifting and falling and swelling into green plains; hundreds of miles of them, tall palms sticking out above the rest like the brushes of chimney sweeps. The huts here, and in all the Bande territory, were circular with a pointed thatched roof overhanging the parti-coloured mud walls, white-washed halfway up. There was one door and sometimes a window; in the middle of the floor were the ashes of a fire which would be lit again at sunset from a communal ember and fill the single room with smoke; the fumes kept out mosquitoes, kept out, to some extent, the fleas and bugs and cockroaches, but not the rats. They were all much alike, these villages, built on a hill-top on several levels like medieval towns; the path one had followed through the bush would drop steeply to a stream where the villagers came to wash their clothes and bathe, then rise abruptly up a wide beaten track out of the shade to a sil-houette of pointed huts against the midday glare. The ground in the villages was scarred by the dry beds of streams. In the centre was the palaver-house and at the limit of the village the blacksmith's forge, both open huts without walls.

But though nearly all the villages at which I stayed had these common properties—a hill, a stream, palaver-house and forge, the burning ember carried round at dark, the cows and goats standing between the huts, the little grove of banana-trees like clusters of tall green feathers gathering dust—not one was quite the same. However tired I became of the seven-hour trek through the untidy and unbeautiful forest, I never wearied of the villages in which I spent the night: the sense of a small courageous community barely existing above the desert of trees, hemmed in by a sun too fierce to work under and a darkness filled with evil spirits—love was an arm round the neck, a cramped embrace in the smoke, wealth a little pile of palmnuts, old age sores and leprosy, religion a few stones in the centre of the village where the dead chiefs lay, a grove of trees where the rice-birds, like yellow and green canaries, built their nests, a man in a mask with the raffia skirts dancing at burials. This never varied, only their kindness to strangers, the extent of their poverty and the immediacy of their terrors. Their laughter and their happiness seemed the most courageous things in nature. Love, it has been said, was invented in Europe by the troubadours, but it existed here without the trappings of civilization. They were tender towards their children (I seldom heard a crying child, unless at the sight of a white face, and never saw one beaten), they were tender towards each other in a gentle muffled way; they didn't scream or 'rag', they never revealed the rasped nerves of the European poor in shrill speech or sudden blows. One was aware the whole time of a standard of courtesy to which it was one's responsibility to conform.

And these were the people one had been told by the twisters, the commercial agents, on the Coast that one couldn't trust. 'A black will always do you down.' It was no good protesting later that one had not come across a single example of dishonesty from the boys, from the carriers, from the natives in the interior: only gentleness, kindness, an honesty which one would not have found, or at least dared to assume was there, in Europe. It astonished me that I was able to travel through an unpoliced country with twenty-five men who knew that my money-box contained what to them was a fortune in silver. We were not in British or French territory now: it wouldn't have mattered to the black Government on the Coast if we had disappeared and they could have done little about it anyway. We couldn't even count as armed; the automatic was hidden in the money-box, never loaded, never seen; it would have been easy when we were crossing one of the fibre bridges to stage an accident; it would have been easy, less drastically, simply to mislay the money-box or to lose us in the bush.

But 'Poor fool,' one could tell the Coast whites were thinking, 'he just didn't know how he was being done.' But I wasn't 'done'; there wasn't an instance of even the most petty theft, though in every village the natives swarmed into the hut where all day my things were lying about, soap (to them very precious), razor, brushes. 'You can have a boy for ten years,' they'd say, 'and he'll do you at the end of it,' and laying down their empty glasses they'd go out into the glaring street and down to the store to see whom they could 'do' in the proper understood commercial way that morning. 'No affection,' they'd say, 'after fifteen years. Not a scrap of real affection,' expecting always to get from these people more than what they had paid for. They had paid for service and they expected love thrown in.

I had hoped to reach the mission at five o'clock; but five o'clock brought us only to another hill, another group of huts and stones, and the forest thick below. The balls of cotton were laid outside the huts to dry and a small tree ruffled a pale pink blossom against the sky. Somebody pointed out the mission, a white building which the low sun picked out of the forest. It was at least two hours away, and the journey became more than ever a race against the dark, which the dark nearly won. It came down on us just as we left the forest and wound through the banana plantation at the foot of Mosambolahun, and it was quite dark and cold as we passed between the huts, the old cook flitting ahead in his long white Mohammedan robe, carrying a trussed chicken. All the fires had been lit in the huts and the smoke blew across the narrow paths stinging the eye; but the little flames were like home; they were the African equivalent of the lights behind red blinds in English villages. There must have been nearly two hundred huts on Mosambolahun, packed together on a thimble of rock, and it stood apart in its remote pagan dirt from the neat Christianized garden village of Bolahun in the cleared plain below. A wide flattened path ran down across the plain to Bolahun and a swaying hammock came up it and a little noisy group of men. The hammock stopped at my side and an old, old man in a robe of native cloth with a long white beard put out a hand. It was the chief of Mosambolahun; ninety years old, he quivered and shook and smiled while his people chattered round him. He couldn't

speak any English, but a boy with a gun whom I found at my
side told me that the chief was on his way home from Tailahun,
where a brother chief had died. He was swept away again by
his impatient hammock-bearers, waving his dried old hand,
smiling gently, curiously, quizzically. He was the explanation, I
later learnt, of Mosambolahun's dirt; he was a puppet of the
younger men, without authority. He had about two hundred
wives, but they would sell him the same wife over and over
again; he was too old to keep count. He knew that he was too
old, he wanted to retire for a younger man, but it didn't suit his
lawless village to lose their puppet. When he became importu-
nate they told him they had made him a bishop, and that
pleased and quieted him.

It was a two-mile walk up to the mission through the village
of Bolahun, through the deep barking of the frogs. The mission
belonged to the Order of the Holy Cross, a monastic order of
the American Episcopal Church. I dumped my loads outside
the long bungalow and waited for the priests to come out from
Benediction. I could hear the low murmur of Latin inside; in
the darkness only the white eyeballs of my carriers were visible,
where they squatted silent on the verandah; everyone was too
tired to talk. But the sound of the Latin represented a better
civilization than the tin shacks of the English port, better than
anything I had seen in Sierra Leone; and when the priests came
out and one led the way to the rest-house, his white robe stirring in the cold hill wind, I was for the first time unashamed by
the comparison between white and black. There was something in this corner of a republic said to be a byword for corruption and slavery that at least wasn't commercial. One couldn't
put it higher than this: that the little group of priests and nuns
had a standard of gentleness and honesty equal to the native
standard. Whether what they brought with them in the shape
of a crucified God was superior to the local fetish worship had
to be the subject of future speculation.

That night, as the filter dripped and dripped in the bare rest-
house living-room, after the carriers had been paid off and the
case of whisky opened, I went outside to find the sick C's partner, Van Gogh. For the prospector's tent was just outside and a

hurricane lamp was burning. 'Van Gogh,' the priest had said, 'you'll like Van Gogh,' and seeing a syphon standing on the boxes by the tent, I thought that I would invite him to bring his soda over for a drink. I raised the flap and there Van Gogh was, lying wrapped in blankets on his camp-bed; I thought he was asleep, but when he turned his head I saw that he was sweating; the pale golden stubble of his chin was drenched in sweat. Five hours before he had gone down with fever, and all that night the German doctor attached to the mission sat up with him. He was bad, very bad; he had spent a lifetime in the tropics, but nine months in the Republic had got him down. Next day they took him to the little mission hospital in our hammock; the boys from his gold-camp in the Gola forest came and packed up his tent and goods and carried him down, sick and swaying under the blazing sun.

SUNDAY IN BOLAHUN

It was Sunday in Bolahun, unmistakably Sunday. A herdsman drove out his goats among absurdly Biblical rocks, a bell went for early service, and I saw the five nuns going down in single file to the village through the banana plantations in veils and white sun-helmets carrying prayer-books. They were English; tea with them (a large fruit cake and home-made marmalade and chocolate biscuits wilting in the heat and delicious indigestible bread made with palm wine instead of yeast) was very like tea in an English cathedral town; it was an English corner one could feel some pride in: it was gentle, devout, childlike and unselfish, it didn't even know it was courageous. One couldn't help comparing the manner of these nuns living quite outside the limits of European protection with that of the English in Freetown who had electric light and refrigerators and frequent leave, who despised the natives and pitied themselves.

A great deal of nonsense has been written about missionaries. When they have not been described as the servants of imperialists or commercial exploiters, they have been regarded as sexually abnormal types who are trying to convert a simple happy pagan people to a European religion and stunt them with European repressions. It seems to be forgotten that

Christianity is an Eastern religion to which Western pagans
have been quite successfully converted. Missionaries are not
even given credit for logic, for if one believes in Christianity at
all, one must believe in its universal validity. A Christian cannot believe in one God for Europe and another God for Africa:
the importance of Semitic religion was that it did not recognize
one God for the East and another for the West. The new paganism of the West, which prides itself on being scientific, is often peculiarly neurotic. Only a neurosis explains its sentimental
lack of consistency, the acceptance of the historic duty of the
Mohammedan to spread his faith by the sword and the failure
to accept the duty of a Christian to spread his faith by teaching.

The missions in the interior of the Republic are, of course,
peculiar in being completely free from political or commercial
contacts. The black Government distrusts them and no European firm has any trading posts in the Liberian hinterland.
Faith in their religion is the only thing which can have induced
American monks and English nuns to settle at Bolahun. There
is no drama to compensate them for the fever, the worms and
the rats; the only danger is the danger of snake-bite or disease.
They are not ascetics, who find satisfaction in cords and hair-
shirts; they have done their best, once settled in Bolahun, to
make themselves comfortable. The fathers have built a little
hospital, they get their chop boxes from Fortnum and Mason,
wine comes in over the French border, vegetables once a month
from Sierra Leone; they have even built a kind of rough hard
court for tennis. They haven't forced Christianity on an unwill-
ing people, they haven't made a happy naked race wear clothes,
they haven't stopped the native dances. The native in West
Africa will always wear clothes if he has the money to buy
them, he will always prefer a robe to a loin-cloth, and to anyone who has spent much time in the bush villages the roughest
native robe will appear aesthetically preferable to the human
body—the wrinkled dugs, the running sores. As for the dances
and the fetish worship, the missionaries have not the power to
stop them if they wished to; Christianity here has its back to
the wall. Converts are comparatively few; there is no material
advantage in being converted; the only advantage is a spiritual

one, of being released from a few fears, of being offered an in-
substantial hope.

And in Bolahun particularly there were material disadvan-
tages in Christianity. No white man is allowed to own land in
the Republic, the missions are at the mercy of the Government,
and nine miles away at Kolahun lived Mr Reeves, the District
Commissioner. Mr Reeves was a Vai, a Mohammedan; he belonged, psychologically, to the early nineteenth century, to the
days of the slave trade. He hated Christians, he hated white
men, especially he hated the English language. With his seal-
grey skin, dark expressionless eyes, full deep red lips, dressed in
a fez and a robe of native cloth, he gave an effect, more Oriental than African, of cruelty and sensuality; he was gross, impassive and corrupt. His wife was a Miss Barclay, a member of
the President's household, and it was said among the natives
that when he was appointed the President promised him that
he would be a District Commissioner forever. He was sent first
to Sanoquelleh at the other end of the country and an unpleasant story had followed him to Kolahun, a story of some
Mandingo traders whom he was said to have caught smuggling
goods over the border from French territory, and to have shut
in a hut and burned to death. It was impossible in the Republic
to investigate a tale like that, but there were other stories of
cruelty and despotism for which I found plenty of evidence:
stories of his house built by forced labour and paid for by the
seizure of the natives' produce; stories of how his messengers
flogged the men working on the road, how no man from Christianized Bolahun dared show his face in the town. The nuns
one day had seen him pass hurriedly by in a hammock, his messengers whipping the carriers on. So many stories leaked down
to Monrovia that even a Government separated by ten days'
rough trekking was forced to take notice, and the President
was on his way, at this very time, to Kolahun to listen to the
chiefs' complaints.

One had to remember that background to Benediction in the
little ugly tin-roofed church. The raised monstrance was not a
powerful political symbol: 'Come unto me all ye who are heavy
laden and I will give you commercial privileges and will

whisper for you in the ear of a Minister of State.' It offered, like early Christianity, stripes from the man in power and one knows not what secret oppression from the priests of the fetish. There were not many at Benediction: Christianity here was still the revolutionary force, appealing to the young rather than the old, and the young were on holiday. A tiny piccaninny wearing nothing but a short transparent shirt scratched and prayed, lifting his shirt above his shoulders to scratch his loins better; a one-armed boy knelt below a hideous varnished picture. (He had fallen from a palm-tree gathering nuts, had broken his arm, and feeling its limp uselessness had taken a knife and cut it off at the elbow.)

A CHIEF'S FUNERAL

A few days after our arrival Amedoo fell ill. All through the night I heard his racking cough, and in the morning the German doctor examined him and found one lung affected. He lay on the doctor's couch dumb with terror, but he agreed to go into the hospital; he was frightened, but he was still the perfect servant. His illness introduced me to Mark. Mark was a Christian schoolboy; he came down from the mission to help Laminah and the cook; he was dirty and lazy, but he was amusing. He had a great sense of drama and a high neighing laugh; he soaked up gossip like a sponge, and he had this characteristic in common with white boys of his age, that he was the hero of imaginary adventures.

On the fourth morning early, there was a stir in the village below, a blowing of horns which faded slowly on the northward road. Long before anyone else Mark knew what had happened and he told it with malicious glee because he hated Reeves. Reeves with the chiefs had gone down to the limit of the road to meet the President, but the President had slipped quietly up by other paths to Kolahun and arrived at an empty compound: the horns and the shouts were Reeves's party returning as quickly as they could to Kolahun. So I sent Mark off with a letter to the President asking for an interview, and while I and my cousin sat at supper, Mark dramatically returned, bursting in at the door, holding himself poised at the entrance with his hand raised, before he delivered the reply, stuck in a cleft stick, that the President had already moved on from Kolahun to Voinjema. You could tell that he was dramatizing the whole affair, he had persuaded himself that he had escaped by the skin of his teeth from the wicked DC.

Mark, because he was a Bande and could speak English, acted as my guide round Bolahun. A chief had died at Tailahun two miles away and Mark led us over to the village to see what we could of the funeral ceremonies. It was a tiny place perched on an uneven rock mound. The grave was in the centre of the village among the flat stones which marked the other graves; a mat was spread on it, and a middle-aged woman sat there, the youngest mother among the chief's wives. She was shielded from the sun by a roof of palm branches, and a pile of fuel and a cooking-pot stood there at the spirit's disposal. Christianity and paganism both marked the dead man's grave, for there was a rough cross stuck on the mount to propitiate the God whom the old chief had accepted on his deathbed, while in a pit close by, following a pagan rite, sat eight wives, naked except for a loin cloth. Other women were smearing them with clay; it was rubbed even into their hair. The majority were old and hideous anyway, but now, in the pale colour of the pit in which they sat, they looked as if they had been torn half decomposed from the ground. They had lost with their colour their mark of race and might have been women of any nation who had been buried and dug up again. There was pathos in the bareness of these symbols, the cross, the clay, the youngest mother. One felt that two religions here were appealing on the simplest terms: splendour and the big battalions were on neither side. There must have been scenes very like this, I thought, in the last days of pagan England, when a story about a bird flying through a lighted hall into the dark played its part in the conversion of a king.

It was the third day after the burial. The next day the women would wash off the clay, oil their bodies and be free again, there would be dancing for three days on end, and again at the end of forty days. The girls were getting their hair frizzed out for the funeral dances instead of wearing it in the usual way gummed down in a neat pattern of ridge and parting. The local 'devil', Landow, from Mosambolahun, had entered the village for the funeral, and it was really to see him dance that I was there. I had caught one glimpse of him at dusk in Bolahun striding by in his long raffia skirts and his wooden snouted mask. From each village on the way he collected irons, for on entering Tailahun he must pay the new chief a tribute of several bundles.

The new chief dozed in his hammock in the tiny palaver-house. I dashed him two shillings; it was the heat of the day, and he was bored and embarrassed by the visit. Two chairs were fetched for us, and about thirty people crowded into the cramped hut; the insects were hopping on the floor. Presently two men with long drums arrived; dangling below each drum a metal disc. They wore red caps with gold stars on them and a long tassel very like the caps of the Frontier Force I had seen at Foya. They stamped their bare feet among the jiggers and tapped their drums and metal discs with little curved hammers. More musicians slowly gathered in the cramped hot hut at the sound of the drums. Three women came with varying sizes of rattles— gourds containing grains of rice which they shook in nets, and a man with a harp of five strings made of palm fibre, attached to half a gourd which he pressed to his breast (the faint sweet twanging could only be heard when the drums and rattles were still). Last came a man with an ordinary big drum, which did give a kind of sexual urgency to a music hard for a European to understand. The music was continually mounting to a climax as the drummers beat their feet and sweated and the women rattled and swayed, but nothing ever happened. It seemed only one more meaningless climax when the devil at last appeared.

'THE LIBERIAN DEVILS'

I call him 'devil' because it is the word most commonly used among the whites and English-speaking natives in the Repub-lic. It is no more misleading, I think, than the word 'priest' which is sometimes used elsewhere. A masked devil like Landow (of what are known as the Big Bush Devils I shall have some-thing to say later) might roughly be described as a headmaster with rather more supernatural authority than Arnold of Rugby ever claimed. Even in the Sierra Leone Protectorate, where there are many missionary schools, most natives, if they are not Mohammedan, will attend a bush school, of which the masked devil is the unknown head. Even the Christian natives attend; Mark had attended, though the Christians are usually favoured with a shortened course because they cannot be fully trusted with the secrets of a bush school. And the bush schools are very secret. All the way through the great forest of the interior one comes on signs of them: a row of curiously cropped trees before a narrow path disappearing into the thickest bush: a stockade of plaited palms: indications that no stranger may penetrate there. No natives, girls or boys, are considered mature till they have passed through the bush schools, and the course in the old days lasted as long in some tribes as seven years, though now two years is the more usual period. There are no holidays; the children are confined to the bush; if a child dies his belongings are deposited outside his parents' hut at night as a sign that he is dead, and he is buried in the bush. When the children emerge again they are supposed to be born anew, they are not allowed to recognize their parents and friends in the village until they have been introduced to them again. One definite mark they bear with them from the bush, the mark of 'tattooing'. The tattooing varies with the tribes: in some tribes a woman's body from the neck to the navel is elaborately and beautifully carved. 'Carved' is a better word than 'tattooed' to convey the effect, for tattooing to a European means a coloured pattern priced on the skin, but the native tattoo marks are ridged patterns cut in the flesh with a knife.

The school and the devil who rules over it are at first a terror to the child. It lies as grimly as a public school in England between childhood and manhood. He has seen the masked devil and has been told of his supernatural power; no human part of the devil is allowed to show, according to Dr Westermann, because it might be contaminated by the presence of the uninitiated, but it seems likely also because the unveiled power might do harm; for the same reason no one outside the school may see the devil unmasked for fear of blindness or death. Even though the initiates of his particular school, who have seen, as it were, the devil in his off-moments, know him to be, say, the local blacksmith, some supernatural feeling continues to surround him. It is not the mask which is sacred, nor the blacksmith who is sacred; it is the two in conjunction, but a faint aura of the supernatural continues to dwell in either part when they are separate: so the blacksmith will have more power in his village than the chief, and the mask may continue to be reverenced, even when discarded, and fed by its owner like a fetish.

Mark, when I knew him better, told me a little of his own experience. As a Christian boy he spent only a fortnight in the bush, and all he did, he said, was to sit and eat rice. He was in the mission school one day when the devil, this same Landow, came for him. There had been no warning. His teacher told him not to be afraid, but the devil, through his interpreter (for the devil does not speak a language the native can understand), said, 'I'm going to swallow you.' He was not allowed to go home first; he was bound hand and foot and his eyes were bandaged and he was carried into the bush. He was very scared. Then they flung him on the ground and cut him with a razor, but he said it didn't hurt much. They made two little ridges on his neck, two under the armpit, two on the belly. I asked him if he was beaten, for Dr Westermann, writing of the Pelle tribe in Liberia, has described a kind of Spartan training. He said he was beaten once: one day the devil told the boys they were not to go outside their huts all day whatever they heard; of course they disobeyed and were beaten. At the end of a fortnight he was dressed in white clothes and taken back to the village in the dark. He admitted at last rather reluctantly that the devil, who didn't wear his mask in the school, was the blacksmith at Mosambolahun: so perhaps they were wise to teach him nothing, but just to let him sit and eat rice for a fortnight. In any case they are easy-going, lazy, not very religious in Bande country. It was to be different among the Buzies.

THE MASKED BLACKSMITH

It was the blacksmith of Mosambolahun then who now swayed forward between the huts in a head-dress of feathers, a heavy blanket robe, and long raffia mane and raffia skirts. The big drum beat, the heels stamped and the gourds rattled, and the devil sank to the ground, his long faded yellow hair billowing in the dust. His two eyes were two painted rings and he had a flat black wooden snout a yard long fringed with fur; when it opened one saw great red wooden tusks. His black wooden nose stuck up at right angles between his eyes which were almost flat on his snout. His mouth opened and closed like a clapper and he spoke in a low monotonous sing-sing. He was like a portmanteau word; an animal, a bird and a man had all run together to form his image. All the women, except the musicians, had gone to their huts and watched Landow from a distance. His interpreter squatted beside him carrying a brush with which, when the devil moved, he kept his skirts carefully smoothed down lest a foot or arm should show.

The devils need an interpreter because they do not speak a language the native can understand. Landow's mutterings were fluent and quite unintelligible. Anthropologists, so far as I can gather, have not made up their minds whether it is a real language the devil speaks or whether the interpreter simply invents a meaning. Mark's explanation has the virtue of simplicity, that the Bande devil speaks Pessi, that the Pessi devil speaks Buzie; the Buzie devil, on the other hand, he continued with a convincing lack of consistency, spoke Buzie, but in so low a tone that no one could follow him.

The devil was paying his respects to the chief and to the strangers, so the interpreter explained in Bande, and was ready to dance for them. There was an uneasy pause while I wondered with the embarrassment of a man in a strange restaurant whether I had enough in my pocket. But a dash of a shilling was sufficient and the devil danced. It was not so accomplished a dance as we saw later by a devil belonging to a woman's society in Buzie country; the lack of religious enthusiasm in the Bande tribe, if it allows them to lead an easier life, less under the fear of poisoning, diminishes their artistic talent. Vitality was about the only quality one could allow Landow; he lashed a small whip; he twirled like a top; he ran up and down be-

tween the huts with long sliding steps, his skirts raising the dust
and giving his progress an appearance of immense speed. His
interpreter did his best to keep up with him, brushing him
when he was within reach. The spirit was definitely carnival; no
one above the age of childhood was really scared of Landow;
they had all passed through his school, and one suspected that
the blacksmith of Mosambolahun, the slack grimy town, had
not maintained very carefully his unmasked authority. He was
a 'good fellow', one felt, and like so many good fellows he went
on much too long: he would sit on the ground and mutter, then
run up and down a bit and sit down again. He was a bore as he
played on and on in the blistering afternoon sun, hoping for
another dash, which I simply hadn't got with me. One woman
ran up and flung down two irons and ran away again, and he
cracked his whip and raced and turned and spun. The villagers
stood in the background smiling discreetly; it was a carnival,
but it wasn't a carnival in the vulgar sense of Nice and the Bat-
tle of Flowers; it wasn't secular and skittish; like the dancing in
the Spanish cathedral at Easter, it had its religious value.

I remembered a Jack-in-the-Green I had seen when I was
four years old, quite covered except for his face in leaves, wearing a kind of diving-suit of leaves and twirling round and
round at a country crossroads, far from any village, with only
a little knot of attendants and a few bicyclists to watch him.
That as late as the ninth century in England had religious significance, the dance was part of the rites celebrating the death
of winter and the return of spring, and here in Liberia again
and again one caught hints of what it was we had developed
from. It wasn't so alien to us, this masked dance (in England
too there was a time when men dressed as animals and danced),
any more than the cross and the pagan emblems on the grave
were alien. One had the sensation of having come home, for
here one was finding associations with a personal and a racial
childhood, one was being scared by the same old witches. They
brought a screaming child up to the devil and thrust him under
the devil's muzzle, under the dusty raffia mane; he stiffened and
screamed and tried to escape and the devil mouthed him. The
older generation were playing the same old joke they had

played for centuries, of frightening the child with what had frightened them. I went away but looking back I saw a young girl dancing before Landow, dancing with the sad erotic appeal of projecting buttocks and moving belly; she at least didn't know it was the blacksmith of Mosambolahun as she danced like Europa before the bull, and the old black wooden muzzle rested on the earth and the eyes of the blacksmith watched her through the flat painted rims.

MUSIC AT NIGHT

That night Gissi, a Buzie man, came up to play the harp. A row of black heads lined the verandah, while he sat with dangling legs picking out of the palm fibres light melancholy monotonous music, beautifully superficial music which just tickled the surface of the mind, didn't tiresomely claim any deep emotion whether of grief or exaltation, the claim which fixes strained masks on the faces in a concert hall. This was the music of a cigarette-box; it was sad, but it didn't really care, everything would always be the same. The little recurring notes plucked with four nails died out and began again unvaried against the night, the black faces, the hurricane lamp and the moths that drove by in swarms to shrivel their wings against it. Mark shovelled them from the table in handfuls, and Gissi didn't watch his harp or his fingers or his friends; he looked away smiling gently at the hopping wingless moths. He was not a handsome man, he was beautiful as a woman can be beautiful, without effeminacy. His round skull and tiny ears, projecting lower lip and long curling eyelashes had nothing in common with the buck negro type, who represents Africa to the European lounging round the bars off Leicester Square, beating the piano in dance orchestras. His chin was very gently moulded, his hair fitted his head like a skull-cap; he was more Grecian than African, early Grecian before the decadence. He wore an elephant-hide bracelet and a silver ring.

The goat-herd came and danced, stamping and flinging out his arms, and one by one the men came out of the dark on to the verandah, into the lamp-light, hurling themselves this way and that, sending the shadows flying from their arms and legs.

Their faces were strange but soon they were to become familiar, for these were the labourers whom Vande, my newly-
appointed headman, had found for me, to carry fifty-pound
weights for four weeks on end, for three shillings a week and
their food. It sounded to a stranger next door to slave labour,
but these were not slaves stamping up and down with a controlled wildness and an unconscious grace. There was Amah,
my second headman, a tall sullen humourless Mandingo with a
shaven head in a long blue and white robe; there was Babu, a
Buzie man like Gissi with the same delicate cultured features, the
features of a tribe sensitive to art and fear, weavers of exquisite
cloth, in touch more than any tribe with the super-natural,
makers of lightning, poisoners; Fadai, a gentle-mannered boy
from Sierra Leone with soft sad eyes, infected with yaws; there
was one-eyed shaven shifty Vande Two.

They didn't speak a word as they swayed and stamped; each
improvised, dancing alone with no reference to the others; it
was only the music and the shadows which lent them unity. I
was to see these improvised dances again and again during the
long trek. The slightest hint of a tune would set them off; if
there was no music someone would tap a twig on an empty tin.
They were more easy to appreciate than the communal dances.
They had obvious dramatic qualities and one could see hidden
under the personal idiosyncrasies the germ of the Charleston.
But to the native, I suppose, the communal dance was on a
higher, more subtle level; only one hadn't oneself got a clue to
their appreciation. I saw such a dance in the village. A band of
youths with drums chanted an air, while about seven boys shuf-
fled in a small circle with their hands at their sides, one foot
forward, the other brought up beside it, then forward again.
Presently three girls joined them and the circle became smaller
than ever: a girl's nipples bulged against the back in front, her
buttocks were pressed by the girl behind. Round and round
they went to the monotonous beat, a snake eating its own tail.

That night of dancing on the verandah was specially memo-
rable because it was the last at Bolahun. The next day the real
journey was going to begin. Amedoo had returned from hospi-

tal; even Van Gogh, pale as a ghost under his bleached gold stubble, a curiously intellectual sensitive face for a prospector (he treated the natives with a harsh lack of consideration one would never have guessed existed behind the horn-rimmed glasses), had staggered over for a cup of tea. Long study of the manuscript maps the Dutch prospectors had made of the Western province, consultations with the German linguist, had decided us to take a different and longer route. I wanted to deliver my letter to Chief Nimley, and so I planned to walk down to Sinoe and Nana Kru, first striking along the northern border to Ganta, where an American medical missionary, Dr Harley, might be expected to know something of the route. Nobody in Bolahun had been so far as Ganta, but the German doctor at the hospital had been to Zigita, and there one might expect to get more information. The fathers with a saintly trust in human nature cashed my cheque for £40 in small silver on a trading firm in Monrovia and sold me two hammocks which could be carried by two men apiece. With these light hammocks I hoped to economize in men and time.

The first stop, so at first it was decided, was to be Pandemai, and I sent off two carriers ahead to warn the chief, but as we talked at tea, the distance to Pandemai seemed to increase while the kindness one might look for from the chief in Kpangblamai became more desirable. The truth was, I couldn't help being a little scared. I wanted to break the strangeness and wildness gently.

Mark and I had decided to add to the company as interpreter, jester and gossip. I hadn't been able to resist the letter he thrust on me one day over the verandah.

Sir In honour to ask you that I am willingly to go with you down Monrovia please kindly I beg you. Because you love me so dearly I don't want you must live me here again, and More over I am too little to take a load. I will be assisting the hammock till we reach. Me and the headman. Please sir don't live me here again. I was fearing to tell you last night please Master, good master and good servant. I am yours ever friend Mark.

It proved always possible, however tired and vexed and sick I felt, to gain a little of the old zest at second-hand through Mark, for Mark had never seen the sea nor a ship nor a brick house. It was the greatest adventure he was ever likely to have and he was still only a schoolboy. One could see in his avid gaze at new people and new customs the dramatizing instinct at work: he was going to have stories to tell when he got back to school.

Now on the verandah, with the dancers, apprehensions gathered. This was the last rest-house we would occupy for a long while. It was to be native huts after this. I remembered what the sisters had said of the rats which swarmed in every native hut. You couldn't, they said, keep them off your bed; the mosquito net was useless; once a sister had woken to find a rat sitting on her pillow savouring the oil on her hair. But you soon got used to rats, they said. They were right, but I didn't believe them. I had never got used to mice in the wainscot, I was afraid of moths. It was an inherited fear, I shared my mother's terror of birds, couldn't touch them, couldn't bear the feel of their hearts beating in my palm. I avoided them as I avoided ideas I didn't like, the idea of eternal life and damnation. But in Africa one couldn't avoid them any more than one could avoid the supernatural. The method of psychoanalysis is to bring the patient back to the idea which he is repressing: a long journey backwards without maps, catching a clue here and a clue there, as I caught the names of villages from this man and that, until one has to face the general idea, the pain or the memory. This is what you have feared, Africa may be imagined as saying, you can't avoid it, there it is creeping round the wall, flying in at the door, rustling the grass, you can't turn your back, you can't forget it, so you may as well take a long look.

A dog ran whining across the verandah, between the dancers' legs, and off down the path to the convent. Some instinct told it to keep moving; it slathered and whined and ran; it had been bitten by a snake. The sisters had called in a medicine man who had poured medicine down its throat and tied sticky charms to its legs, but these the sisters had removed when the man had gone. It was still alive, but it had to keep on running.

It wasn't so good when the dancers went. Neither of us felt too happy; I couldn't help remembering C and Van Gogh. My cousin had been bitten all over (if by mosquitoes, then malaria might easily find us less than half-way through the forest). I had a rash over my back and arms like the rash of chicken-pox. I didn't feel so well: perhaps I had drunk too much whisky. There did seem to be an air of sickness about the prospect; Amedoo's lung and Van Gogh's fever contributed to it. After dinner I went out to the last pail-closet I should see before Monrovia; the wooden seat, of course, was swarming with ants, but I realized by this time that it was luxury to have a closet at all. We had discovered we hadn't enough lamps with us. The boys needed both lamps while they were washing up the dinner things, which meant that we must sit in the waning light of our two electric torches. The mosquito-netting over the windows and door was broken, and anything came in, large horse-flies, cockroaches, beetles, cockchafers, and moths. Now and then to save light we sat in darkness. It was a grim evening and our nerves were rather strained. Big spiders dashed up and down the wall, the filter in the corner slowly and regularly dripped, a tom-tom was beating somewhere some message, probably about the President's coming, and a big black moth the size of a bat flapped against the walls. The only thing to do was to go to bed early and sleep well.

But that was impossible; a great storm of rain beat upon the roof and afterwards it was too cold to sleep properly, just as in the day it had been too hot to walk. I dreamed uneasily I was present at the assassination of the President. It took place in Bolahun close to one of the green leafy arches they had raised in case he passed that way, between the borders of the path where the pineapple plants were sprinkled with white powder which meant 'There is joy in our hearts at your coming.' He was shot in a carriage by one of the drummers I saw at Tailahun and I tried in vain to send the story to a newspaper. At four I woke and got out of bed, without putting on my shoes, and found my vest, it was so cold. I knew some days later that I had caught a jigger by my carelessness, the small insect which burrows into the toe under the skin and lays its eggs and goes on

multiplying until it is cut out. I slept again and had more restless dreams: that there was a case of yellow fever in Bolahun
and I was put in quarantine and my diary was burnt; I woke
weeping with fury. I began more than ever to wish I hadn't got
to go at dawn. The process of psychoanalysis may be salutary,
but it is not at first happy. This place was luxury, it was civilized in a way that I was used to and could understand. It was
foolish to be dissatisfied, to want to penetrate any further. People had made their home here. I thought of the five sisters who
had come from Malvern; I thought of the young German doctor with his duelling scars and his portrait of Hitler. He was the
best kind of Nazi; he had been given the strength and the enthusiasm and the hope, and he hadn't been in Germany to see
the dirty work done. His wife, dark and thin and lovely in a
fierce tired way, had borne her first child at the mission three
weeks before. Bolahun in the early morning of the last day
seemed a lovely place, where oranges were twelve a penny and
mangoes three for a farthing and bananas so cheap that one
hadn't time to eat them before the ants and flies got into them.
These were what I remembered most clearly through the monotony of the forest: the lovely swooping flight of the small
bright rice-birds, the fragile yellow cotton flowers growing
with no stalk directly out of the canes, something like a wild
rose, transparent primrose petals with a small red centre and a
black stamen; butterflies, palms, goats and rocks and great
straight silver cotton trees, and through the canes the graceful
walking women with baskets on their heads. This was what I
carried with me into new country, an instinctive simplicity, a
thoughtless idealism. It was the first time, moving on from one
place to another, that I hadn't expected something better of the
new country than I had found in the old, that I was prepared
for disappointment. It was the first time, too, that I was not dis-
appointed.

NEW COUNTRY

Coming into Riga three years before, I had deceived myself into
thinking I was on the verge of a relationship with something
new and lovely and happy as the train came out from the

Lithuanian flats, where the peasants were ploughing in bathing-slips, pushing the wooden plough through the stiff dry earth, into the shining evening light beside the Latvian river. I had left Berlin in the hard wooden carriage at midnight; I hadn't slept and I'd eaten nothing all day. There was a Polish Jew in the carriage who had been turned out of Germany; he couldn't speak any English and I could speak no German, but a little stout Estonian girl who had been a servant in London could speak both. She was an Estonian patriot, she hadn't a good word for Riga, she regarded the grey spires beyond the river with firm peasant contempt.

And there *was* something decaying, 'Parisian', rather shocking in an old-fashioned way about the place. One could see why someone so fresh and unspoiled was disgusted. The old bearded droshky drivers and their bony haggard horses at the station were like the illustrations to a very early translation of *Anna Karenina*; they were like crude and foxed wood engravings. They must have dated back to the days when Riga was a pleasure resort for Grand Dukes, a kind of aristocratic Brighton to which one slipped away from a duchess's bed with someone from the theatre, someone to be described in terms of flowers and pink ribbons, chocolates and champagne in the slipper, of black silk stockings and corsets. All the lights in Riga were dimmed by ten: the public gardens were quite dark and full of whispers, giggles from hidden seats, excited rustles in the bushes. One had the sensation of a whole town on the tiles. It was fascinating, it appealed immensely to the historical imagination, but it certainly wasn't something new, lovely and happy.

Even the street women were period. They were not, poor creatures, young enough to be brazen under what little light there was, though they had a depraved air of false youth as if they knew their only hope was to appeal to the very old. Their manners too, one felt, dated back to the Grand Dukes. Their allure was concentrated in an ankle, a garter, which they would bend down to adjust with a dreadfully *passé* gesture of allurement. Their street manners were infinitely more elegant than the street manners of London, but they weren't in the picture any longer. There were no more Grand Dukes on the spree to be attracted by their immature girlish legs, their corseted waists, their slipping garters, their black silk stockings; unless perhaps one of the old droshky drivers was a Grand Duke. It was not improbable. At Tallinn a Baron carried luggage at the airport. And there could be no more suitable ending of an evening than for a street-walker to go home with the droshky driver; the garter with the long grey Franz Josef whiskers.

You couldn't really pity them. They belonged so completely to a different world. A war and a revolution came between, left you on one side, with the little stout Estonian peasant girl who spoke English and German and didn't trouble to flirt, and left them with the ikons in the second-hand shops, the Orthodox priest selling pictures on the pavement, a wilderness of empty champagne bottles . . .

It was a late winter evening when I drove through into the Nottingham suburb from the station, round streets quite as dark as Riga's, down and down below the castle rock and the municipal art gallery with the rain breaking on the windows. I had a job, it excited and scared me, I was twenty-one, and you couldn't talk of darkest Africa with any conviction when you had known Nottingham well: the dog sick on the mat, the tinned salmon for tea and the hot potato chips for supper carried into the sub-editor's room ready-salted in strips of newspaper (if you had won the football sweep you paid for the lot). The fog came down in the morning and stayed till night. It wasn't a disagreeable fog; it lay heavy and black between the sun and the earth; there was no light but the air was clear. The municipal 'tart' paced up and down by the largest cinema, old and haggard and unused. Her trade was spoilt; there were too many girls about who hadn't a proper sense of values, who would give you a good time in return for a fish tea. The trams creaked round the goose market, and day after day the one bookshop displayed a card in the window printed with Sassoon's poem:

> Have you forgotten yet? . . .
> Look up, and swear by the green of the
>   Spring that you'll never forget.

Somebody must have put it in the window for Armistice Day, and there it stayed, like the Poppy Day posters in Freetown, through the winter months, black sooty dripping months.

In Nottingham I was instructed in Catholicism, travelling here and there by tram into new country with the fat priest who had once been an actor. (It was one of his greatest sacrifices to be unable to see a play.) The train clattered by the Post Office: 'Now we come to the Immaculate Conception'; past the cinema: 'Our Lady'; the threatre: a sad slanting look towards *The Private Secretary* (it was Christmas time). The cathedral was a dark place full of inferior statues. I was baptized one foggy afternoon about four o'clock. I couldn't think of any names I particularly wanted, so I kept my old name. I was alone with the fat priest; it was all very quickly and formally done, while someone at a children's service muttered in another chapel. Then we shook hands and I went off to a salmon tea, and the dog which had been sick again on the mat. Before that I had made a general confession to another priest: it was like a life photographed as it came to mind, without any order, full of gaps, giving at best a general impression. I couldn't help feeling all the way to the newspaper office, past the Post Office, the Moroccan café, the ancient whore, that I had got somewhere new by way of memories I hadn't known I possessed. I had taken up the thread of life from very far back, from as far back as innocence.

2
His Excellency the President

'BOSS OF THE WHOLE SHOW'

Mark called me at five in the morning, scrabbling against the mosquito-wire. I was sending him ahead with the Mandingo Amah to warn the chief at Kpangblamai of our arrival, of my need of a hut and food for about thirty men, and to ask him to send a messenger to the chief at Pandemai to warn him that I should not be coming after all. I packed my Revelation suitcase and Amah took it, striding off down the path into the village. He wouldn't be home for weeks, but all his belongings were tied up in a rag the size of a workman's handkerchief.

It was seven-thirty before I followed. The long column of carriers slipped down from the mission hill into the mist. Vande, the headman, left the column for a few minutes and disappeared between the huts to say good-bye to his wife. He had a cloth cap, a loose shirt and shorts; he carried no load, taking with him for a few days his young brother to carry his bundle; he was very like an English foreman, cheerful, unexacting, a pipe-smoker. When he wasn't smoking he was shaking a rattle made of two tiny gourds filled with seeds. He kept to the trail of the column staying behind with any man who needed a rest.

For the first mile along the wide beaten way towards Kolahun a piccanninny followed at a jog-trot. He was about two feet high; he carried an empty sausage tin and an empty Ideal milk tin, one in each hand. Men turned and told him to go back, but he wouldn't obey; he had to run to keep up, but he kept up. He wanted to go with his father. The men laughed and shouted up the line and presently his father turned back and ordered him home. The line passed them and went on: they stood there, the tiny child sullen and unhappy and obstinate, the father telling him to go back as one says 'Home' to a dog. At last he left him there, stubbornly planted.

The broad red clay road had been improved for the President's coming, the trees had been cut down on either side and the trunks tipped into the great palmy ravines. The heavy mist lay low between the hills; one couldn't see how close one was to the great forest. A deer sprang across the road, a little brown deer which might have belonged to an English park, not the royal antelope which lucky travellers may still see in the Republic, no larger than a rabbit, except for its slim legs, ten inches high with horns of less than an inch. The road was all right so long as the mist held, but all the shade had been cut away, and I hurried to leave it behind before the sun had reached the middle sky. It was half-past nine when the road came to an end in Kolahun, the headquarters of Mr Reeves.

It occurred to me that though I had been told that the President had gone, and Mr Reeves presumably with him, it would be wise at least to inquire for the Commissioner. The town seemed empty, the green triumphal arches for the President were dusty and wrinkled with heat; a two-storeyed concrete house stood apart from the huts in a compound where the star and stripes dangled from a post. This was the house built, according to the natives of Bolahun, with forced labour. That extra storey gave it a formidable air; it stood there above the town as if it watched and knew all that happened; it would be unwise to pass it by with such a long caravan of men; it couldn't help noticing.

Everything was very still, very Sabbath; nobody left the huts to see us come in, which was odd (the town might have been sacked), but I noticed when we were nearer that there were about a dozen soldiers, in the scarlet caps with the gold star, marching up and down in the compound. At the other end of the town on a hill was a kind of garden shelter and I could see the scarlet cap there too. A small yellow-faced half-caste in a black fez came down from the compound and waited for me. Yes, he said, the Commissioner was there, and immediately led the way back into the compound between the sentries, leaving the carriers and the servants outside. I had the impression that we had been expected; and how could we not have been if it were anyone's duty to watch the road from the first storey?

A gramophone was playing, and Miss Josephine Baker's voice drifted across the compound with an amusing and sophisticated melancholy. It made everything for the moment rather unreal: the carriers sitting in the dust, the quiet drift of huts, the forest edging up over the horizon became no more than a backcloth for a lovely unclothed cabaret figure. One couldn't really believe in Mr Reeves, who appeared in a sinister melodramatic way from behind some curtains dressed in a scarlet fez and a long native robe; his heavy black Victorian side-whiskers, his thick grey skin, his voluptuous mouth were just part of the Paris revue. But somebody turned the gramophone off upstairs, and we were removed at once from the dour company of Mr

Reeves by a smart miniature black officer with glittering gaiters. He said, 'Won't you come upstairs? The President will see you in a moment.'

It was quite unexpected. I hadn't asked to see the President, I had believed that the President was in another part of the country, and I was a little taken aback. I was in a shirt and shorts with a water-bottle at my side; I was very conscious of the dust I had collected on the way, and I remembered all the stories I had heard of the Liberian rulers, how they liked to keep a white man waiting and demanded that he should always be suitably clothed for an interview.

We sat down in a tiny upper room and a soldier with a revolver holster changed the record. Miss Edith Olivier's *Dwarf's Blood* lay on the table. The black officer was very neat, very gentle, very attentive; he was like a china figure which has been kept carefully dusted. Presently a young woman came in; she wore European dress: she looked more Chinese than African. She had slanting eyes and a quality of deep repose. She didn't speak a word, though the officer presented her as 'one of the President's entourage', but sitting down beside the gramaphone she took up a pack of cards and began to shuffle them. Her father, I learnt later, had been made a justice of the supreme court: there is a distinctly Stuart air about the civilization of the Liberian Coast.

She was the loveliest thing I saw in Liberia; I couldn't keep my eyes off her. I wanted to talk to her, somehow to express the pleasure the sight of her gave in the empty sun-cracked place. Josephine Baker's voice couldn't compete with her, whining out at the end of the record before the soldier could change it. It was as if suddenly one saw what Africa might be if she were left to herself to choose from Europe only what would beautify her; she promised more than the frozen rhetoric in the declaration of independence. I never spoke a word to her ('Very hot marching in this weather,' the little shining officer said politely, making small talk), I only saw her once again from a distance when she stood on the President's balcony in Monrovia watching the Krus demonstrate their loyalty below, but she remains the kind of vivid memory which draws one back to a place, even after many years.

Then the President came in: a middle-aged man called Barclay with curly greying hair in a thick dark suit, a pinned and pinched old school tie and a cheap striped shirt. Africa, lovely, vivid and composed, slipped away, and one was left with the West Indies, an affable manner, and rhetoric, lots of rhetoric. But there was a lot of energy, too: he was a politician in the Tammany Hall manner, but I never saw any reason to change my opinion that he was something new on the Coast. He might be out to play his own game, but he was going to play it with unexampled vigour and the Republic would at least pick up some chips from his table. I asked him whether his authority was much the same as the American President's. He said it was more complete. 'Once elected,' he said, 'and in charge of the machine'—words ran away with him; something candid and childlike and excited continually peeped through the politician's dignified phrases—'why then, I'm boss of the whole show.'

Liberian politics were like a crap game played with loaded dice. But in the past it had been the custom to give the other fellow a chance with the dice. There was a kind of unwritten law that the President could take two terms of office and then he had to let another man in to pick the spoils. It was a question of letting, for, as Mr Barclay said, the President was boss of the whole show; the newspapers were his; most important of all, he printed and distributed the ballot papers. When Mr King was returned in 1928 he had a majority over his opponent, Mr Faulkner, of 600,000, although the whole electoral roll amounted to less than 15,000. But Barclay was altering that; he wasn't playing fair in his opponent's eyes; he was treating politics seriously and he has some claim to be known as the Republic's first dictator. The term of office had hitherto been four years, but Mr Barclay was to hold a plebiscite at the same time as the presidential election and increase the term to eight years. He could use the same means to put that through as he could put through a fabulous majority: he had the printing press. He had, too, the Civil Service. He explained to me, beaming with

gold-rimmed benevolence, how he had cleaned it up and removed it from political influence, had instituted examinations
in place of nominations. What he failed to mention was the
small string he kept in his fingers. When candidates of equal
merit were presented—and that was very easy to arrange—the
President himself had the right of choice.

But one had to admit that this man had energy and courage;
he was worth a dozen Kings, and his hands were comparatively
clean. He had been Mr King's secretary of state, but the League
of Nations commission, which had found the President person-
ally responsible for shipping forced labour to the little dreadful
Spanish island, Fernando Po, and for countenancing the mild
form of slavery that enabled a man to pawn his children, had
exonerated Barclay. The only real blot in the eyes of the outside
world on his administration was the Kru campaign described
in the Blue Book from which I have quoted, and for that the
man on the spot was chiefly responsible, Colonel Elwood Davis,
the black mercenary from North America. No President before
Barclay had dared to tour the interior. Mr King had travelled
rapidly down from the Sierra Leone border with two hundred
soldiers, but the President now had with him only thirty men. I
could see almost the whole lot of them marching up and down
the compound. The tribes, of course, since Mr King's day, had
been disarmed by Colonel Davis, they had no more than a few
guns in every town, but they had swords and spears and
cutlasses.

The President, it is true, didn't linger. He travelled very rapidly, forcing the pace, up paths he was not expected to use, and
his inquiries were very brief. I have said that the natives in Bolahun had no hopes that Mr Reeves would be ever brought to
book. Their doubts were justified, for I heard later that when
the President arrived, the chiefs, who had been bribed or in-
timidated, had no complaints to make. He was able to return
as rapidly to Monrovia as he had come. He said that everywhere the population had been enthusiastic but dances are easily arranged and it is not much trouble to build triumphal arches
of greenery and sprinkle white powder. I never came across a
single native in the interior who had a good word for the politi-

cians in Monrovia. If they preferred one ruler to another it was simply because they were happier under one Commissioner than another. Everywhere in the north I found myself welcomed because I was a white, because they hoped all the time that a white nation would take the country over.

This attitude is unreasonable, but their minds do not move on the level of reason. To accept a black overlord offended some deep communal instinct which was unaffected by the fact that under the worst black Commissioner they had not suffered what the natives in French West Africa had suffered under white Commissioners. They did not take into account at all from what they had been saved by the nominal nature of black rule. In that rough, unmapped country, if they were twenty miles from a Commissioner's headquarters, they were fifty years away. They were left alone to their devils and secret societies and private terrors, to the paternal oppression of their chiefs. They weren't interfered with as they would certainly have been interfered with in a white colony, and one was thankful for their lack of education, when one compared them as they were in Buzie country, striding along the narrow forest paths, the straight back, the sword with an ivory handle swinging against the long native robe, with the anglicized 'educated' blacks of Sierra Leone, the drill suits and the striped shirts and the dirty sun-helmets. Every head of a family in this tribe had his sword and wore it when he left his village, every young man had his dagger, and even the tool of the men working on the farms, the broad-bladed cutlass in its beautifully-worked leather sheath, had an air of chivalry, of an older civilization than the tin shacks on the Coast. Even the poorer tribes beyond the Buzie country, the Gios and the Manos, with their loin-cloths and sores, were not more neglected than were the natives of a Protectorate under the care of a single sanitary inspector.

HOSPITALITY IN KPANGBLAMAI

His Excellence the President talked for more than an hour in the little room above the Sunday-stricken town. He was very courteous, and it went against the grain to deceive him and give the impression that Zigita was the farthest extent of the journey

I intended to take. The Commissioners in the Western Province had been warned of my coming, and I wanted as quickly as possible to slip over into a province where I was not expected. As quickly as possible . . . but it was not easy to stem the rolling tide of the President's hopes, the roads, the aeroplanes, the motor-cars. It was a paradoxical situation; a black preaching progress to a sceptical white, but the white had come out of the busy bustling progressive scene and he had noticed there nothing more lovely than the Buzie cloths the President spread for his inspection. There was nothing crudely peasant, nothing art and crafty, nothing to remind one of stalls at bazaars and dear ladies with pale-blue bulbous eyes, about these cloths: they were sophisticated in their design, but the sophistication had a different source from ours. It sprang directly from a deeper level; it wasn't tinged by the artistic self-consciousness of centuries.

There was a world of difference between these cloths and the Mandingo cloths from French Guinea, one of which I had bought in the market at Bolahun and which can be bought, too, at double the price, on the Coast, at Freetown and Monravia. The Mandingo is a trader, his line of country is immense when it is computed less in mileage than in difficulty: in forest, swamp, river and flood. One finds him in the ports, one finds him five hundred miles in the interior in places where no white man has been seen in living memory. He is unmistakable: his height and shaven head, his Semitic features, his air in his scarlet fez and his long robe, a verse of the Koran hung round the neck, of a long trading lineage. He rides the only horses to be seen in the interior, but more often he does the journey on foot. In French Guinea I met a Mandingo who could tell me the whole route to the Coast at Cape Palmas or Grand Bassa. He made the wild four weeks' journey as regularly as a traveller in silk stockings who catches the Brighton Belle once a week. But the cloths, the swords and knives they carry with them are not superior to the peasant arts of Central Europe; they have the same crude tourist stamp; lozenges of bright crude colours on the heavy cloth. And this is interesting when one considers that there are no tourists in French Guinea, and few white men at all in the far corner of the colony which touches Liberia. The trade goods have to be carried through hundreds of miles of forest to reach the kind of public which enjoys the bogus gaudy article.

It was all against the proper White House etiquette, I felt, but it was I who had to make the move to end the interview, for I began to fear that it would be dark before I reached Kpangblamai. I was still following roughly the route which Sir Alfred Sharpe took in his journey through Liberia in 1919. All the way along this northern border the ground is high, generally about sixteen hundred feet, and the ground broken. Sir Alfred Sharpe wrote after his journey that he had never been in any part of Africa where the going was so bad, but at least it isn't monotonous like the way through the central forest, where there is no variation in the narrow paths, the dull tangled greenery, where there is nothing to see for hours on end but the carrier's feet and the tree-roots. Here, between Kolahun and Kpangblamai, there were hills to scramble over, the Mano River to cross on a wide bridge of twisted creeper, the great swallow-tailed butterflies swarming at the water-courses, tiny winged primroses resting on the damp sand and rising in clouds round our waists, and once a little ferny, brackeny glade, warm and sweet like an English summer.

These first few days of trekking had a beauty that later one completely missed: everything was new, the villages with the women pounding rice, the cluster of stones where the chiefs were buried, the cows rubbing their horns along the huts; the taste of warm, boiled and filtered water in the dried mouth; the sense, above all, that one was getting somewhere, that one was going deeper. It made me walk fast, faster than my carriers and my companion. A march, this first week, was a dash; my hammock-men, as I didn't use my hammock, kept my pace, and an evasive half-relationship developed from shared oranges, the rests at the water-courses, where they drank out of the empty meat tins they carefully preserved and I from my bottle . . .

Babu was one of these men, the Buzie: he played the harp tentatively when we rested; he couldn't speak a word of English, but he had amused friendly reliable ways of showing that he was on your side in the arguments which soon came thick and fast. He was one of the few carriers who smoked a pipe, a small clay pipe, and one could imagine him a season-ticket-holder, the reliable support of his mother and sisters in a remote sad suburb. For there was an undertone of sadness which grew as the trek went on; he wasn't strong enough for the work; he didn't complain, he was completely reliable until he was simply too sick to go farther. He was at first the only Buzie man with us; he didn't mix easily but sat apart with his pipe, sometimes coming up to the door of my hut to smile his good wishes and go away again.

The other man on the first day who went ahead with me was Alfred. Alfred was another type altogether, in his cloth cap and shorts. He had learnt to read and write, he knew English; he thought he was out for a jaunt. Plump and sweaty and horribly ingratiating, he managed to be the one who carried the harp and not the empty hammock. He pointed out everything which he considered of interest, he hung around; but among the men he was the focus of discontent; he always knew that a town was 'too far', I could hear his fat grumble doing its work whenever a group gathered together to voice their complaints, and a moment later there he would be, back at my side, doing me a little service, oily and friendly and proud of his English.

Kpangblamai was about four and a half hours' march from Kolahun. It appeared quite unexpectedly towards the end of the worst heat on the usual hilltop, and there was Mark running dramatically down to meet us at the stream. He had a school friend with him, Peter, the chief's son, and he said he had 'plenty plenty fine house' covered with pictures. So it was: rectangular, like a small stable with two stalls and a verandah. The stalls were bedrooms, containing native beds, platforms of beaten earth spread with matting. The walls were papered thickly with old advertisements and photographs out of illustrated papers, most of them German or American. Over a chair made out of an old packing-case was an article by General Pershing on Youth; beautiful women showed their teeth brushed with Chlorodone, handsome men displayed their ready-made suitings, somebody wondered why she wasn't a social success, and a man in uniform denounced a clause of the Treaty of Versailles. It was a really fine house, the only one like it in the town; we didn't have another lodging in a native town so good before Monrovia.

The chief at Kpangblamai was overpoweringly hospitable. I hadn't time to sit down and rest and take a drink before the old man arrived, wizened and reserved, in a turban and a kind of liberty robe which was like the tea-gowns worn at Edwardian literary teas. He brought with him his headman, who wore a robe of the ordinary blue and white striped native cloth and a battered bowler hat. He was even older than the chief, they neither could speak a word of English, but while from the chief's manner I gathered an impression of a rather sad tired benevolence, the headman was full of shrewdness, satire, salacious humour. He giggled in a sly way; he had, I felt sure, the low-down on the whole town; he wasn't, like the chief, an idealist; if he had belonged to another race, he would have been one of those elderly men who pinch girls' bottoms on buses in a friendly, harmless way. Chief and headman were inseparable; they went everywhere together like the higher and the lower nature.

Now they had brought with them a basin full of eggs (every one of which proved to be bad), a huge basket of oranges, and three gourds of palm wine. For the first time I was thirsty enough to enjoy palm wine; I drank one gourdful not realizing the danger of dysentery if it wasn't fresh or the gourd was dirty; it was the colour of stone ginger beer and had a soft flat taste like barley water. The chief and the headman sat down on the native bed and I gave them cigarettes. Nobody spoke. Presently they got up and went away, but a minute later the chief returned with a chicken. That first day I didn't know the right etiquette; I dashed back for each present when it arrived; and the presents multiplied rapidly. Later I learnt from Amedoo that I should dash once only at the end of my stay.

I was longing for a wash and I hadn't had time to shave before I left Bolahun, but the hospitable chief kept me on the run. No sooner had he gone after presenting the chicken than his son came in to say that the devil would dance for the visitors:

so with the chief and the headman we sat out in the blazing sun and waited for the devil to appear. This time it was a devil belonging to a woman's society, a devil from Pandemai in Buzie country, who was travelling to Kolahun to dance before the President.

It came out between the last huts at the end of the wide little whitewashed town, then swayed and simpered forward in a country robe, swinging a great raffia bustle, nodding its black mask. The bustle swung up and showed huge pantaloons of fibre, like a caricature of a Victorian dress. One remembered Miss Tilly Losch in a Cochran revue hesitating before a pillarbox with just this air of coyness, the sophisticated copy of something young and artless. This devil seemed to a European to have a mock female, mock modest manner, which was curiously and interestingly gross when combined with the long cruel mask, the slanting eyes, the heavy mouth. It turned and turned, swinging the bustle above the pantaloons, and the interpreter ran round and round carrying a small whip. There was something about it of the witch of one's childhood; perhaps because it remained so feminine even while it was unrecognizable as a woman; perhaps because of its curious head-gear; the tall tufted pole taking the place of the sugar-loaf hat. It sank on to the ground and recited its greetings on a low gushing note. It was a far more accomplished dancer than Landow. To compare Landow's wild rushes, matching the great crude muzzle, with the simpering silly sinister gait of this woman's devil was like comparing brutality with cruelty. It may have been a tribal difference: no Bande craftsman could have made this mask. Landow's was a mask of childish fancy running in the vein of nightmare: this was a work of conscious art in the service of a belief.

After the dance the chief's son, Peter Bonoh, said that his father wished to show the visitors his town. The whole length of Kpangblamai cannot have exceeded a hundred and fifty yards, but before we had seen all the activities of that small settlement, I felt much as a member of the royal family must feel after a tour of an industrial fair. I had been allowed no rest after the march, the palm wine was lying heavy in my stomach, there

was no air on the baked plateau, and I thought that I was going to faint before I reached the end. Five weavers were at
work, each under his own little shelter of palm branches; a man
was cutting leather sheaths for daggers; and in the smithy they
were making blades, one man working a great leather bellows,
another beating out the white-hot blade (I would have paid
them more attention if I had known then the importance of the
smith, how frequently he is the local devil and his word more
powerful than the chief's). In front of another hut two women
were spinning a kind of top upon a plate, working the thread
out of a mass of cotton. In a little wooden enclosure a woman
was boiling the leaves of a forest plant in a great caludron to
make a dark-blue dye. The smell of the cauldron, the pressure
of the crowd fingering my sleeves and the cloth of my trousers,
the necessity of keeping my face fixed in a bright cheerful interested mask made me feel weak and ill. There seemed no end
to the parade of industry. It was a tiny plateau, not much larger
than the Round Pond in Kensington Gardens; wherever I looked,
between the shoulders of the crowd, I saw the huts give way to
trees, and above the trees the high forested ridge of the Pandemai hills; but in the hot stuffy evening it seemed as endless as a
maze of which one doesn't know the clue.

Two women sat on the ground smoothing out cotton as it
came from the pods; a group of women were extracting the
thick yellow oil out of the palm nuts; another weaver. . . . At
last we were back at our hut; the chairs and tables were out;
and another present arrived from the chief—a kid; it escaped
and led a howling chase between the huts before it was brought
back and tethered. My cousin went to bed, she couldn't stand
the thought of food, and I had my very English meal from our
stores alone, sardines on toast, a steaming hot steak and kidney
pudding, a sweet omelette washed down with whisky and orange. I was only half-way through the second course when Peter Bonoh put his head through the screen to say his father was
outside, and there the old chief was sitting in his chair at the
entrance in his tea-gown and turban. He had brought an orches-
tra with him and all through dinner they played their monotonous tinkling tunes. The chief hadn't anything to say; he sat

there quite proud and happy and ignored, while the headman giggled salaciously somewhere in the dark near by, until at last he slipped away into the moonless night carrying his chair.

But there was one thing I had to know before I went to bed—where to go next. The doctor at the mission had spoken of an easy day's march to a place he called Dagomai, a long march the day after to Nicoboozu, and then Zigita. That was as far as he had been on the way to Ganta, but south of Zigita, at Zorzor, there was a Lutheran mission where someone might know something of the way beyond. The maps of the Dutch prospectors didn't cover the ground so far east.

The trouble was, no one had heard of Dagomai. Peter Bonoh hadn't heard of it, neither had his father or the old headman. The only town they could suggest between Kpangblamai and Zigita was Pandemai. But that wasn't far enough for a day's march, and besides I didn't expect too friendly a reception from the chief there, who had been expecting me that night. Dagomai, Dagomai, I kept on repeating in the hope that somebody would have heard of the place. Presently 'Duogobmai,' the chief said doubtfully. It sounded very nearly right, it was on the way to Nicoboozu, and I decided that it must be the place the doctor had meant. 'Too far,' Alfred said, joining in, 'too far'; the carriers clustered round and he whispered to them how far it was; they hadn't begun to work together yet, they were full of jealousy and suspicion; he had the right material to his hand. But I didn't believe him; even the doctor's wife had done the march to Dagomai; and now I quite firmly believed that Duogobmai and Dagomai were the same place. It wouldn't pay me not to believe it; time was money, and it wouldn't do to lose myself my first day loose in the Liberian interior.

For hours as I lay in bed I heard the faint music of the harps, the low sound of Alfred talking to the carriers; I wondered what I'd do if they refused to obey me. I suppose it is the thought which strikes every new prefect at school, but I had never been a prefect; I had never before so abjectly depended on other people's obedience. I was glad afterwards that I hadn't for a moment imagined that Alfred, oily, smart, ingratiating, mutinous Alfred, might be right.

It was the first time I had slept in a native hut, and foolishly, for the sake of privacy, I kept the door closed, as the natives do themselves for fear of wild animals from the forest. I had never before experienced such heat; it was like a blanket over the face, even the thin muslin mosquito-net took the breath. But at any rate there were not yet rats; only a few rustles in the roof, and in the end I fell asleep in spite of Alfred's whisper, the music and the heat and the strangeness.

THE PRIMITIVE

I was called at five by Mark and Amah, whom I again sent on ahead to warn the chief at Duogobmai. It was just as well to get Amah out of the way; Vande had chosen him as second headman, but already I could tell how unpopular he was. He was the only Mandingo among the carriers, and for the first week of the march tribal differences caused almost continuous trouble. He was strong, reliable, the best-looking man of a rather weedy set, but he had no sense of humour and they teased him mercilessly until he got into a sullen rage.

Mark and Amah had nearly three hours' start, for the chief's hospitality was by no means over. He gave my cousin a hideous leather satchel made in the village in the bright crude colours of Italian leather work, and his son gave me a bundle of knives from the smithy. Unfortunately his hospitality included the carriers and he provided them with a large meal before they started.

The character of a carrier is childlike. He enjoys the moment. He cannot connect cause and effect. He is used to one meal in the day at evening, he lives on the edge of subsistence, and it would be a hard master who grudged him the unexpected pleasure of an extra meal. The chief's kindness made them for a few minutes gloriously happy, and when almost immediately they suffered from walking with heavy loads on a full stomach, they didn't connect their suffering with their pleasure. They simply felt with minds clouded with indigestion that somebody was treating them badly. It was always the same throughout the four weeks of marching; whenever they had a breakfast they worked badly, grumbled and made palavers; when food became scarce they worked well and were happy. On one occasion they spent nearly forty-eight hours without food and at the end of that time they were fresher than they had ever been.

I had been warned of this; I knew what to expect; the food hadn't been in their bellies five minutes before rebellion stirred. But they could be distracted, too, as easily as children, and when a man presented me with a small grey monkey on a string they were temporarily happy again. They liked something to torment. They poked it with sticks. They turned it upside down. They dragged it head first in the dust. They tickled its private parts, and the little brute screamed at them and tried to bite and turned its bloodshot eyes this way and that for an escape. When they left it in peace for a moment it sat with its head in its wrinkled hands as if it were weeping. Laminah and Alfred were its chief tormentors, they were like bullies at school with a new boy who couldn't hit back; the other men were amused and tormented it occasionally when they were bored, but sometimes they were kind to it, offering it pieces of banana or kola nuts, and after a while they forgot it. Even Laminah gave up teasing it in the end, and Mark became its companion. After the first four days it went everywhere with him; it sat on his shoulder all the way through the forest until at Ganta it escaped; it rested its hands on his head and searched his hair for insects. It never tried to bite him; he never talked to it; they accepted each other in silence.

It was eight o'clock before the men had finished eating and were ready to start. They were very slow and quarrelsome, and I went on ahead with my two spare hammock-men. Alfred walked in front dangling the monkey, and Babu walked behind carrying two harps. Almost immediately we were in the forest, but it was only the edge of the great waste of bush which covers the Republic to within sight of the sea. I felt rather absurd with my two companions, climbing up out of the forest, over the crest of a small cracked hill covered with round huts while the natives came to the door and stared at the sight of the first white man they'd seen for months. One really needed to be a minor prophet to emerge suddenly like this, almost unaccompanied, with two harps and a monkey . . .

On a narrow path we met three men with long curved cut-lasses cutting away the bush; Alfred spoke to them; they came from Pandemai. They said the chief had expected the white man the night before; he had swept a hut and cooked food for thirty men. Alfred suggested it would be a good thing to spend the night with the chief. He would be offended otherwise. Duo-gobmai was too far, too far. . . . He asked the men about it. They shook their heads. He said that it was more than a day's march from Pandemai. But I couldn't speak the language, and Babu, whom I trusted, couldn't speak any English, and Alfred I be-lieved to be a liar. But liars sometimes speak the truth.

A little later a tiny stream, a patch of sand, a cloud of butter-flies, marked the boundary between Bande country and Buzie country, and soon after we came out into a broad sun-drenched clearing below Pandemai. A concrete house was being built be-side the path with a fence and a garden gate, and a black man in a European suit with an old white topee came out to meet me and laughed and lifted his hat and laughed again. He was a middle-aged man with a hard mean face which he had covered defensively for the occasion with an expression of silliness and subservience. He said, 'Mr Greene, we were expecting you last night.' He had the name pat, he laughed in a nervous servile way after every sentence, and there was something unmistak-ably clerical about his manner. One felt the Sermon on the Mount was somewhere about, though it had gone sour. He was a missionary from Monrovia, and now he was engaged in building his new mission. Like Mr Reeves he believed in con-crete and like Mr Reeves he kept his brother blacks well in hand.

He said, 'The chief had everything prepared for you last night,' and again he laughed as much as to say, 'I know I'm laughable, I'm only a black and you are a white, you are laugh-ing at me, but you needn't think I don't laugh too.' He led the way up to Pandemai, laughing and complaining all the way, not taking himself seriously, with a bitter humility which didn't really disguise the hardness and meanness below it. I wanted to go straight through; I was afraid of trouble with the carriers if they once put down their loads, but the missionary was too ready to accept my refusal as one more sign that he was despised. I couldn't give him that excuse, and now that my cousin had joined us, I let the missionary lead the way to his two-roomed hut in the town. The place was bug-ridden; we had only sat on the porch for a minute, while we ate the bananas he brought in a wooden bowl, before he realized that.

Sir Alfred Sharpe passed through Pandemai, 'an old war town', in 1919, and was received with great hospitality by the local chief. Perhaps the black missionary had not then arrived: now the town seemed dead: the chief when he came, a sullen suppressed man who presented his dash of a chicken and a pail of rice as if they had been exacted from him by force. The missionary ruled him. When, thinking of the wasted chop and the trouble he had taken the night before, I prepared to dash him five shillings in return, the missionary caught my hand. He said he couldn't allow it; there was no need to give the chief anything; I was the guest of the country. At last he allowed two shillings to pass to the chief, who stood by with a beaten smouldering air like an honest man who watches, without the power to intervene, two racketeers squabbling over his property.

The missionary calculated that Duogobmai was still six hours away. That was disquieting, for we had already marched for more than two hours, but nothing would induce me to stay. It wasn't only the unfriendly chief and the bugs in the hut; I was still planning my journey by European time: the listlessness, the *laissez-faire* of Africa hadn't caught me. I had planned to reach Duogobmai that night and to fail to reach it seemed to put back everything. I wasn't confident enough to see the journey as more than a smash-and-grab raid into the primitive. . . . There was a dream of a witch I used to have almost every night when I was small. I would be walking along a dark passage to the nursery door. Just before the door there was a linen-cupboard and there the witch waited, like the devil in Kpang-blamai, feminine, inhuman. In the nursery was safety, but I couldn't pass. I would fling myself face downwards on the ground and the witch would jump. At last, after many years, I evaded her, running blindly by into sanctuary, and I never had the dream again. Now I seemed to be back in the dark passage:

I had to see the witch, but I wasn't prepared for a long or careful examination.

So I wouldn't be delayed, and though the carriers grumbled and Alfred whispered again into my ear, 'Too far. Better stay here. Too far,' I insisted on going on. Rather recklessly I pledged myself that it wasn't far to Duogobmai. I nursed the idea that a black always exaggerated, when the fact was they had so hazy an idea of time that they were just as likely to minimize. I said, 'It's only about five hours from here. I know. The white doctor at the Holy Cross told me.'

Only five hours, I thought, as the midday heat came nearer, striking up from the dry ground, catching the feet as much as did the roots of trees beating down on one's helmet so that for moments at a time it was cooler to raise it and take the full sun on the skull. We were in the forest now, but it was still the edge where it flattened out towards the Mandingo plateau to the north: the dead dull edge of it which didn't shelter sufficiently. A few birds moved overhead, out of sight, their wings creaking like unoiled doors. A monkey ran along a branch of a great grey cotton tree, which was buttressed on the ground like a tower. It flung itself into the air at the height of a cathedral spire, dropped fifty feet and out of sight behind the palms and ivy, the tangle of greenery. The boy with the harps leapt aside at a slither in the grass. That was all the life there was, except for the long sullen chain of carriers, dropping farther and farther behind. I wondered whether they would stay the journey; if they left us I hadn't the money to reach the Coast. Would I have the nerve, I wondered, if it came to a showdown, to refuse to pay them or would we go tamely back with them to Bolahun?

The bush got thicker; the paths narrower. It was difficult to keep one's feet among the roots. My cousin and the carriers were out of sight and hearing. Nothing seemed to live but the snakes and birds, and they were invisible, and the ants. It was a country made for ants. Their great yellow tenements, twelve feet high, broke through the bush, enchained the villages. Their swarms drove across the paths, like Carthaginian armies; the route on either side was lined with sentries; one could imagine

the heaving at tiny ropes, the cracking of infinitesimal whips.
Sometimes near water there were other ants, guerilla ants this
time who whipped at one singly through the air and fastened
their pincers in the skin: stockings couldn't keep them out: their
nip was like the cut of a knife. These, one sometimes felt, were
the real owners and rulers of the bush, not the men in the villages one passed every two or three hours above their scanty
streams, ringed with a little plantation of kola trees, the leaves
turned upwards in great ugly yellow bowls like brass *épergnes;*
not certainly the few white men who had passed this way and
left in a little cleared space beside the path an abandoned gold-
working: a deep hole the size of a coffin, a few decaying wooden
struts above a well of stagnant water, the ivy already creeping
up. This was the ruling passion of most white men in this dead
bush, a passion just as secret, needing as much evasion, kept
perhaps with as much fear, as the secrets of the bush houses
which stood away from the path behind a row of stunted
charred trees like funeral cypresses or a fence of woven palm
leaves. A few banana trees at the edge of one village were
fenced in: 'the devil's bananas'.

It was odd in this shabby lost bush to be told by one's guide,
pointing to a tiny path, that that was the 'road' to Voinjema.
The carriers were still near their own country, and though the
paths were sometimes as numerous and apparently as random
as a child's criss-cross scrawlings on a sheet of paper, Babu knew
his way. He didn't have to hesitate; to show the route to those
who came behind he would close the wrong paths with sprays
of leaves. These were the only road signs in the bush.

Under the vertical sun we reached another village, I and my
two spare hammock-men and Amedoo. They led me to the
palaver-house, the low thatched barn in the middle of the village where the old men were drowsing out their siesta. I sat
down in a hammock which was slung on one side, and the old
men ranged themselves opposite and blinked and scratched. It
was too hot to talk. A woman lay in a patch of shade, on her
face in the dust, and slept. The chickens scratched on the floor
for the grains of rice which sometimes fell between the slats of
the roof. A long time passed; I wanted to scratch too. I wasn't

bitten; it was a nervous reaction. The old men blinked and scratched their armpits and heads and thighs; they burrowed inside their loose robes to find a new spot to scratch. It was too hot to be really curious about anyone, though a few of the younger men of the village stooped under the thatch and sat down and stared and began to scratch. The delay irritated me. I wanted to eat my lunch and get away, but it was nearly an hour before the carriers began to stumble in, tired and stubborn, suspicious and complaining. Alfred went round among them, urging them to rebel, gathering evidence from the villagers as to how far Duogobmai was.

But I still persisted in believing that they were wrong. I was without experience. All the white men I had met in Sierra Leone had told me how blacks must be driven, how they lied and humbugged, and it was not unnatural that I should believe they were lying now, 'trying it on', like schoolboys who are testing a new master's discipline. And as a weak master who knows his own weakness bluffs it out with a new form, unable to recognize who is truthful and who is not, alienating the honest by classing them with the dishonest, I became all the more stubborn. I ate my food very fast, so that the men might have only a short rest, I told Vande to make Alfred one of my cousin's hammock-carriers so that he might be forced to work, I wouldn't listen to their arguments.

Laminah said softly behind my chair, 'Amedoo's feet very bad.'

At least I had the good sense not to alienate my boys. I depended on them for any comfort that could be wrung out of the country; it was they who, however tired they were, saw first to putting up our beds and chairs, to preparing our food, to boiling water for the filter. I said, 'If his foot's really bad, we'll stay.'

Laminah said, 'Amedoo go on. He say he no humbug.'

'It'll be only three hours from here,' I said. 'Only three hours, the doctor said so.' They didn't believe me, but they went about among the carriers repeating what I said; they put up a good pretence of believing. It is one of the curious things about a black servant, the way in which he includes loyalty in his service.

I am not praising him for that. One ought not to be able to

buy loyalty. It enabled me to victimize my carriers. I walked straight off out of the village with my two spare men and left the carriers behind. I was paying them three shillings a week and that sum paid, not only for an eight-hour day or more of heavy carrying, but for their loyalty. The poor fools when I left them had the money-box, I was a foreigner, my servants were foreigners, they could have shared the money out and gone home. But I was almost certain, though I had known them only two days, that they would follow. I ought to have despised them, as I would have despised the little tame employee at home who puts his office first. But after a while I began to love them for it. Perhaps there is a difference. There was no trait of cowardice in their loyalty, no admission that the richer is the better man. They *did* sell their loyalty, but it was a frank sale: loyalty was worth so many bags of rice, so much palm oil. They didn't pretend an affection they didn't feel. Love was quite one-sided as it ought to be.

So they followed after me, though a long way behind. Three hours went by and there was no sign of Duogobmai. The worst midday heat wore off soon after four. Another village offered hospitality I wouldn't take. Babu and Kolieva stayed and drank water outside one of the ragged huts, but I went stubbornly on to where the forest began again. A man followed me. He had a few words of English: he said we would never reach Duogobmai before dark. There was still another village between. But I went on: I couldn't bear the thought of waiting; I had been walking now for more than eight hours, but I had gained my second wind. One of the two men dropped behind; I was alone with Babu and the harps; it was not only the heat that was fading out of the air, the ferocity of the light between the branches was tamed.

Suddenly Babu sat down by the side of the path and changed his vest. He smiled shyly, winningly; we were coming to a town; he had to clean himself, just as much as any season-ticket-holder who straightens his tie before he gets to the City. As the light went out the forest began to rustle; one wondered whether after all it was so dead as it had seemed. I couldn't help remembering that the man in front was in the greater danger from a snake, but the man behind from a leopard, for leopards, one is told, always jump at the back. Another village lifted itself on the skyline at the green tunnel's end: the sky was grey, the huts so black that quite suddenly one realized how close night was. It would have been wise to stay, but it was a tiny village, not more than thirty huts on a little cracked hill-top. The thatch was falling in, a few horrible tiny dogs with bat ears came barking out and three old women sat on the very edge of the hill, sorting out cotton seeds, dirty and scarred and naked, like disreputable Fates. The hill dropped straight below them. They were just on the margin of life. I didn't believe there was rice enough in the place to feed my men.

Below the hill a wide river lay flat and heavy in the evening light. It was the Loffa, which flows down into the sea about thirty miles above Monrovia. None of these Liberian rivers have been traced from their source in the French Guinea hills to the sea; their upper course is represented in the British War Office map with dotted and inaccurate lines. They usually fall in rapids about fifty miles from the coast and so commercially are of little value, but even in these calm upper reaches they are not used at all by the natives of the Republic: the only canoes one sees are ferries, and these almost all on the French border. One would expect villages to cluster round these rivers, but actually they flow through the wildest and least inhabited part of the bush until within a few days' trek of the Coast. The way over the Loffa that evening was by a great hammock bridge. It was a really lovely architectural sight, seventy yards of knotted creeper swinging down from an arboreal platform fifteen feet in the air and out and up ten yards above the Loffa to another tree on the opposite bank. The foothold was about a foot wide, but it was railed on either side with creepers to the height of a man's shoulders. Sometimes the creepers had given way, and one had to stretch across the gaps while the whole bridge swung like a rope ladder.

Half-way across Mark was standing with a chicken in his hand. He was sick and tired and hungry. He could hardly stir another yard. But Amah, who had been carrying a load all day since they left more than twelve hours before, was quite fresh.

He was waiting for Mark on the other side. He had taken off his robe and was naked except for his loin-cloth. He picked up the Revelation suitcase and swung it up to his head as if he were only beginning the day's march. He was admirable when things went wrong; he sulked and grumbled only on a day of rest or after a short march. It amused him that I should have overtaken them, and he strode up the path from the Loffa laughing and chattering in Bande.

Duogobmai came in sight, a line of blackened huts at the top of a long red-clay slope. A strange pink light welled out of the air, touching the tall termite mounds which stood along the path. It seemed to have no source in the darkening sky, it gave the whole landscape, the ant-heaps and the red clay and the black huts of Duogobmai on the hill-top camp, a curious Martian air. Men ran out of the huts and looked down at us, climbing up out of the dusk and the forest.

It was quite dark when we came into the town and felt our way between the huts to find the chief's. Duogobmai looked very old and very dirty. It was like a Tudor town in its cramped crowded way; the thatch of the huts touched, one had to stoop between them, and the narrow paths were blocked with creamy moonstruck cows like Jerseys with twisted horns standing in their turd among the hens and dogs and small fierce cats and goats.

The chief was a middle-aged man with thick lips and little cunning eyes who looked more Oriental than West African in his red fez. He sat in a hammock before his hut. I couldn't tell whether he was friendly or not. He just sat there and listened to Amah speaking, to Amah asking for huts and food for thirty men. He was a slow thinker and he was startled by our sudden appearance. He hadn't seen a white face for years. I still believed that this must be the Dagomai the doctor had directed me to, but no, the chief said, no white people had stayed here since they had begun to pay hut tax, and that was as far back as memory took him. In his slow way he was immensely tickled; it was as good as a circus. He sent some men to clean a hut.

It was quite dark: there was no moon. The blacks moved between the huts with smouldering torches, but the little cheerful embers lit only wretchedness and dirt. A few carriers tottered in and sank immediately to the ground beside their loads with their heads in their hands. There was no humbugging; they were completely exhausted. Amah led me to the hut which had been chosen for us: a small round hut with a native couch at one side, where there was just room for two beds. The chief's lamp, the only one in the village, stood on the floor and the sweepers raised clouds of dust which rose and settled again: there was a burnt-out fire in the middle. Somebody put a box on the floor and I sat down to wait. I was anxious: I couldn't imagine how my cousin and the carriers could get across the long hammock bridge in the dark, avoiding all the gaps where the creepers had given way. I sent Amah with the lamp down the hill to see if he could find them and sat in the dark and heard the first rustle of the rats above. I dropped into a doze, and nearly an hour later voices roused me, a lamp swaying between the huts, a sudden pack of worn-out men. Amedoo rushed like a whirlwind into the hut, lashing with his stick at the legs of the few blacks who sat there with me: he could never remember that he wasn't any longer in the British Empire. He was worn out and in a despairing rage because half the carriers, he said, had stayed at the village the other side of the Loffa, refusing to cross the bridge in the dark. There were no beds, no mosquito nets, no lamps, no torches, no food, and worst of all in the blasting heat of the hut, no filter.

Old Souri, the cook, appeared in the doorway in his black fez and his white robe which had been torn in the forest. He had a chicken in one hand and a bare knife in the other. He said, 'Where de cookhouse? Where de cookhouse?' Nothing, no seedy village, no ten hours' trek, could quench the old man's ruling passion.

There was nothing to do but have our hammocks slung and lie all night in them fully dressed and wrapped in blankets to keep away mosquitoes. While Amedoo and Amah prepared the hut we stumbled out of the village to relieve ourselves. We had no light, we lost our way in the coil of little huts, it was a pitch-black night except for the quivering sparks of fireflies. We struck endless matches, making water in the dry pitted ground.

And suddenly I felt curiously happy and careless and relieved. One couldn't, I was sure, get lower than Duogobmai. I had been afraid of the primitive, had wanted it broken gently, but here it came on us in a breath, as we stumbled up through the dung and the cramped and stinking huts to our lampless sleeping place among the rats. It was the worst one need fear, and it was bearable because it was inescapable. Only one thing worried me a little: it seemed likely after a night without nets we should both go down with fever when we were farthest from both Bolahun and Morovia, though luckily our quinine was on the right side of the Loffa.

There was no water to drink because there was no filter, and it was appallingly hot, lying covered by blankets over our clothes. My cousin was wise and bore the thirst, but in this village there was so much chance of disease that one wasn't adding to it much, I thought, by drinking two dirty gourds of palm wine. Then I had to fall back on neat whisky. The hut was too short for the hammocks to be stretched at full length; we had to sit in the dark bolt upright waiting for the rats to come. There was a bat somewhere in the roof, and I had noticed before the lamp went out a few huge cockroaches flattened against the wall.

And then luck changed. It was as if fate had been merely curious to see how the worst would affect us. Suddenly the carriers arrived with Vande grinning and happy and proud in the rear. Somehow he had persuaded them to cross the river in this pitch darkness, and there they were with the beds and nets and food and filter, sinking to the ground by the hut too tired to grumble. So after all one was protected, protected from the flies which stayed awake all night, from the mosquitoes, the cockroaches and the rats, by one's net. But it wasn't easy to sleep. Outside, the carriers sat round the lamps and had their chop and I heard vitality come slowly back to them and Alfred's voice sowing dissension. When their lamp went out the rats came. They came all together, falling heavily down the wall like water. All night they gambolled among the boxes, and the cows snuffled round the wall and made water nosily. A jigger burrowing under one of my nails burned like a match flame. By half-past five the village was awake again.

3
Into Buzie Country

THE HORRIBLE VILLAGE

I wasn't surprised when the carriers struck work next morning and demanded a day's rest. They said Nicoboozu was a full day's journey away. I sent for the chief and Mark interpreted. The chief said Nicoboozu was seven hours off; he was lying or Mark was lying. But I had stood out against the carriers once before and had been proved wrong. Now they didn't believe me: they believed I was driving them hard on purpose, and so I granted their demand promptly to try to win their confidence again. But it took me more than one day to do that. They were like children who have caught a grown-up lying to them.

It wasn't a place I would have chosen to rest in. It was a really horrible village. The only thing to do in it was to get drunk. I noted in my diary, 'A woman goes round scraping up the cow and goat dung with her hands, children with skin disease, whelping bitches and little puppies with curly tails and bat ears nosing among the food Souri is cooking for us in the dust outside a hut, skinny chickens everywhere, dust getting into the throat. Roofs touching. Indelible pencil all over the hands. Damp pages. Lot of trouble with the carriers. A long walk to get away from the village to relieve oneself.'

It would have been stuffy anyway in the narrow space between the huts, but all day a crowd of villagers crushed out what little air there was. They had never before had a chance of examining white people closely. I couldn't take out a handkerchief without a craning of heads, nor raise a pencil without a pressing forward of watchers who didn't want to miss a thing. This intent unamused stare got on the nerves. And they were so ugly, so diseased. The thought of disease began to weigh on my mind; I seemed to swallow it in the dust which soon inflamed my throat; I couldn't forget where the dust had come from, from the dung and the bitches and the sores on the feet.

Only a few of the women broke the monotonous ugliness of the place. The adults had been beautifully and elaborately cut in bush school; the patterns were like metal plaques spread from the breasts to the navel; and there was one small girl in a turban with slanting Oriental eyes and small neat breasts who did appeal to a European sexual taste even in her dirt. To their eyes she was probably less attractive than the village beauty who gazed at herself all day in a little scrap of cracked mirror, a girl with swelling buttocks and smeared and whitened breasts which hung in flat pouches to her waist. It was curious how seldom they did appeal: perhaps sexual vitality was lowered by the heat and the marches, but it was partly, I think, their lack of sexual self-consciousness. They weren't, until we came near to the Coast and 'civilization', interested in the sex of their visitors, but only in their colour or their clothes. The nakedness, too, was monotonous; it brought home how few people, and for how short a period of their lives, one can see naked with any pleasure.

There was something shifty and mean about Duogobmai, even apart from its dirt. It was the only place, until I got into Bassa country where the coastal civilization had corrupted the natives, in which I found nothing to admire. The chief was a Mohammedan, but no sooner had I produced a bottle of my whisky than he arrived with a present of palm wine and some eggs, all of which were bad. I gave him half a tumblerful of neat whisky and he tossed it down as if it were lemonade, then rolled away towards his hut. An agreeable and depraved old man with thin white hair twisted into tiny pigtails brought two eggs; he was the oldest man in Duogobmai, the owner of the hut; and he explained through Mark that he didn't want a dash. He sat down close by, his reward was a ringside seat, and watched the show: the white man writing, drinking, coughing, wiping the sweat from his face. Presently I gave him a swig of

whisky; it went immediately to his head. One moment his lip
was on the glass, the next he was swaying and giggling in senile
tipsiness. He tried to smoke a cigarette, but the smoke got in his
eyes. He was like a withered plant one has tried to revive with
spirit; it begins immediately to open and flutter its petals, but a
moment later the spirit has run its course and it is more dead
than ever. In the middle of lunch the chief arrived again to in-
troduce his brother, a fourth lieutenant in the Liberian Frontier
Force, through whose village we would pass next day. He was a
young simple brutal man in a fur cap with a small metal Liberian flag on it. They had obviously come for whisky and I gave
it them; it sent the chief back to his hut for the rest of the day.

He was quite right; there was nothing else to do but drink.
The difficulty was to get drunk; the spirit ran out in sweat almost as quickly as one drank it. The race between the night and
drunkenness became furious as darkness fell. For I still feared
the rats: I wanted something to make me sleep; but drink was
quite useless for that purpose and most of the night I lay awake
listening to the rats cascading down the walls, racing over the
boxes. I had already learnt that one could not touch the
earthen floor with naked feet without catching jiggers under
the nails; now I learned that at night anything left outside a
case would be eaten—by cockroaches or rats. They would eat
anything: shirts, stockings, hair-brushes, the laces in one's shoes.

RATS

Rats indeed take some getting used to. There are said to be as
many rats as human beings even in England in the large towns,
but the life they lead is subterranean. Unless you go down into
the sewers or haunt the huge rubbish dumps which lie beyond
the waste building lots under a thin fume of smoke, you are unlikely to meet a rat. It needs an effort of imagination in Piccadilly Circus to realize that for every passing person, there is a
rat in the tunnels underneath.

They are shy creatures; even while I slept among them, and
heard them round me all night, I never *saw* one until I arrived
in Ganta, where they were bolder and didn't wait till dark.

Flash a torch: they always avoided its beam; leave a lamp burning: and they played just as furiously in the shadow outside the range of light.*

I remembered the first live rat I ever saw. I had returned with my brother from a revue in Paris to a famous hotel on the left bank near the Luxembourg. It was about one o'clock in the morning; my brother went upstairs first; and lolloping behind him, like a small rabbit, went a rat. I could hardly believe my eyes as I followed them; it didn't go with the dapper lounge, the wealthy international guests. But I wasn't drunk; I could see quite distinctly the rough brown fur at its neck. I suppose one of the million or two rats in Paris was reconnoitering. Its appearance had a premeditated sinister air. I thought of the first Uhlans appearing at the end of a Belgian country road.

The next rat I saw was dead. I had taken a cottage in Gloucestershire and the country scared me. Something used to make a noise in the thatch every night, and I thought of rats: I knew the villagers went ratting along the hedge at the bottom of my garden. The rat-catcher, a rat-like man himself in old army breeches who was said by cruel village rumour to have allowed his first wife to starve, came with his ferrets; they scrambled along the thatch, rearing at the chimney stack like tiny polar bears; one of them couldn't keep his footing and continually fell off until he had to be put back in the bag. There weren't any rats, the catcher said, and refused payment. He had a pride in his profession and would only be paid by results, at the rate of a shilling a rat. But that night there was a knock on the door. A village woman stood in the door and held out a dead rat, jumping with fleas. She said, 'I thought maybe you might like to see a rat. We've caught twenty down the hedge,' dangling the body under my lamp.

It is not, after all, unreasonable to fear a rat. The fear of moths, of birds and bats—this may be nerves, but the fear of the rat is rational. To quote Hans Zinsser, 'It carries diseases of man and animal—plague, typhus, trichinella spiralis, rat-bite fever,

---

*Perhaps town rats are bolder. In Freetown in 1942 I would lie awake under my mosquito-net and watch them scamper across my dressing table and swing upon my black-out curtains. (1946)

infectious jaundice, possibly trench fever, probably foot-and-mouth disease and a form of equine 'influenza'. . . . They have nibbled at the ears and noses of infants in their cribs; starving rats once devoured a man who entered a disused coal-mine.' It wasn't in the least comforting to remember that there are forty million rats in England; the thought of the one rat which the sister at Bolahun had found sniffing at her hair was enough to hinder sleep.

And lying awake and hearing the rats play among our boxes, I couldn't help remembering, too, the list of diseases I had read in England: leprosy, yaws, smallpox. . . . They were all, I felt certain, to be found in Duogobmai, and it was no comfort to know that leprosy was hardly at all contagious and that none of these diseases could be transmitted by fleas in a rat's fur. One felt that even the dust in the cramped dirty town was poisonous, no less than fleas.

And yet all the time, below the fear and the irritation, one was aware of a curious lightness and freedom; one might drink, that was a temporary weakening; but one was happy all the same; one had crossed the boundary into country really strange; surely one had gone deep this time.

BUZIE COUNTRY

If we seldom sank as low as Duogobmai we seldom rose as high as Nicoboozu, which we reached next day after an easy cheerful trek of only three hours. Alfred had gone home; he had decided that the journey was not going to be a holiday; and in his place Vande had taken a friend of Babu's, a Buzie man called Guawa. Guawa was an asset; he had the carriers singing before Duogobmai had slipped behind the trees. He sang and he danced, danced even when he carried a hammock or a load; I could hear his voice down the trail, proposing the line of an impromptu song which the carriers took up, repeated, carried on. These songs referred to their employers; their moods and their manners were held up to ridicule; a village when the carriers pressed through in full song would learn the whole story of their journey. Sometimes a villager would join in the chant, asking a question, and I could hear the question tossed along the line until it became part of the unending song and was answered.

At the village before Nicoboozu the fourth lieutenant waited to greet us; he led us to his hut, and his brother brought a present of a large cockerel and a dozen eggs. The fourth lieutenant brought out his weapons, a long spear with a leather grip softened by fur and with a leather sheath, and a sword with goatskin at the hilt. He showed me his warrant as a fourth lieutenant dated 1918, and a letter from his commander recommending him for personal bravery and stating that, though he was completely illiterate and unable to learn the new drills, he was a good officer in peace and war. He said he had fought the Grebos and the Krus, and there was a young naïve brutality in his manner of touching his sword, a pride in killing and death.

Nicoboozu was a clean little town, the huts wide apart, and the chief was old, hospitable and incurious. He dashed us a chicken and a hamper of rice, saw that the hut we were to sleep in was swept, and then retired to his hammock and shade from the midday sun while we had a bath in a tin basin and the jiggers were cut out of our toes.

Nicoboozu was as favourable an example as we could find of a village touched by the Buzie culture. Here the women wore little silver arrows in their hair and twisted silver bracelets, beaten by the blacksmith out of old Napoleon coins brought from French Guinea, and heavy silver anklets; the men wore rings, primitive signet rings with a flattened side, and decorative beaded rings and rings twisted to match the bracelets. The weavers were busy, and every piece of craftsmanship we saw was light and unselfconscious. There was an air of happiness about the place which next day we did not find in Zigita. Zigita is the principal town of the Buzie tribe, it is a town where even the commonest bush cutlass is beautiful, but it isn't happy. It is Buzie in another fashion, the fashion of witchcraft and fear.

The village women danced to us that evening in starlight to the music of rattles. It was not a lovely dance; they were not lovely dancers but emaciated old women slapping their pitted buttocks in a kind of Charleston; but they were cheerful and happy, and we were happy, too, as they slapped and rattled and laughed and pranced, and we drank warm boiled water with whisky and the juice of limes, and the timelessness, the irresponsibility, the freedom of Africa began to touch us at last.

It wasn't easy to analyse the fascination behind the dirt and disease, but it was more than a personal fantasy, satisfied more than a personal need. Different continents have made their call to different ages, and people at every period have tried to rationalize in terms of imperialism, gold or conquest their feeling for an untouched land, for a country 'that hath yet her maidenhead, never sacked, turned, nor wrought, the face of the earth hath not been torn, nor the virtue and salt of the soil spent by manurance; the graves have not been opened for gold, the mines not broken with sledges, nor their images pulled down out of their temples'.

The old women danced and were cheerful, with the sores on their breasts and the silver arrows in their hair. There were mines in Nigeria broken by sledges: over the border in Sierra Leone were other mines. Justice ruled on the north, the east and the west: here there were injustice, massacre, exaction, but the forest stayed forest, it was hardly pitted at all by the little holes the white prospectors had dug, the steep paths to Zigita sparkled with mica, but the minerals remained where they were in the soil of the country, and the images had certainly not been pulled down out of the temples.

That Zigita proved, the Buzie town reached by forest paths so steep that I hardly had to bend to use my hands in climbing. The President might speak of building motor roads through the Republic: these paths proved what difficulties lay before him. He had forgotten or never trodden this way, as hard and rough, according to Sir Alfred Sharpe, as any in Africa, which leads to Zigita sprawling across a high plateau, surrounded by forests and higher hills, five and a half hours' trek from Nicoboozu. Zigita itself is nearly two thousand feet up, and to the northwest, Ongizi, a thimble of almost perpendicular rock, rises another thousand feet, the home of evil spirits. But all round Zigita are hills and forest; it is overlooked from every side but one, and on nights of storm the lightning runs along the top of the hills, circling it with green flame.

THE BIG BUSH DEVIL

In Zigita it is quite easy to believe that there are men in Buzie country who can make lightning. The use of lightning is little more than a postgraduate course to be taken when the ordinary initiations of the bush school are over, just as the women may take poisoning as *their* post-graduate course. About six years ago the old blind chief of Zigita lost his wife. She ran away to the hut of a younger man, and when the chief sent to him to claim the proper fine, they had gone. This flight, this failure to pay the customary fine, made the couple guilty, not their adultery. A year later the chief travelled down to Monrovia to a conference with President King. He heard that the young people were living in the town with their baby. He was a forbearing man and again he sent to them to demand that the fine be paid. When the young man refused, the chief, who was a member of the Lightning Society, made artificial lightning which struck the hut, killed the man and the woman, but left the baby, who lay in the bed between them, unharmed. This story is believed by everyone in Liberia, white and black. I heard it from several sources, and it never varied. The old chief I did not see, because he was away at Voinjema meeting the President.

A Liberian District Commissioner is stationed at Zigita: the compound lies up the slope of a hill above the town, above the long field of thatched and pointed huts like stooks of bound bean-stalks. The town chief, who brought to my hut in the compound a crowd of men with swords and daggers and jewellery for sale, seemed young and downtrodden. He was ordered about by the DC's clerk (the DC was away at Voinjema), but if the DC had the chief well under his thumb, there was a higher, though more secret, authority than the Commissioner's: the Big Bush Devil, in Dr Westermann's phrase the Grand Master of a Bush Society, whom it is death or blindness for an uninitiated native so much as to see and who must be distinguished from the devils we had watched dancing in grotesque masks, the mere heads of the local bush schools. A new hut was being fenced in for him by the townsfolk as my carriers climbed the slope to the compound: this was a force ruling by terror and poison, which had already driven away one District Commissioner, the other side of the Buzie medal to that which now, as we sat on the verandah with the town chief and the clerk, so richly displayed itself.

The servants did the bargaining. Bracelets and daggers were sold for a few shillings apiece; a sword with a carved ivory hilt was bought from a fat man with the authoritative air of an Eastern eunuch for eight shillings. He lost his temper with Laminah, who, he said, was spoiling the market. He had a few words of English; he said, 'yes'm' and 'no'm'; there was something servile and baleful in his manner. He was one of the richest men in the town. I met him in my stroll that evening and he asked to have a picture taken of him. 'Which is your hut?' I said. 'I'll take you in front of it.'

'That my hut,' the fat man said, pointing past a black bull. 'Yes'm. And that. And that. And that. Yes'm. And that,' marking out half the town with his plump finger. Next day, the terrified Laminah, who remembered how his bargaining had angered the stranger, learnt that he was the headman of the devil.

The sales continued until late: all the finest swords and spears were bought last by men who slipped quietly in behind the lowered reed screens which at mosquito-time made the verandah into a little private room. One owner, at the chief's command, unwillingly brought a lovely sword in a worked leather sheath, with a hilt of ivory and brass. He didn't want to sell; he loved the sword; it had been his father's. It was pathetic to watch the struggle in his mind between his love for it and the wealth he was offered. I raised my bid to twenty-two shillings and the man nearly gave way. That sum of money would have fed him, and fed him well, for more than three months. He lifted up the screen and ran from temptation, back down the hill into the village, carrying the sword. The carriers laughed at him as they lay sprawling on the verandah.

For we led a patriarchal life on trek. Only the places in which we slept were free from intrusion. If the hut had a verandah or a room to eat in, it belonged to the carriers too. They sat round, on the floor, in the hammocks; they slept in corners. It was assumed that I would always be glad to see them there, to attend to their wants even in the middle of a meal, giving them iodine or Epsom salts. At Zigita a leprous man from the town came, with the sellers, to be healed, standing dumbly, holding out his rotting hands. Passive misery had been stamped on his face for a long while, but he had seen the carriers take medicine from me and one could tell that behind the misery a spark of belief had been struck in miracles. It was no good destroying hope and admitting there was nothing I could do. I gave him a few tablets of boric acid to dissolve and bathe his hands with.

At half-past six when the leper and the men with swords to sell had all gone home, the mosquito-screen was lifted and a stranger slipped in. We were drinking whisky and lime; the hurricane lamp was turned low to save oil; we couldn't understand what the man wanted when he spoke urgently to us from the shadows. We called Mark to translate. It was a command from the devil in the town that no one should go outside; no one must even look through a window, for the devil proposed to leave his hut. The servants came in from the cookhouse and listened; the man slipped away again into the dark and left them scared. I tried to sound the servants; it was disquieting to see how grave and frightened Laminah had become, although the longest march never stilled his tongue for long. He stood there silent and gloomy in his shorts, his little white waiter's jacket which the forest had torn, his woollen cap with the red bobble. He believed, one could not doubt it, that if we so much as saw the devil through a window we would go blind. The warning reached the carriers who were gathered in the cookhouse, and suddenly all the voices were turned low like lamp flames. One could hear the silence welling up the hill from Zigita into the compound. I looked from under the mosquito-screen; the compound was quite empty; the sentry who usually guarded the gateway had disappeared; the screens were down in the clerk's house and the windows shuttered.

I said: 'But if we go outside, do you really think that anything . . . ?'

They watched me carefully, trying to make out if I were serious. Mark was a Christian boy, he wouldn't answer directly, he was ashamed of his fear, but he said he thought we oughtn't to go. Amedoo broke in excitedly with a story it was difficult to follow about what had happened in 1923 at dinner one night at a District Commissioner's in Sierra Leone: 'The DC he sit here, his wife she sat there, Mr Trout he sat here, Mrs Trout she sat there and the devil passed through.' He said that if we went and saw the devil, the devil would put a medicine on the town and there would be no white man after we had gone with better medicine. The boys went into the two rooms and drew the mosquito-screens over the windows; after they had cleared dinner they sat with the carriers in the cook-house with the blinds pulled down; we could see the lamp shining on the floor through the slats and the shadows of the silent figures.

But the needs of the body had to be satisfied, and taking our electric torches we went out through the compound to the edge of the forest. The town of over two thousand inhabitants might have been deserted; the pale sickle of a new moon, a sky luminous with stars, circle after circle of shuttered huts. The place had an eerie air after Nicoboozu and Duogobmai, where music and dancing, laughter and cries went on till midnight, for it was not yet nine. But as we returned up the path out of the forest and flashed our torches on the town, we lit up two human figures who were standing silently outside the devil's hut. Perhaps the devil had set a watch on Zigita to see who moved or peeped, because for some time after we returned to the rest-house we could hear feet moving in the compound, lightly stirring in the dust outside. As we undressed the devil's music began in Zigita, the pulse of a drum. We turned out the lamps and lifted the screen from the window which faced the town, but there was nothing to be seen from the direction of the devil's hut; no lights moved. 'When once,' Saki wrote, 'you have taken the Impossible into your calculations its possibilities become practically limitless.' We had the creeps that night; there were no doors and anyone could slip into the house under the mosquito-screens. I very nearly took the automatic out of the money-box to load it; only self-consciousness prevented me.

I had expected the atmosphere in the morning to clear. This was the day of rest which the carriers had looked forward to, but they showed no sign of enjoying it. They lingered in the rest-house, avoided the town. Mark said it was a bad place where they fought with poison and not swords, and I remembered uneasily how simple it would be for the devil to poison the carriers' food and teach the sceptical whites a lesson. Thunder kept wandering along the hills; two carriers complained of their heads and one of his belly, and I sent off a messenger to the Lutheran mission at Zorzor warning them of our coming next day, although I had meant to stay another day at Zigita. All the morning the building of the fence round the new hut went on, a line of women carrying pails of water up and down the hill from the river to loosen the soil. The noise was like that of a distant rugger match; every now and then there were screams of delight as if a try had been scored. Once the headman arrived on the verandah and asked for some oil, and if I had not stopped him, Laminah would have given him the greater part of our supply.

Again a warning was brought to the compound that the devil was leaving his hut. After the drums had sounded, no one was to go outside. The fat baleful man appeared with him at the gateway of the compound. He had with him a little old man with a white goatee beard who wanted us to buy some crude leather pouch. 'Yes'm,' and 'No'm,' the fat man said at intervals. 'And this devil,' I said, 'why can't I see him?' He laughed evasively and Laminah plucked at my sleeve. He knew who the fat man was and he was scared. The fat man turned and saw him. He became boisterously funny, but without any humour showing in his little sunk eyes. He said, 'You want to see devil, eh?' gripping Laminah's arm, and he began to talk to him in his own tongue.

When Laminah got away he was stammering with his fear. The fat man, he said, was the devil's headman and the old man with the goatee beard his medicine man. The headman had frightened him badly in revenge for his bargaining over the sword; he had told him that he would be carried away into lot of trash to sell, and I, not knowing then who he was, chaffed the bush for seven years and forcibly initiated into the Bush Society. The thunder rumbled round the hills and the clouds broke up. Amedoo joined us. He said, 'England good place. You have one God and no devils. I have one God too but plenty devils.' He was a Mohammedan. He began all over again the story about the English DC. He wanted to prove that it wasn't safe to laugh in private at a Big Bush Devil. They could make themselves invisible; they could hear everything.

Then the rain came washing down, a vertical wall of water, while the thunder rumbled. We ran for shelter. Mark met us on the verandah, anxious to impress us, too, with how bad a place it was. The DC, Amedoo began to tell us all over again, had been having dinner. 'Mrs DC sat here, Mr Trout there.' The DC had laughed and said that he would like to see the devil, and immediately the devil had passed invisibly through the dinner-table splitting it in half. Through a window we could see a man standing outside the devil's hut in the pouring rain fanning the thunderstorm away with a switch of elephant hair, fanning it away from the devil's hut towards the compound and the hills. He stood there for more than two hours in the rain, fanning.

The storm continued all the evening and well into the night. It certainly kept away from Zigita; the hills and the huts leapt up in green light; the thunder travelled all the way along the rim, the lightning screwing down into the forest. There was no sound from the devil's hut. The stage was magnificently set for a supernatural act. I had promised the boys we would not look outside, but we kept watch on the hut through a crack in the shutter. It leapt and receded before the green flames; something should have happened to crown the wild night, but nothing did. The devil never stirred and the great natural preparation went on too long without a climax; the storm became a bore.

That night the rats came leaping into my room like large cats; they knocked things over; they made too much noise for me to sleep, though they always evaded the eye of the torch. A tin went crashing over; once I could have sworn that the lamp itself had gone. But curiously, when daylight came, nothing was out of order; even the biscuit-tin I had heard fall was in its usual place.

There was certainly something bad about Zigita. I never felt quite well again until I reached the Coast. It was not that I believed in the devil's power so much as in the power of my own mind. The suggestion of malice and evil here was so great that I could imagine it influencing my mind until I half believed, and a half-belief can be strong enough to affect the health.

So in a way I was just as glad to leave Zigita as the carriers were. They broke into song as soon as they got beyond its boundaries, and made fast time on the wide treeless track south to Zorzor. We couldn't see twenty yards ahead at first because of the deep wet fog which dropped softly round us, but when the sun had sucked it up, we experienced the real ferocity of Africa on the shadeless road. It staggered and sickened me even through a sun-helmet. Once a beautiful little green snake moved across the path, upright, without hurry, bearing her bust proudly forward into the grasses like a hostess painted by Sargent, poisonous with gentility, a Fabergé jewel.

At lunch in the only shade the wide gorge provided the messenger arrived from Zorzor with a note to tell me that I could have a house in the compound of the Lutheran mission.

KINDNESS IN A CORNER

I had expected something better of a mission than this parched playground on a hill-top opposite Zorzor: the deserted houses, nobody about, the dusty plants, and at last the fat American woman trailing forward through the afternoon heat in a green-flowered dress, the pattern tightly expanded across the hips, a white topee. She whined at us dismally that this was the house: the dusty rambling shuttered house stuffy with the smell of vermin, torn mosquito-wire across the windows. She couldn't find the keys and gazing through the windows I could see stacks of missionary literature on wobbly tables and piles of broken filters against the peeling walls. 'You see, I'm all alone here,' the American woman wailed, trailing around the building looking for the keys, but she checked herself, when she had taken another look at my dirty shorts, my dirty face and unshaven skin, and when a little later I insisted, 'Are you really quite alone?' she wouldn't answer the question, scared, I suppose, for her goods and her honour.

If Duogobmai was the dirtiest place in the Republic, Zorzor

was the most desolate. It hadn't been left to itself; the whites had intruded, had not advanced, had simply stuck and withered there, leaving their pile of papers, relics of a religious impulse, sentimental, naive, destined to failure. Mrs Croup's husband had been drowned at Monrovia: the other man in the mission had gone off his head. Mrs Croup had been alone now for six months. I heard her voice whining away across the compound, as I hypocritically called after her some expression of my pleasure at sleeping in a house after the native huts, 'Well, I guess we try to keep it free of bugs.'

But she was a kind woman, and her whine had its excuse. I found next day that I was whining too. It was the heat. One hadn't the energy to finish forming words; the voice trailed out, like bad handwriting, after the first syllable. She was kind, courageous, practical and a little bizarre. She sold me a cracked lamp from the mission stores at a great deal more than its value, and she kept a black baby in her house and a cobra in her garden. The cobra she fed with a live chicken every day; she had always meant to watch it as it swallowed the chicken, but somehow, though she guessed it would be interesting, she had never thought to watch through the lid of the hutch at the right time. She said enigmatically, 'I'd have sent you an invite to dinner, but I'm going home in six months,' an excuse which became even more difficult to understand when later in the evening, learning that we were leaving next day, she said: 'Oh, if I'd known you were going that soon, I'd have sent you an invite.'

That evening I had a conference at her house. She had advised me to cut across the corner of French Guinea to Ganta, making my first stay at Bamakama. As usual the carriers said it was too far. So I took Amah down to her, as the spokesman of the men, and Vande slid in at the door with a dour silent carrier who always trailed at his heels. They sat on stools and the baby crawled about their feet and Mrs Croup stoked up a roaring fire in the tiny stuffy tropic room lined with photographs in Oxford frames.

But as Mrs Croup talked, I became more and more doubtful whether she really knew anything about the route. She always travelled in a hammock specially made to carry her weight, with eighteen hammock-carriers. She drove them hard: a ten-hour trek was nothing to her. She sent out for a man who knew the route, but he had never been farther than Bamakama and then he had taken two days over the journey; he believed there was a short way by Jbaiay, but he wasn't sure whether it was passable, whether the chiefs had mended the bridges since the last rains. I could see the carriers' doubts growing; they were thinking that again I was going to force them into too long a trek. So I told them that we would go next day to Jbaiay and there discover the road to Bamakama; if it was too far we would spend the night at Jbaiay. They assented to the plan with suspicious alacrity . . .

There were no rats that night: only cockroaches, ready to eat anything available. They lay there, while the light was on, flat-tened like large blood blisters against the wall, but when it was extinguished they flashed faster than lizards on the hunt. Sir Harry Johnston, who knew only the coast districts of Liberia, never penetrating, I believe, much farther inland that his rub-ber plantation at Mount Barclay outside Monrovia, speaks of these cockroaches as 'obviously harboured and bred in the heaps of refuse which accumulate' in the Americo-Liberian set-tlements. But really they can be found everywhere in the Re-public. 'These insects,' he wrote, 'do not hesitate at night to attack human beings who are asleep. They creep to the corners of the mouth of the sleeping person to suck the saliva. They eat the toe-nails down to the quick, and above all, they gnaw at any sore place or ulcer on the skin. . . . Dr Büttikofer relates that he only saved his body from attack at one time by placing bowls of rice and sugar in his bedroom as a counter-attraction. . . . The present writer has been attacked in a some-what similar way, but on board dirty and uncomfortable steamers on the West Coast a good many years ago. In the bunks of these steamers cockroaches swarmed, and there were of course no mosquito curtains to shield the unfortunate pas-senger, who would wake in the dead of night, in black dark-ness, to find two or three large cockroaches clinging to his lips.'

This, as I grew more tired and my health a little failed,

seemed to be what I would chiefly remember as Africa: cockroaches eating our clothes, rats on the floor, dust in the throat, jiggers under the nails, ants fastening on the flesh. But in retrospect even the cockroaches seem only the badge of an unconquered virginity, 'never sacked, turned, nor wrought'. In Sierra Leone, in the bright electric Hill Station, one was conscious under the fans beside the iced drinks of how the land had been subdued; but even in the capital town of Liberia one was aware only of a settlement, a very chancy settlement that might be wiped out at any time by yellow fever. White and black, they were living here for a short while on the surface of the land, but Africa had the last say, and it said it in the form of rats and ants, of the forest swallowing up the little pits the Dutch prospectors had made and abandoned. There is not so much virginity in the world that one can afford not to love it when one finds it.

4
Black Montparnasse

THE CARRIERS' STRIKE

Next morning we entered France: so the colony was known among the natives of the Republic. One of the men reported sick before we started, was paid off and left behind. The number of carriers had now almost reached a minimum. My cousin used a hammock and needed four carriers, but I reduced my hammock-men to three: I hadn't used the hammock yet and unless I went sick I saw no reason why I should ever need to use it.

The country was stamped as French from the first village we stayed in, which was neither Bamakama nor Jbaiay as I had intended: French in its commercial sense, in its baits which I should have believed to be intended for tourists, if there had been any hope of tourists. It was astonishing what a difference the invisible boundary made. You could not have mistaken this land for Liberia. Tourists would have been quite at home here among the round huts and the scarlet fezes of the Mandingo traders. For these traders were indistinguishable, except that their dignity was less tarnished, from the men who sell carpets in the Dôme and the Rotonde. The only difference was we had followed them home. It was as if we had shadowed them all the way from the Boule Miche, sitting in third-class carriages, travelling steerage, riding up the long way from Conakry on horseback.

In 'France' the trouble with the carriers came to a head. Their complaints, the phrase 'too far', 'too far', had got on my nerves. To be deserted altogether, I began to think, might be preferable to this recurrent bickering, this pressure to go more slowly than I could afford. The trouble was I did not know the extent of my authority and I did not know which of them I could trust. Vande I suspected; the headman was a cheerful rogue with his pipe and his cloth cap and his rattle; but it sometimes seemed to me that he let the carriers have their own way too often. I trusted Amah, because Amah was unpopular with the other men; I trusted Babu, the Buzie, and his friend Guawa; I thought I could trust my hammock-man, Kolieva, who went ahead with me on each day's march.

But it was Kolieva who led me effectually astray the first day in France. We took the wrong path from the first: the carriers had evidently talked in Zorzor with the inhabitants and decided that the way to Bamakama by Jbaiay was too long and rough. No one ever knew the name of the town we reached about two hours later, across the upper reach of the St Paul. It sounded like Koinya. It was distinguished from the Liberian villages by a kind of town-planning. The huts of the chief and his wives were enclosed by a high wall in the centre, round which the town circled. The whole place was rather like an encampment of traders on the road.

When Amah arrived he interpreted what the chief had to say: that Bamakama was a full day's trek away and that he was uncertain whether the paths between them had been cleared or the bridges opened after the last rains. He was a man of great dignity, a little below the average Mandingo height with a black beard and a scarlet fez and a country robe and that Semitic expression in the dark eyes above the hooked nose of being open to the commercial chance. The men in the village had their hair curiously cut into patterns and tufts: I had seen nothing of the kind in Liberia. Their heads were often completely shaved except for two tufts, at the crown and the nape; they looked like poodles, and a poodle of course is a French dog. The women in French Guinea, too, lived up to the standard of a country which provides the handsomest whores and the most elegant brothels; their hair was gummed into complicated ringlets like watch-springs round the ears, they were sometimes painted on the face with blue and ochre, as well as the usual white stripes, and this gave them the thick rather unfinished look of a modern portrait.

It was no good going on after what the chief had said. He promised a guide for the next day and had the only square hut in the village swept out. This was another peculiarity of the French colony, that every town had to supply a rest-house for travellers. The idea would have been a better one if travellers had been more frequent, but these rest-houses (usually, though not in Koinya, a little outside the towns in a compound of their own) had almost always fallen to decay with spiders building across the doors, the thatch dropped in and the cook-house a ruin over the ashes of old fires. In Koinya, perhaps, the inhabitants were far enough from the route of any French Commissioner to use the rest-house themselves, with the result that it was clean and well cared for.

No sooner were we settled in the hut than trade began. Everything was for sale. There was no such thing as dashing here. The dash, though it has become a convenient method of extorting money, must have originated in a gesture of courtesy and hospitality, in a generosity rather alien to the modern Mandingo mind. All the junk of civilization had been washed up in the village like the last line of seaweed on a beach. One could get porcelain pans and pails, knives crudely decorated with silver alloy and brass to catch a stranger's jackdaw eye; even the common curved cutlass for hacking a path through the bush was offered gaudily got up, its handle covered with the alloy from Napoleonic coins, the blade as blunt as wood. It must have been the pure spirit of commerce which led them to manufacture these objects (they could not have encountered white tourists here twice in ten years), or perhaps this was the obscure factory from which the gimcrackery on sale in Conakry and Dakar, in Paris itself, came; we had stumbled on an industrial centre in the furthest corner of one of the least known of the French colonies. Perhaps even the cannibals on the Ivory Coast were now chiefly occupied in manufacturing baits for tourists.

The carriers had only marched for half a day, but they had eaten before they left Zorzor and there was trouble in the air. They kept sulkily apart from my hut, all except Babu and Amah, talking in high angry voices. I was no longer a patriarch among my retainers; I was the unjust employer; there was bad blood somewhere which had to be let out. It worked a little on the nerves not knowing what complaint they would make or when they would bring it to me; and the worst of it was that I could not lose my temper. I must remain cheerful and good-humoured, I had to laugh at them however much I wanted to curse them.

In the afternoon I lay down, but I couldn't sleep. A little while before sundown, when I was sponging myself in my tin bath, Amedoo came into the hut. He said, 'The labourers say they want more money. Massa say no.' He was the perfect manservant; he advised me how to meet a mutiny with the calmness and firmness of Jeeves advising Bertie Wooster on the choice of a tie. But it was sometimes a strain to live up to him: his loyalty, his honesty and his complete reliability demanded so much in return: a master, too, who was reliable as he understood reliability, in the imperial manner. He had lived with District Commissioners; he completely failed to understand any other than the official attitude of a man to his carriers. It was a relief to me when in the last week of the trek even Amedoo's morale began to weaken.

I lingered as long as I could in my bath; it was embarrassing to know that Amedoo would judge me by my conduct now; it would have been so disgracefully easy to have given way. For, after all, the carriers were disgracefully underpaid. At last I had to go outside, sit down, pretend to write my diary. I was aware of them watching me, judging the moment to strike. I felt like a fly on the wall and they held the whisk. Then Kolieva came for-

ward, and about fifteen carriers drifted up in a close group behind him. I hadn't expected Kolieva to be one of them. He was
embarrassed and that helped me; he was exaggeratedly sullen
and falsely dignified, his heavy lip drooped, he beat at his toes
with a stick and spoke thickly. He was the only one of the mu-
tineers who knew a few words of English. It occurred to me as
I counted the number of the strikers that I could never reach
my objective without them, paying at every town for new carriers at the Government rate. If they remained firm and took
their pay and left us, we should have to cut straight through the
forest towards Monrovia. I wasn't sure that my money would
last even then. If they had only known it, they had all the aces
in their hand.

Kolieva said they wanted to talk to me. They wanted more
money. I pretended not to understand him. I said I was willing
to lend anyone a little money on his wages. Vande had already
borrowed sixpence at Zigita. How much would they like?
Kolieva grew more embarrassed; he said the Government wage
for a carrier was a shilling a day. He was quite right of course;
the proper wage was a shilling, though I believe it was legal to
contract over a period at a smaller rate, and actually no one in
Liberia, except a few unfortunate travellers taking carriers from
town to town, ever pays the proper wage. Certainly not Government officials, who can generally get carriers for no payment
at all.

I said the Government wage didn't include food, and I was
paying for their food. They could not tell that their food only
came to about twopence a head; but they stood in a surly circle, not really listening to anything. It was no good arguing the
merits of the case. Besides, the merits were all on their side. I
was exploiting them like all their other masters, and it would
have been no comfort to them to know that I could not afford
not to exploit them and that I was a little ashamed of it. I pretended to be puzzled, to understand nothing of what they
meant; they had contracted . . . I told somebody to fetch Vande
and when he came I asked him what it was they were arguing
about; I had understood from him that they had agreed to
work for three shillings a week.

Then I bluffed. There was nothing else to do. They had me on the spot. Babu and Amah were on my side and of course my servants; Vande, too, I thought, from the way he spoke to them, though I couldn't understand a word of Bande. I said, 'Tell them they can go home. I'll give them their pay, but they won't get any dash, I'll take new carriers here.' He talked to them, they shouted things at him, after what seemed a long while he smiled. He said, 'They no want to go.' It was the moment to strike harder. Kolieva seemed to be the ringleader; I told him to go. I'd pay him off. I thought to myself all the while: if I can keep them together for a fortnight more they will be in a country as strange to them as to me; they won't want to leave. There was a tribe, about a week ahead, which was still supposed to practise cannibalism on strangers; they wouldn't want to be paid off there. But I had won: Kolieva explained it was all a mistake, grinning with shame; and a moment later they were laughing and joking as if there had been no disagreement; they were like children who have tried to get an extra holiday but bear no grudge because they have never really believed they would succeed. The dispute had let out most of the bad blood; for two more days there were to be continual arguments, which wore my temper to threads, and then quite suddenly they began to work together happily and smoothly.

Vande asked whether they could kill the kid I had been given in Kpangblamai, and it seemed the right moment for conciliation. I said 'yes', not expecting the immediate slaughter there in front of the hut: the little kid held down on the ground by its legs like a crucified child, the knife across the throat and the screams through the flow of blood. The kid took a long time dying, the blood welling out across the earth, gathering in pools on the baked unporous ground, as the light went and someone in the chief's enclosure began to shake a rattle. And it was good to know that one had not been deserted.

BAMAKAMA

The next day wasn't so good. We were out on the trail with a guide from Koinya by seven, but the paths were very rough for the carriers, and they and my cousin fell a long way behind.

There was a multiplicity of little paths and the country was slowly changing from the Liberian hills and forest to a plateau covered with tall elephant grass twice the height of a man, a plateau which I suppose stretches northward to what Mungo Park called the Mountains of Kong, and then on again to the Niger. On one of these tiny paths I saw the only horse, with the exception of the bony mare in Freetown, I saw in West Africa; an old Mandingo with a white beard and a turban sat it and watched us go by through the grass. A boy carried all their gear upon his head. He may have come from very far away, perhaps from the Sahara.

After three and a half hours' march we reached the St Paul River again, or the Diani as this upper reach is called. On either side the forest followed it, a slow shadowed river, seventy yards across, under the huge trees. It was only at the watersides that nature was ever beautiful: away from the rivers it was too dry and shrivelled and lifeless for beauty. But here there was faint movement, depth and gleam: refreshment, too, in the thought that the great slow stream was moving down to *our* destination, though by a quicker route, and would come out two hundred miles or so farther, past the great central forest, into the flats and mangrove swamps of Monrovia.

A ferry took us to the other side, a raft built of the trunks of trees lashed together and pulled across on a creeper rope. Amedoo was with me and Amah and about ten of the carriers; the others were somewhere behind with my cousin. After half an hour I was anxious, but my anxiety was small compared with Amedoo's. He had been ordered in Sierra Leone by Daddy to take care of us and never to show his face again in Freetown without us, and the responsibility weighed on him. He walked restlessly up and down the high bank above the river, shouting, but the sound died out a few yards away among the trees. There was nothing we could do if they had lost their way, and my cousin's lot really would have been happier than mine. My cousin had Laminah and the cook and Vande, the beds and mosquito-nets, and most of the food and more than half the carriers. I tried to make up my mind what I should do; it would be no use chasing each other all over French Guinea. I decided to go on, just as my cousin, I learnt later, had decided to go back.

But at last when I was on the point of giving the order to march, for fear we should be caught by darkness in the bush, an answer *did* come, from between the big trees, from across the water, and presently a tired angry band rejoined us. Among the many paths which had to be closed with sprays, one had been left open and they had taken it. The path had narrowed into nearly nothing at all, but they went on, Laminah cutting a way for them with the sword he wore, until they reached a closed wall of greenery and knew they were lost. In such densely overgrown country it was easy enough to be lost completely within a mile of a village and for all they knew they might be ten miles from any other human beings. If it had not been for the river I should have gone straight on to Bamakama without knowing that they were lost, and if Laminah had not found a man who guided them to the St Paul, a piece of luck they couldn't have expected when once they had strayed off the main path, we should have been permanently separated, for my cousin had no idea of the route I intended to follow the other side of the St Paul.

Another four hours' marching along narrow winding trails through thick elephant grass brought us to Bamakama. Here there was a rest-house for travellers outside the village in a small rotting compound, but it was so long since any white man had used it that it was in a horrible state of decay, the hut was full of bugs, and suddenly as we drank our tea an army of flies descended on the compound, settling all over our faces and the food. The monkey sat in a corner moaning like a child, and as the sun declined and the flies left us, the cockchafers came, detonating against the wall. A rat had died under the floor, and the smell of decay settled over the compound. This was the second place where there was nothing to do but get drunk. We looked across the wall with envy towards the airy village. We were enclosed like lepers with the dead rat and the cockchafers.

And again there was the inevitable palaver. That night it was the water-carriers who caused the bother. The water for our washing and for the filter had to be carried up every day from the nearest stream in basins. Kolieva headed a deputation. I couldn't make out clearly what it was about; a tribal dispute seemed to have split the carriers into hostile groups. They complained, I think, that Amah, the second headman, favoured the Bande carriers; they didn't do their share of the water-carrying. They asked that Amah should cease to be second headman. The fight went on a long while and I was glad to be a little drunk. But I slept badly; what Daddy had told me in Sierra Leone came back now when my nerves were tired with the marches and the squabble. I imagined all night that leeches were falling on my face. It was really the plaster ceiling of the pretentious rest-house which the rats were demolishing. I was too drunk to remember that the mosquito-net protected me.

GALAYE

The smell of the dead rat, the cockroaches which had got at our clothes and eaten them into holes, drove us away early. I was anxious above everything to get to Ganta. Mrs Croup had spoken of it as three days away, but the chief at Bamakama seemed to think it was at least another three days off. It seemed to recede rather than approach; nobody at Bamakama really knew the way, because Ganta was in Liberia, another country, and though the Mandingo traders recognize no boundaries, their country stretching from Timbuctoo to the Coast and Paris, across desert and forest, the ordinary tribesman has seldom moved more than a day's march from his town. The boundaries between country and country, as between tribe and tribe, might be no more than a tiny stream the carriers waded through beneath a shower of butterflies, but they could not have been more definite if all the European display of barbed wire and Customs sheds had been visible on either bank.

The chief strapped on a sword and acted as guide. I was glad that he set so smart a pace: if we were ever to reach Ganta, I thought, the men had got to be raced through the villages between. I had promised them a short march of three hours; but I was afraid my temper would give way altogether if I had to argue them on at every village. So we raced ahead, the chief and I and Kolieva, and left my cousin and the men to follow;

I knew the carriers hadn't the resolution to stop behind without me.

It took exactly three hours to get to Galaye, a populous little town with the remains of old mud walls at the back like pieces of abandoned scenery. The rest-house here was in such a state of decay that I wouldn't use it and chose a hut in the village instead. It was a hospitable place; few of the younger people had seen a white face before and they stood all day in the doorway. There was nothing you could do without their noticing it; to draw a handkerchief from the pocket caused a craning of necks. It worked a little on the nerves, this constant stare; but you had to recognize the superiority of their attitude over the white man's to do something strange. We were as good as a circus; they had no wish to stuff us or skin us or put us in cages. The carriers, after one more dispute over the water-carrying, were very cheerful, but I knew better by now than to expect their happiness to last. Their mood changed more rapidly than April weather. They, too, were appreciating something genuinely Gallic, for the girls of Galaye had an air of greater freedom towards strangers than I saw in any other tribe: one girl in particular who, when dark fell and the drums and harps were taken out, joined the carriers' dances, a stamping and thrusting out of the elbows and buttocks, a caricature of sexuality. When they approved of a dancer, the others crowded round and stroked his arms and forehead, a curious intimate tactile applause.

The dancing went on for hours in a close hot circle before our hut. The moon was half full, and the increasing light worked on their spirits. This was one of the revelations of Africa, the deadness of what we think of as alive, the deadness of nature, the trees and shrubs and flowers, the vitality of what we think of as dead, the cold lunar craters. The carriers were aware of the moon with an intimacy from which we were excluded. At Galaye it was already moving in their blood, so that even Amedoo burst into the circle and danced with a sudden wild lapse from dignity. But the most grotesque of the dancers was a moron dwarf. They dropped him into the ring with a couple of piccaninnies of three years old who were as tall as he, and he swayed a great inflated head, like a blister a pin would burst, to the beat of the rattle, and then howled and wept to be released.

I lay in bed while the music went on and held Burton against the mosquito-net to let the lamplight shine feebly through on the page of cheap print. The cover was already going damp, as if the book had been left out in the dew. The word *nigra* caught my eye, as I listened to the feet stamping and the calls I couldn't understand. I suddenly felt, reading the lines of Calpurnius Graecus, the irresistible tug of the familiar, a longing for flowers and dew and scent. It was hard to believe they existed in the same world and that there were emotions of tenderness and regret that couldn't be expressed with a harp, a drum and a rattle, buttocks and black teats.

> Te sine, vae misero mihi, lilia nigra videntur,
> Pallentesque rosae, nec dulce rubens hyacinthus,
> Nullos nec myrtus nec laurus spirat odores.

I put the light out and listened to the moonlit tumult, but when it ceased and the villagers crept into their huts and put up the doors, there was such a rush of rats down the walls that I switched on my torch and saw the shadows racing down. But I had left my door open and they didn't stay. I had the night to myself.

THE DEAD FOREST

The next day was the eleventh of the trek, and we turned back into the great forest with very little idea of where we should spent the next night, except that I was determined it should be at least fifteen miles towards the vanishing Ganta. Examining my diary I find the first expression of a weariness which was more mental than physical. Ganta, which I had thought was two days away from Zorzor, seemed to be receding. I had long given up thinking in terms of hours, but I still clung to time in the sense of darkness and daylight, not admitting yet that to be happy in Africa one must cease to count even the days and weeks and months.

The chief at Galaye told me that Ganta was still three days away, and only after Ganta would we begin to head south. Every march took us farther from the Coast.

It was not that the villages were ever dull to me, and only here in French Guinea were their simplicity and hospitality a little tarnished by the touch of white rule, but the rising in the dark, the hurried breakfast, the seven hours of tramping along narrow paths through the hot-house forest with no view to either side and only occasional glimpses of sky above, this routine became almost unbearable. I was usually alone with a carrier or a guide who couldn't speak English, for Mark and Amedoo could not keep my pace, and I had to try in vain to occupy the mind, to think of things to think about. I would calculate: I can think of this place or that person for so many hundred steps, and I would have a sense of triumph when the thought lasted me for a few dozen steps further than I had hoped. But usually it was the other way; the image or the idea lost interest a long while before I had taken the hundred paces. And this succession of thoughts had to be kept up for six or seven hours on end. I remember for what a long time I was able to think of fruit salts, for far longer and with more longing than I thought of beer or iced drinks. I suppose my digestion was suffering from the tinned foods, rough rice, the dry tough African chickens, and about five eggs a day. For the only way to economize our tinned supplies, which threatened to run short, was to eat off the country, rice, eggs and chicken, for meal after meal.

If the forest had been full of dangerous life the day's marches would have been more supportable. A few monkeys, a snake or two, the sound of heavy birds creaking invisibly overhead, and ants, ants everywhere, this was all the life in the dead forest. The word 'forest' to me had always conveyed a sense of wildness and beauty, of an active natural force, but this forest was simply a green wilderness, and not even so very green. We passed on twelve-inch paths through an endless back garden of tangled weeds; they didn't seem to be growing round us so much as dying; there was no view, no change of scene, nothing to distract the eyes, and even if there had been, we couldn't have enjoyed the sight, for the eyes had to be kept on the ground all the way, to avoid the roots and boulders. It was a relief, a distraction, when a stream broke the path. A carrier would horse one across, for it was dangerous to wet the feet in the tiniest shallow stream because of guinea-worm which the Mandingo traders had brought down from the Sahara. The smell of the carriers had long ceased to be noticeable: I suppose our own smell by that time was bad enough, for fear of the same worm prevented us bathing as the carriers did in the rivers. The guinea-worm makes its way through any sore in the foot, going up as far as the knee. When the foot is afterwards put in water the worm spews its eggs into the water through the sore. The only way to deal with it in the absence of a doctor is to find its end like a thread of cotton and wind it out in a long unbroken length round a match-stick. If the worm breaks, the leg may fester.

It was little wonder, then, that the senses were dulled and registered only acute boredom. I suppose there was some beauty in the forest, but the eye had long ceased to be aesthetic. The great swallow-tailed butterflies which rose in clouds round our waists at the stream sides seemed no more worth watching than the black ants which fastened on the flesh.

Perhaps the Liberian forest is peculiar in Africa for the quality of deadness, for other writers more often complain in *their* parts of Africa of the noise and savagery of the jungle. M. Céline is an example. 'The forest is only waiting for this signal [the sunset] to start to shake, whistle and moan in all its depths, like some huge, barbarous, unlighted railway station. . . .' How we would have welcomed the moans and whistles of that station. You can grow intimate with almost any *living* thing, transfer to it your own emotion of tenderness, nostalgia, regret, so that often of a relationship one remembers the scene with the most affection. A particular line of hedge in a Midland county, a drift of leaves in a particular wood: it is only human to imagine that we receive back from these the feeling someone left with them. But no one had ever transferred to *this* forest any human emotion at all. Like the shell of a house on a bankrupt housing estate it had never been lived in.

That poem of A. E. Housman's which begins

> Tell me not here, it needs not saying,
> What tune the enchantress plays
> In aftermaths of soft September
> Or under blancing mays,
> For she and I were long acquainted
> And I knew all her ways.

had a curious fascination for me during those weeks; it was like a succession of pleasant sounds in a foreign language; it represented the huge difference between this Nature and what I had previously known. I used to reserve it as a last resort for when I could think of nothing else to think about and recite it very slowly to myself, wondering whether I had covered a hundred yards between the first and last verse.

The poem had ceased to mean anything; it was impossible here to think of Nature in such terms of enchantment and nostalgia; it would have been like cherishing a dead weed in a pot, a sign of mental derangement.

> And full of shade the pillared forest
> Would murmur and be mine . . .

So Housman wrote, sharing the feeling of Wordsworth and many English Nature poets, that Nature was something alive which could be possessed as one possesses a friend or a lover, but this forest had never belonged in that way to anyone. Perhaps it was even wrong to think of it as dead, for it had never been alive.

But it was only fair, I suppose, that the moments of extraordinary happiness, the sense that one was nearer than one had ever been to the racial source, to satisfying the desire for an instinctive way of life, the sense of release, as when in the course of psycho-analysis one uncovers by one's own effort a root, a primal memory, should have been counterbalanced by the boredom of childhood too, that agonizing boredom of 'apartness' which came before one had learnt the fatal trick of transferring emotion, of flashing back enchantingly all day long one's own image, a period when other people were as distinct from one-self as this Liberian forest. I sometimes wonder whether, if one had stayed longer, if one had not been driven out again by tiredness and fear, one might have relearned the way to live without transference, with a lost objectivity.

RAIN IN THE AIR

The chief from Galaye acted as our guide back from the plateau into the forest, wearing for the occasion a black tail coat and a green beret, with one of his men to follow him and carry his sword. At a large village, Pala, they told us that the next town was Bamou, a long way off; we should certainly not reach it until six, and we had started the march at seven. There was nowhere in between where we could sleep. The men were grumbling already as they arrived, and I could foresee a long series of angry complaints. But I wouldn't consent to stay at Pala, (that would be to delay our arrival at Ganta too long), so I didn't wait for all the carriers to arrive, to get together and rebel, but walked off with a guide, the hammock-men and Amedoo.

We went for more than three hours without passing a village, and the path was wide enough for the sun to scorch us incessantly; for lunch we had to make a clearing with swords in the bush itself to gain enough shade. But in the small village we reached at last I learnt to my relief of a town not more than an hour and a half away. The village chief was hospitable, bringing out gourds of palm wine for my carriers to drink, and I did not notice in time his unwillingness to offer his hand. Only after I had put out my own and he had reluctantly taken it did I see that it was covered with white sores. It may not have been leprosy, and in any case leprosy is only very slightly contagious, but it spoilt my food for me all that day.

I never knew the name of the place we reached. It cannot have been Bamou, for we must have left that path. It had a guest-house in a little enclosure just outside the town. The chief was sullen and inhospitable, he wouldn't provide a cooked meal for the carriers, nor would he allow them to sleep in the town. He said they would cause trouble there. I bought rice from him at the highest rate I had yet paid and he left again with his headman and a little train of disapproving ancients.

The air was heavy with thunder. The carriers felt it as they lay about in the verandah. I sat listening to snatches of argument, until just before sunset, as the storm gathered and bore down out of the north-west, shouts and bugle-calls brought everyone to the fence. A procession was approaching the compound from the village. A man with an old sporting gun over his shoulder led the way, then a covered hammock borne by four men, attendants running on either side and one of them blowing blasts on a bugle. I thought it must be at least a French Commissioner and hoped that he would not ask to see my papers, for I had no visa which would allow us to pass through a French colony. But it wasn't a French Commissioner who stepped out of his hammock and strutted to the gate with a dog at his heels and a riding whip hung at his wrist. He was a black with tight curled ringlets and black side-whiskers. He wore an old white topee, a Fair Isle jumper, breeches and braces and a belt, gaiters and little white kid boots. He stood swinging his whip, watching us as if we were curious caged animals, with superb arrogance. Somebody said he was the chief from Djiecke, the next town on the track to Ganta. He spoke neither English nor French, but when I asked him through Mandingo Amah how far it was to Djiecke, and told him that I intended to reach the town next day, the answer came, of course, 'too far'. It seemed unlikely, for it was nearly sunset and he would hardly have planned to spend the night in the bush. When he had stared at us for long enough he swaggered back to his hammock and to the sound of one more heraldic blast was borne away swaying into the forest.

A heavy storm broke soon after dark: lightning like one prolonged flickering illumination. The carriers slept on the floor of the verandah. The sound of their breathing and snores was very companionable in the pounding electric night, and they kept away the rats. But the storm worried me. The dry season was supposed to last another month, but sometimes the rains came early. It would never do to be caught in the interior, for on the lower level below Ganta the ways in the wet season were impassable; Central Liberia between the villages became a swamp, and we had not yet even turned towards the south.

CAFÉ BAR

Suddenly in the inconsequent manner of Africa Ganta came close and we left French Guinea behind us. On the last day the colony proved more than ever French. Djiecke took us by surprise after only two hours' march, a neat native school behind a gateway, Ecole de Djiecke, in a tidied park-like plain.

A small fussy black in a topee and European clothes and pince-nez came to meet our train from the school compound. He was very conceited, very inquisitive and we couldn't understand each other's French. When he learned that we were English he became deeply suspicious. He wanted to know where we had come from and when I said Sierra Leone he was convinced that I was lying. I think his geography was vague, for he couldn't understand that we could have come from Sierra Leone by land. He wanted to know what canton we had just left, but I didn't even know what a canton was. I thought it had something to do with Switzerland.

With every question he became more official, excited and conceited. I don't know what impression of a foreign spy he gained from my vague manner. He said we must see the French District Commissioner, a day's march away. He seemed to me dangerous; if he had authority in the town he might hold us up indefinitely. So I was polite, probably too polite, telling him that it was impossible, I must go straight on; for if this was Kjiecke, Ganta was at last very close. I could see his little thin black body swelling under the drill, for he personified the power of France. He asked to see my passports and after a search in the baggage I found them and showed him the word 'France' in the list of countries for which the passport was available. I don't think it quite satisfied him, he had more brains than I bargained for, but at that moment there was an interruption. We were standing close to the chief's compound and a message came from him that we were to enter and rest, while chop was prepared for our men. If we had had a taste of French officialdom, now we were to taste French hospitality.

The chief had shed his oddly-assorted European clothes. He was dour and handsome in his native robe and his sideburns, squatting on the floor of his hut with his daughters and wives around him. The daughters were the prettiest women I had seen in Africa. They lay round and over him like kittens. The schoolmaster left us disapprovingly; there was a distinct atmosphere of sex and relaxation about the scene and it didn't suit his pedagogic mind; but soon after a boy brought in a letter from him in French which one of the girls translated to her father. I think he may have asked the chief to detain us, for it became more and more difficult to get away. Not that I really in my heart wanted to go from the moment that the chief produced a bottle of French white wine, an enamel cup, and a tin of French cigarettes. It was like a dream: ever since we had entered French Guinea our minds had continually reverted to Dakar, to the cafés and the flowers and what seemed to us now the delicious freshness of the place where plague is endemic and the natives die of the want of will to live. I had sometimes tormented myself, washing out my mouth on the march with the warm filtered water—fruit had long since given out—with the thought of a bottle of wine.

And here it was. The chief sat grimly on the floor among his girls, with only the faintest suspicion of enjoyment about his mouth, and poured the warm sweet delicious wine into the enamel cup. He drank and passed it to me; I drank and passed it to my cousin. Back it went to the chief and was refilled. It didn't take long for the three of us to empty the bottle. We were all a little drunk in no time; the heat of the hut, the confused tumble of half-clothed girls helped. As there was no sign of the promised chop for my men, I sent a boy out to fetch a bottle of whisky from my case. The chief had never tasted whisky before, but he had innate taste; he didn't gulp down the neat spirit like the chief in Duogobmai. He sent a daughter for a pail of water and when the water was brought, he smelt it. It didn't pass his inspection, he emptied it on the ground and sent her for more. Then he settled down to drink, became grimly merry without moving from the floor and forced the whisky on his

favourite daughter, until she was drunk too. We grinned at
each other and made friendly gestures.

The favourite daughter could speak a few words of English:
her thigh under the tight cloth about her waist was like the soft
furry rump of a kitten; she had lovely breasts: she was quite
clean, much cleaner than we were. The chief wanted us to stay
the night, and I began to wonder how far his hospitality might
go. The girl was feeling a little sick with the whisky, but she
never stopped smiling. I felt that she would be as unobtrusively
and neatly sick as a cat and would afterwards be quite ready
for more fun. A boy of about sixteen came in and knelt in front
of his father. He pushed the whisky away; he wouldn't drink it;
and now he tried to stop his father drinking. He fetched a bottle and persuaded his father to put away every other drink for
future use.

It became more and more like a blind in Paris; the wine, the
bitter Gallic smoke, the increasing friendliness with someone
you can't speak to because you don't know the language well
enough. You've run across him in the Montparnasse bar and
gone on exchanging drinks ever since: you speak English and
he speaks French, and you don't understand each other. There
are a lot of girls about whom he seems to know and you'd
vaguely like to sleep with, but you can't be bothered because
the wine's good and you are beginning to feel a deep emotional
friendship for the man on the other stool. He seems to know
everyone: you don't understand a thing, but you are happy.

We were there two hours, right into the full heat of the day;
the men had their chop in the end, and the chief began to get
sleepy and forgot that he was supposed to detain us. I don't
really know why we ever went; the schoolmaster was the only
blot on the place; I think we might have been very happy there
all night. Perhaps if I hadn't been a bit drunk I'd have stayed,
but the idea I thought I had lost, that one ought to stick to
time-tables, came up again in the Parisian air, and I was a little
uneasy, too, lest the schoolmaster should have sent a quick
messenger to the French Commissioner and that we might find
ourselves under arrest—the French colonies are very carefully

preserved. So I refused to stay. Before we went I photographed
the girl, but she wouldn't be taken as she was, insisted on putting on her best dress for the picture: the chief would not be
photographed. By that time two men had to support him. He
followed us a little way out of the village, sleepily imploring us
to stay, until we were out of earshot.

It was another four hours' march to Ganta. Soon after
Djiecke we left the forest behind and took a path through elephant grass towards the River Mani or St John, which forms
the boundary line between French Guinea and Liberia and runs
south-west into the sea at Grand Bassa, a hundred and sixty
miles away. That was where we were to end our march, though
I didn't know it then. We were now at last off the route followed by other English travellers, for Sir Alfred Sharpe in 1919
went up northwards into French Guinea, another ninety miles
or so, and then retraced his steps and went down to Monrovia
between the Loffa River and the St Paul.

The Mani here was about forty yards wide with steep banks.
We crossed by dug-out canoe, and the spirit of all the carriers
lifted on the other side. They hadn't really liked France, and
Mark's enthusiasm as he stepped on shore, the monkey clinging
to his skull, infected them. 'Now we are in our own land
again.' It was an unexpected example of national feeling, for
they were certainly not among their own tribe; they were in the
land of the Manos, where ritual cannibalism practised on
strangers has never been entirely stamped out. Amah ran up
and down the line of carriers with a load on his head encour-
aging them to a longer stride because this was Liberia.

One came to Ganta through a series of leopard traps, winding maze-like paths between walls of plaited reed, and then out
on to a beaten road, beside a straggling line of huts across a
wide treeless plain, up the side of a hill and down again, with
the Liberian flag flying above a whitewashed compound and
more people than we had seen for weeks, Mandingos and soldiers among them. There were stores here, the first we had seen
in Liberia, with the goods laid out on the ground, but the
whole appearance of the place was as nomadic as a forest market. It looked as if it had been built up overnight and might be

shifted next morning. It was the plain, I think, which gave it that air. One was used to villages circumscribed by a hill-top, with the burial stones and the palaver-house in the centre, looking as old as the rock itself and the cracked soil. This ribbon development along a highway which was being driven north and south had a raw look. Only the District Commissioner's compound at one end and the little group of mission buildings a mile down the road at the other had a stable air, as if the next rains wouldn't wash them away.

As our caravan came out on to the road from the river path and the leopard traps, a group of yellow-faced Liberians in European clothes, more like Italians than Africans, turned to watch us. One of them, the only dark-skinned one, took off his topee. Later in Tapee-Ta I was to get to know him better, and those soft sad lustrous seeking-a-friend eyes of his. He was called Wordsworth. He watched us yearningly as we toiled up the bare scorched road towards the Methodist mission. Already he was intent on joining that odd assortment of 'characters' (the Grants and the Kilvanes) one collects through life, vivid grotesques, people so simple that they always have the same side turned to one, damned by their unself-consciousness to be material for the novelist, to supply the minor characters, to be endlessly caricatured, to make in their multiplicity one's world.

PART THREE

Mission Station

THE LOWLANDS

Mr Somerset Maugham, I suppose, had done more than anyone to stamp the idea of the repressed prudish man of God on the popular imagination. There was an earlier time when Stevenson's *Open Letter* allowed us to recall Father Damien; *Rain* has impressed the image of Mr Davidson over the missionary field: the Mr Davidson who said of his work in the Pacific Islands, 'When we went there they had no sense of sin at all. They broke the commandments one after the other and never knew they were doing wrong. And I think that was the most difficult part of my work, to instil into the natives the sense of sin': the Mr Davidson who slept with the prostitute, Sadie Thompson, and then killed himself.

I remember at school finding it a little hard to reconcile the popular idea of missionaries with the thin tired men who used to stand on a platform rapping with a small stick while the starved-looking bodies of black children slid across the screen. They seemed to be less biblical than Mr Davidson; they seemed to be more concerned with raising a few shillings for the support of the hideous tin church which was projected as a grim climax onto the sheet than with the sense of sin. The sense of sin lay far deeper across the altar steps of our own school chapel. Here was all the prudery and pornography one needed. These visitors from Africa, I felt, were not only innocent beside our own masters, they were innocent among the blacks they taught. There they stood, in their ruined health and their worn simplicity, begging for our shillings for a new altar cloth, a silver cruet stand; I couldn't believe they had done much harm among the alligator societies, the human leopards, nor corrupted very effectively those men whose secret ritual it is to sacrifice a child once a year to the great python.

In Liberia I discovered another kind of missionary. I do not imagine Dr Harley, the Methodist medical missionary, is unique in Africa: a man with a body and nerves worn thread-bare by ten years' unselfish work, cutting away the pus from the huge swollen genitals, injecting for yaws, anointing from craw-craw, injecting two hundred natives a week for venereal disease. He had made his home in this corner of Liberia with his wife and two children, curious little elderly yellow-faced boys; he had lost one child, who was buried at the mission.*

All the way along the Liberian border I had heard of him; he was the man in Liberia who knew most about the bush societies—the little time that the long hopeless fight against disease allowed him was devoted to those investigations. But he did not care to talk about them before his servants for fear of poison.

We had been lent a house a hundred yards from the mission, a luxurious little house it seemed to us by this time, for it was built of wood with a tin roof, the floor raised to escape the ants. At one end was a dispensary, and just outside was the open hospital building, long wooden benches under a roof of thatch. The forest came up at the back, like a small private wood. Ganta scared me: there was a smell of chemicals, of sickness and death about the place. Quite suddenly we had dropped down from the highlands, and the air had changed. It was heavy and damp. There were palms about and a sense of drenched ground, flies and ordure. I would never have believed that a climate could so completely change in the course of a day's march. It had an immediate effect on the health: all energy left me: that night it was difficult to walk as far as the mission house for dinner; my stomach quite suddenly ceased to function.

I remember a rather grim dinner. Dr Harley had been out all day and was tired and ready to fall asleep where he sat; it was the dead boy's birthday. When he heard that I had walked from

*Dr Harley has now completed more than 20 years at Ganta. (1946)

the Sierre Leone border without using a hammock, he said I was mad to do it; he had just sent a man—Dr D—home dead who had made the comparatively short trek from Monrovia on his feet. Nobody could walk long distances in this climate without danger. I tried to turn the conversation to the bush societies, but he sheered away from them. He said that Sinoe, which we had planned to reach, was at least four weeks away. The pain I had been feeling for some days now in my stomach seemed to get worse at the news. I could have been happy enough settled in one place for months, but the thought of four more weeks of physical exertion, of rising before dawn and walking for six or seven hours through the dreadful monotony of the forest, I could not bear.

On the way back to our house I remember we hadn't taken our quinine for two days. The rats had been at the hairbrushes and gnawed the bristles. They ran along between the wall and the roof in my room without even waiting for me to put out the light. I took a handful of Epsom in the warm boiled water from the filter which was dripping regularly in the corner and watched them scamper along the narrow crack above my head. I didn't care a damn about the rats any longer, the sisters at Bolahun were right; I was scared in the same way as I had been in England when I suddenly found that my plans had gone too far for me to back out of the Liberian journey; I could remember reading the British Blue Book and thinking, 'In three weeks I shall be *there*,' 'there' meaning the long list of diseases and of Colonel Davis's atrocities. I got no thrill at all; I was just scared. I comforted myself, 'I shan't try for Sinoe,' but I knew I hadn't the moral courage to make straight for Monrovia. The rats jumped down when I turned out the lantern, but I wasn't any longer afraid of rats. I was discovering in myself a thing I thought I had never possessed: a love of life.

LIBERIAN COMMISSIONER

Of course by daylight I felt better; it is difficult to believe in death before sunset. But a four weeks' longer trek to Sinoe was beyond me, especially as I hadn't enough men with me now to use the hammock. There was one other excuse, too; no money. I had no means of getting more money at Sinoe and I should not have enough to pay the carriers after the longer trek.

We thought it politic to walk up through Ganta to call on the DC. He wore a well-cut tropical suit, a small military moustache, his skin was slightly yellow; he looked more Latin than African. He had a reputation for fairness, honesty and efficiency. Now he was engaged in driving the Sanoquelleh-Ganta road south. Once again we were encountering Liberian patriotism. This time it was of a more European brand. There was not a carrier who would not have welcomed white intervention; patriotism in their minds had nothing to do with who ruled them, it was love of a certain territory. But Commissioner Dunbar was one of the rulers. His patriotism was like a European's; to him the thought of white interference was hateful and because England's attitude to the Kru rebellion suggested a danger to Liberian independence, he suspected and disliked the English. He was courteous and reserved and it was hopeless to try to convince him that our journey had no political motive. I felt our amicable expressions becoming shrill in the effort to convince, beating hopelessly against the hard courteous surface of his mind. There was no need to convince him; but he was a man with such admirable qualities that one wanted to leave him with a good impression. But the more we struggled to leave that good impression, the more our voices sounded in our own ears false and hypocritical.

I tried to make him express some of his suspicions by mentioning the town on the forbidden coast-line, but he contented himself with saying that it would probably take us another five weeks to reach Sinoe. Should we have to wait long for a boat to Monrovia? Perhaps a month, he said, leaning back in his wicker chair, the blazing sun over the compound behind giving his yellow handsome face a blurred black outline. It was a politic inaccuracy, because, as we learnt later, there was a weekly launch. I suggested Grand Bassa as an alternative and he encouraged the idea: we could do it in ten days, he informed us, but that was an exaggeration. He didn't know the road himself, it was used only by the Mandingo traders; impassable in the rains, it would be a very rough way through the biggest bush, but ten days should see us on the Coast.

The Commissioner had other reasons than patriotism to distrust the white man. There was a Catholic priest at Sanoquelleh, his headquarters, and the previous Commissioner had been married to a Catholic. The priest had resented the difference between Dunbar and his predecessor; Dunbar had stood strictly to the letter of the law, allowing the priest no privileges. The priest tried to get rid of him, writing letters to the President of Monrovia; and the heat and desolation worked on both men. The priest saw his chance when one of the men working on the roads fell sick. He took him into the mission and the man died there. Immediately the priest wrote a letter accusing Dunbar of having starved his workers and beaten one to the point of death. Dunbar acted with admirable promptitude; he arrived at the mission with a squad of soldiers before the man was buried and carried both the body and the priest over the eighteen miles to Ganta, where he asked the American doctor to examine the body. Dr Harley exonerated him and the priest was expelled from the Republic. As for Dunbar, he had been made to realize that whites were not only hypocritical in their attitude to the Republic, they could be crooked in their dealings with individuals.

THE SECRET SOCIETIES

That afternoon the doctor came in to talk about the bush societies. His investigations were the only enthusiasm he had kept after ten years, but he wanted to be sure that my boys were out of the house. I went and looked in the kitchen where they slept. It was empty. Laminah was sitting in the shade of the hospital looking sick. The doctor had drawn a tooth of his in the morning: I had heard the painful dog-like howls through the wooden wall: and now he was afraid that he was going to die because the gum still bled. He was too sophisticated to paint himself with native medicine, but he had brought a pot of cold cream with him from Freetown and was smearing it all over his face and neck and scalp.

I am not an anthropologist and I cannot pretend to remember very much of what Dr Harley told me: a pity, for no white man is closer to that particular 'heart of darkness', the secret societies being more firmly rooted in Liberia than in any other country on the West Coast. The Government have put up the feeblest of resistances: though Colonel Davis, so he told me later, had court-martialled and shot fifty members of the Leopard Society in a village near Grand Bassa. Indeed, they could not properly resist because they *believed*. President King himself was rumoured to have been a member of the Alligator Society. When the League of Nations Commission was appointed to inquire into Liberian conditions, Mr King and several members of his cabinet—so it was believed in Monrovia—had sacrificed a goat. After the sacrifice, which should traditionally have been a human one, a boatload of young Krus had been drowned close to the beach at Monrovia, and it was generally felt that the alligator was dissatisfied with the goat.

It is a grim world, this of the societies, of the four men who, Dr Harley said, came to Ganta a year or two back from the north looking for a victim. Everyone in Ganta knew they were there, with their ritual need of the heart, the palms of the hands, the skin of the forehead, but no one knew who they were. The Frontier Force were active, searching for strangers. Presently the fear passed. The Manos round Ganta knew what the men were seeking, for they have their own cannibalistic societies, and though I had said nothing of this to my boys and there were no Manos among the carriers, Laminah and Amedoo knew all about it. Laminah said to me one day, 'These people bad, they chop men,' and they were happy to leave the Manos behind. This is the territory the United States map marks so vaguely and excitingly as 'Cannibal'.

The Terrapin Society of the women and the Snake Society of the men, of course, are not peculiar to the Manos. There is the ordinary snake society, a kind of postgraduate course in handling snakes, in curing their bites and dancing the snake dance, and the secret society which does actually worship a python, to which one baby should be sacrificed each year by the fully initiated. This was a common terror once: we came across the memory of what I suppose was a related cult at the sacred waterfall beyond Ganta; now only in Liberia, where the secret societies are so immune from interference, do cases of child murder or disappearance occur with any frequency.

Dr Harley was particularly pleased with having discovered the nature of one devil, the most sacred in the women's eyes, whom it is death for a woman to see. He found it was not an individual at all, but a circle of young warriors who had entered bush school at the same time as the chief's son. The women were warned by drums that the great devil was out, and the young men danced fully armed beating the ground with staffs.

Among all these devils, Dr Harley said, there was one supreme devil, whose fiat ran the length of the Coast and who had the power to stop war between tribe and tribe. He could appear simultaneously in places far apart: he was known by his distinctive mask and robes. These were probably stored in every place of importance along the Coast, above the palaver-house or in the blacksmith's hut. For the blacksmith of Mosam-bolahun, it appeared, was not peculiar in being the local devil. Dr Harley was inclined to believe that the craft of blacksmith was always linked with the status of devil.

It is a curiously Kafka-like situation: headmasters who wear masks and turn out to be the local blacksmith. . . . One reaches the village at the foot of the *Schloss*, to discover that almost anyone may be the master of the *Schloss*; his agents are everywhere . . . there is an atmosphere of force and terror . . . occasionally beauty . . . 'meaning behind meaning, form behind form'. I can imagine that after seven years of investigating this formal but Protean religion, one may still despair of an interpretation. Olga in Kafka's novel, it will be remembered, tried to construct 'out of glimpses and rumours and through various distorting factors' an image of Klamm. 'He's reported as having one appearance when he comes into the village and another on leaving it, after having his beer he looks different from what he does before it, when he's awake he's different from when he's asleep, when he's alone he's different from when he's talking to people, and—what is comprehensible after all that—he's almost

another person up in the Castle.' Take the case of the rich and
sinister headman at Zigita: for all anyone knew he might be the
devil himself . . . or was the devil the blacksmith? or was there
a devil in the sense of an individual at all, any more than the
group of young warriors had been a devil, was it perhaps a
fraud practised by the initiates? But it was a mistake to suggest
that the young warriors were frauds: in their composite form
they *were* the devil.

Then take the masks. I had asked Mark whether he feared
Landow when he was out of his mask and just the blacksmith
of Mosambolahun; and it was obvious that he feared him less,
but that even then the blacksmith retained an aura of something not quite human. Did the supernatural rest in the mask?
No, one person would say, it was in the combination of the
two, but on the other hand old disused masks were often retained as charms and 'fed', and there *were* masks, even apart
from the man who wore them, which it was fatal to a woman
to see: fatal presumably because the devil's agents would exact
retribution, with the knife or with poison, but to what extent
was this human punishment also supernatural?

'Devil', of course, is a word used by the English-speaking native to describe something unknown in *our* theology: it has
nothing to do with evil. One might equally call these big bush
devils angels—for they have the angelic properties of alacrity
and invisibility—if that word contained no element of 'good'.
In a Christian land we have grown so accustomed to the idea of
a spiritual war, of God and Satan, that this supernatural world,
which is neither good nor evil but simply Power, is almost beyond sympathetic comprehension. Not quite: for those witches
which haunted our childhood were neither good nor evil. They
terrified us with their power, but we knew all the time that we
must not escape them. They simply demanded recognition:
flight was a weakness.

That night Dr Harley showed us a grotesquely horrible collection of devils' masks. Each one had obviously been made by
a conscious artist. No effect was accidental. Here were the two-
faced masks of a woman's society; here male masks which
women were forbidden to see. These were different from the

masks worn by the dancing devils. Those had been part human, part animal, these were modelled closely on human features. There was one with a thin beard made of chicken's
feathers, and another, the oldest (it looked at least three hundred years old), had the thin nose, the high brow of a European. It was quite different from any other mask I saw. It might
have been modelled on the features of some Portuguese sailor
wrecked or marooned on the West Coast, or it may have gone
back no further than a slave-trader at the beginning of the last
century, a man like Canot whose autobiography is set on this
Liberian coast, a hanger-on perhaps of his Portuguese employer,
Dom Pedro Blanco, who built his extraordinary palace on the
debated marshy land between Liberia and Sierra Leone, near
Sherbro, where the cargo steamers of Elder Dempster still
sometimes call, to their crews' discomfort, a palace with separate islands for his seraglio, with billiard rooms and all the ad-
vantages, of both European and African civilization. The man
on whom the mask was modelled, of course, was as dead as
Canot, as the Liberian forest which some urgent motive had
caused him to penetrate—perhaps the desire for gold or slaves:
but all the power of his motive had gone into the mask. I do not
think it was greed: it was a fanatical curiosity which leant out
of the empty eyeballs.

A SACRED WATERFALL

Before we left Ganta I learned of a sacred waterfall in the forest near the village of Zugbei. If we made a detour on the way
to Sakripie, our next big town, we would pass the village. One
of Harley's pupils at the mission school was chief there, and
though the existence of the waterfall had been kept secret from
Dr Harley for many years, his pupil had lately shown signs of
willingness to guide him to it. Human sacrifice had once been
offered at the falls, but now the paths were no longer kept
open.

Next morning, as we were about to start along Dunbar's new
road north-east to Zuluyi, I heard that Babu could go no further, he was sick. He had been one of the few men, though he
spoke no word of English, with whom I thought I had some

contact. I had known him to be completely dependable; he had not joined with the carriers who had struck for more pay. I think he was genuinely sick; he had been given heavy loads the last few days and he was not strong, and none of the carriers would have chosen by this time to stay behind alone among a strange tribe, at least ten days' trek away from his own people. I should have liked to dismiss him with a handsome present, but it would only have encouraged others to go sick. I had to pretend anger and pay him off with a very small dash. I felt guilty of a meanness; he had no friends among the carriers, except Guawa, the other Buzie, and they taunted him. I would have lost any of them more willingly.

But it was awkward to lose any man when I was beginning to feel that I might soon need a hammock badly. There were not enough men now to carry even an empty hammock. I had to tell them to take the heavy pole out and leave it behind and add the hammock to one of the lighter loads. I could see the doctor watching me, critically; he didn't have to tell me what he was thinking.

It was about two hours' walk to Zuluyi. The chief there had been one of Harley's pupils and came to guide us to Zugbei. We passed through a thick steep forest country, up the slopes of what the natives believed to be a holy hill. Tiny fairy people, the chief said, had lived on this hill and they used to come down and help the Manos in war. Harley was interested; it was the first he had heard of any pygmy traditions in Liberia. There might be remains . . . I think he was picturing to himself reports, excavations, wall paintings, and the only kind of glory his altruistic spirit could appreciate. There was a big hole, the chief said, pointing up a path which disappeared a few feet away into the trees and underbrush, where the small people used to live. Boys used to go once a year with gifts into the hole. The last boy who had gone to the hole was still alive, an old man, in Zugbei. He had had his head shaved, but when he came out his hair was dressed in ringlets. Now no one went into the hole any more, but gifts were still brought

We reached Zugbei, a tiny village, in the fiercest heat of the day: a worse heat than we had had in the highlands; the air was already saturated with the coming rains. The villages were no longer perched on thimbles of rock above the forest. One came straight into them from the bush; they were like little dried-up airless pools.

The chief led us to the waterfall. None of us expected to see more than a thin trickle or water over a few boulders, for some of the large rivers were so low that the carriers could wade through them and the dug-out canoes lay on the banks cracking for want of use. We walked straight into the thickest wall of forest. The chief and another man led, clearing a path with cutlasses. It was impossible to tell how they knew the way. They walked along fallen trees, scrambled down slopes at an angle of forty-five degrees, cutting all the time; there was no sign of a path. Then suddenly at the bottom of the steepest hill we came out into a dell full of the sound of water, which streamed under feathers of foam over a fall sixty feet deep. All the slopes became alive with people, girls with the pretty horn-shaped breasts of the Manos, men with cutlasses. The whole village seemed to have come with us, but the forest had been so thick we had seen only the chief and his companion. They sat on the slopes staring at the incredible bounty of water. Within the young chief's memory there had been human sacrifices at the fall, the feeding of a slave at the end of each dry season to a snake, a hundred feet long, who had lain below the fall. It was the myth of the rainbow snake which one finds as far afield as Australia: the materialization of the rainbow shimmer in the falling water. The sacrifice had ended when the present chief was a child. The slave, though his hands were tied behind him, had grasped the chief's robe and carried him over the edge of the fall. That had been the end of the sacrifice and the snake had gone down the river to the St John and lived now in a pool, very close to where we crossed, between Ganta and Djiecke.

We said good-bye to Dr Harley in Zugbei. We could have slept there, but I couldn't bear the thought that we had not yet turned south. I wanted at least the sensation of moving, however short a distance, towards the Coast. So we went on for half an hour due south to a dull village of which I couldn't learn the name. It sounded like Mombei. The chief would have no chop cooked for the men, but he dashed me a hamper of rice and they cooked their own. As usual there was no peace when we arrived. I was feeling sick and tired. The scramble in the heat to and from the waterfall had exhausted me more than a long trek, and it angered me that, directly I sat down, a carrier called Siafa came to show me his venereal sore. He had had it for three years, he hadn't shown it to the doctor, who could have injected him, and I felt he might have kept it for a few more weeks untended. But there was one thing I couldn't afford to do, show my impatience or my lack of knowledge. Daily after that I went through the farce of dressing the sore. Afterwards I dosed myself heavily with Epsom and went to bed; suddenly I felt hopelessly tired of rats; we were no longer short of kerosene, so I left my lamp burning, but it made no difference. There were always shadows for them to play in. The Epsom brought me out of my bed in the night to the edge of the forest. It was almost full moon and the huts stood out in a bright greenish daylight. It was absolutely quiet: not a sound from the dark dead forest. Every door was closed and the goats were the only living things in sight, as they wandered sleeplessly between the huts. I thought even then that the scene was beautiful, but the thought did not alter my impatience to be gone. The spell would only work after many months; now all I wanted was medicine, a bath, iced drinks, and something other than this bush lavatory of trees and dead leaves where at any moment I might crouch upon a snake in the darkness.

MYTHOLOGY

I dreamed that I was two thousand miles away from the mud hut and someone was outside the door waiting to come in. Perhaps a goat stumbling across the threshold and the dead fire caused the dream, or maybe a memory of the masks on Harley's table, bobbing up one after another into the sleeping mind, like grotesque balloons at a carnival released towards the ceiling, each with its individual expression of terror and power.

It is the earliest dream that I can remember, earlier than the witch at the corner of the nursery passage, this dream of something outside that has got to come in. The witch, like the masked dancers, has form, but this is simply power, a force exerted on a door, an influence that drifted after me upstairs and pressed against windows.

Later the presence took many odd forms: a troop of black-skinned girls who carried poison flowers which it was death to touch; an old Arab; a half-caste; armed men with shaven heads and narrow eyes and the appearance of Tibetans out of a travel book; a Chinese detective.

You couldn't call these things evil, as Peter Quint in *The Turn of the Screw* was evil, with his carroty hair and his white face of damnation. That story of James's belongs to the Christian, the orthodox imagination. Mine were devils only in the African sense of beings who controlled power. They were not even always terrifying. I remember that at the age of sixteen it was a being with the absurdly symbolic title of the Princess of Time who haunted my sleep. The poisoned flowers, the Tibetan guards, the old Arab whom I think of now as someone like the Mandingo chief at Koinya, were all in her service. I can still recall the dull pain in my palms and my insteps when I deliberately touched the flowers, for I was always trying to escape her, her kindliness as well as her destructiveness. Once I was incited to kill her: I was given a book of ritual, bound in limp leather like an Omar Khayyám at Christmas-time, and a dagger. But she survived into many later dreams. Any dream which opened with terror, with flight, with falling, with unseen presences and opening doors, might end with her cruel and reassuring presence.

It was only many years later that Evil came into my dreams: the man with gold teeth and rubber surgical gloves; the old woman with ringworm; the man with his throat cut dragging himself across the carpet to the bed.

2
'Civilized Man'

FULL MOON

Along the northern border we had been walking through the edge of the enormous bush; now we moved steadily lower and deeper into its heart. The deadness was sometimes broken by the squabble of monkeys; a baboon once crossed the path, running bent like an old man with the tips of its fingers just touching the ground; a leopard's pads had marked the sand by a stream, where a snake had come to drink. And outside the first village, Yeibo, there was a round shallow pond under thorn trees with great carp-like fish lounging lazily in the shadows. It was still early morning, I was happy with the sense that every step was towards home, there was something peculiarly English about the fish, the pond, the quite small trees. It was a foolish mind that had come all this way to find pleasure in a sight so vaguely, so remotely English, a pleasure I felt again when we came out of the forest into a stretch of land like a Midland park; a small stream, a long undulating pasture, a few cows, and groups of trees, like elms, in the long grass. A quarter of a mile away the forest wall set a limit to England, and across the stream in single file came a few men, naked except for their loin cloths, carrying bows and steel-tipped arrows. It was like the world of Miss Nesbit, where odd savage people appear in country lanes; they might have been coming through the Amulet out of the African forest into an English park. We passed them, going ourselves into Africa, while they with their bows and arrows, their naked cicatrized bodies, went on into the park, towards the great house and the butler's pantry.

Six hours brought us to Peyi, where the chief was friendly and the hut clean and the village very poor. Nearly everyone was old and diseased, withered, goitered, with venereal sores. The chief had no authority; he was making a mat when we arrived, and when he had finished the villagers crowded on to it, pushing the chief off. There they lounged outside our hut until the full heat of the afternoon dispersed them, watching everything we did, and a girl had her hair deloused by an old woman with sores over her hands.

Eighteen of the carriers approached the hut; I no longer feared a strike or desertion: they were too far away from their own homes for that. And they had developed a kind of pride in their journey. It was a rare adventure in a country where carriers were usually employed from village to village by the day. I heard them sometimes on the march answering proudly 'Bo-lahun' to questioners. It didn't matter that these strangers had no idea where Bolahun lay. *They* knew through what miles of forest and river they had come, how they had even passed through France, and presently were going to reach the sea.

Now they wanted to borrow threepence each out of their wages. At Ganta they had borrowed two shillings from the cook to buy a goat with, and he demanded sixpence interest, a rate of about fifty per cent a week. The rest of the money they were going to spend on palm wine and extra soup (the name they had for the horrible anonymous wedges of meat or fish with which they cooked their rice). The chief took their money, but he gave them nothing in return, and in this poor village he could find them only one pail of rice for their chop.

But, curiously enough, this didn't matter. They bore no malice. It was the night of full moon. They had very little to eat, they had nothing to drink, the moon and its deep green sight made them happy. They even shared their small meal with the chief and until very late the village was full of song and laughter and running feet. They were crazy with pleasure in the small moon-filled clearing. One could only envy them: we, the civilized, had lost touch with the real lunar influence. It meant to us self-conscious emotion, crooners and little sentimental songs of lust and separation; at best a cerebral worked-up excitement. It couldn't mean this physical outburst, this unthinking tidal urge to joy. Mark said to me on the next day's march, 'Last night we were so happy.' Next night to our eyes the moon would be just as full, they had no calendars to tell them that the moon was on the wane, they didn't need calendars. Night after night they had felt the tightening of the influence that binds us to the cold empty craters; now they felt it loosen. Every month the world turned back into its empty sky.

STEVE DUNBAR

A young man in a Boy Scout's hat and native robe came to meet us next day in the wide clean streets of Sakripie, where there were stores and Mandingo traders in turbans and soldiers of the Frontier Force: a Paramount Chief's town.

The Paramount Chief was away, but this was his son who came and led us to a guest-house in the chief's compound, a huge square with a flag-pole surrounded by whitewashed huts belonging to his wives. He had the ingratiating air of a motor salesman, but he was harassed all the time because he had no authority; he was a joke, no one troubled to obey him. He had a faint hope, I think, as he sat with me on the verandah of the guest-house that our coming would give him prestige. He sent for a chicken and some eggs but nobody brought them. He swore at everyone he could see; he was almost in tears with vexation.

'My name,' a voice said softly behind me, 'is Steve Dunbar. I am very pleased to meet you. These chairs are yours? They are very nice. I have been looking at your beds.' I looked round. A middle-aged Mandingo in a scarlet fez and a native robe nodded and smiled. He spoke excellent English. He said, 'You are travelling through our country. I hope you have my hospitality everywhere. Your chairs are very interesting. I have not seen anything like them.'

'They fold up,' I said.

'That is very interesting. I will buy one of them.'

He told me again, 'My name is Steve Dunbar. I am interested also in your bed. And this table' (it was a card-table bought for three and elevenpence). 'That too folds up? I will buy that.'

I said, 'I'm sorry. You see, we've got to get to Monrovia. I can't possibly sell them before that.'

He changed the subject quite suddenly. 'This chief,' he said, 'is a good young man. If you want anything done tell me.' I said I wanted chop for the men; I would pay a good dash for it in the morning. He told the chief. 'The chief,' he said, 'agrees.'

'I want the chop quite early,' I said. 'They didn't have much food last night.'

The chief fanned himself with the Boy Scout cap. He was hot and excited. He sent several men off in different directions.

'You are going to Ganta?' Steve Dunbar said.

'No, no,' I said. 'To Monrovia. But first to Grand Bassa. And Tapee-Ta. How do we get to Tapee-Ta?'

'You want to see elephants?' Steve Dunbar said. 'You will see plenty. Hundreds. You go to Baplai. There is a civilized man at Baplai. He is a friend of mine. Mr Nelson. You will find him very agreeable. You may say you are my friend. From Baplai you will go to Toweh-Ta. You will see lots of elephants. They will run backwards and forwards all the time over the path.' Across Steve Dunbar's shoulder I caught sight of Laminah's startled face. Steve Dunbar said, 'I will leave you now, but I will see you again in Monrovia and we will talk about the bed and the chair.' He stepped inside and looked at the bed again and then made off across the compound followed by his boy; he had the air of a well-established firm. The chief and I sat in silence. He had his eye on the bottle which Amedoo had put out on the card-table. Presently I could stand his sad covetousness no longer; I gave him a few fingers of neat whisky and he went away.

Almost immediately Laminah was at my side. He was excited (his woolen cap and bobble were all askew), and when he was excited it was almost impossible to understand him. I gathered he wanted a goat. 'For chop?' No, it wasn't for chop. He said something about elephants. Amedoo came forward and explained that our path from now on would be through the biggest bush, that there were lots of elephants, and the labourers wanted a goat. I still didn't understand. He explained that elephants were frightened by the noise a goat made; it need only be a very, very small goat. It seemed a tall story, but if it made them feel safer to have a goat, I didn't mind paying for one. Goats had only cost two shillings at Ganta. I told the Paramount Chief's messenger, who still hung about the verandah, that we wanted to buy a goat. About an hour later a piccaninny, not more than three and a half feet high, arrived with a tiny kid slung across his shoulders. The owner wanted six shillings for it; goats were, apparently, at a premium on the edge of elephant country. The carriers were indignant; they wanted a goat, but they would lose face if their employer paid too much; they would rather dare the elephants without protection. So I refused it, even when the price went down to four shillings. The carriers had never been outside the borders of their northern tribes before; they could never understand that prices varied according to supply and demand. When the price of rice, from Sakripie onwards, began to advance, they were shocked and indignant; they felt were being humbugged.

I learned the origin of the goat idea later at Tapee from Colonel Davis, the Kru coast warrior. Apparently a goat once made a bet with an elephant that he could eat more at a meal. The elephant ate and ate and fell asleep. When he awoke the goat was standing on the top of a high rock. He said he had eaten everything around and was now going to start on the elephant. From that day all elephants have feared the voice of a goat. I'm not sure whether Colonel Davis believed the story or not.

When the sun was low a clamour of voices brought me from bed. The population of Sakripie was pouring into the compound behind two huge stilted and masked devils. They must have stood more then eighteen feet high. They wore tall witches' hats rimmed with little shells; their faces were black, the masks looked as if they had been made out of old cotton stockings, they wore striped pyjama jackets, with the sleeves sewn up to hide the hands, and pyjama shorts, while the stilts were wound with a thinner striped material. Their performance was humorous and sophisticated. They sat down on the roof-tops and idly fanned themselves with their legs crossed, then stretched a leg right across the thatch and pretended to fall asleep. They had a sense of climax which would have earned the applause of the most sophisticated music-hall audience as they leaned back their whole stiff inarticulated length at an angle of about twenty degrees and just recovered as they began to fall. They had the usual interpreter with them. He lay on the ground while they hopped on one stilt towards him, so that it seemed almost inevitable that the wooden hoof would be planted on his face; but always at the last moment they cleared him. When the entertainment was over, they left the compound by the wall; the gateway was too low for them. They sat on the ten-foot wall and lifted over each stiff leg in turn like old men crossing a stile, and for a long while after their witch hats were visible bobbing away above the huts towards their own compound.

It was dusk when they had gone, and I began to be impatient for the carriers' chop. It was nearly forty-eight hours since they had eaten a really good meal. I sent a messenger for the chief, who said that the chop was at that moment being cooked. I made the mistake of giving him whisky, thinking it would make him more ready to do what I wanted, but it only made him sleepy and confused and less able than ever to deal with his disobedient townspeople. When it was quite dark and we were sitting in the compound squeezing limes into our whisky, he returned with a pretty nubile girl who was one of his two wives. His father the Paramount Chief, he said, had fifty-five. He drank more whisky and became rather fuddled. I was aware of the carriers hovering miserably out of range of my hurricane lamp; I wanted to impress them that I was doing something about their food, I was feeling guilty sitting there drinking whisky, waiting for my own chop to be served. I told the chief he was lying, that he had done nothing about the men's chop, and he leapt up, dignified and drunk and a little too plausible, like the motor salesman he should have been. He said he would show me that he was not a liar; the chop was cooking now—I had only to follow him, and he set off with long strides towards the town. I called out into the shadows for Vande and pursued him at the run. It was a very lovely night; I had never seen so many stars; the whisky made me want to be at peace with all the world; I was quite ready to take the chief's word when he halted outside one of the furthest huts and pointed to a circle of women, their faces lit by the slow low flames of the wood fire on which they were boiling a great cauldron of rice. 'Is it enough?' I asked Vande, and Vande said, Yes, it was enough. Neither of us could speak the language and ask the women whether the food was really intended for the carriers. A few sullen notabilities of the place loitered at the edge of the dark, hating us, hating the young drunk chief. We returned and presently I went to bed. After an hour or two someone moved in my hut. It was Amedoo come to tell me that the carriers had received no chop at all and had gone hungry to their beds.

THE TAX-GATHERER

The dry weather *was* breaking: in a few weeks the way to Grand Bassa would be impassable. When I woke at half-past five the rain was pouring down, the empty compound was lit by green lightning. The chief's cows, great cream-coloured beasts with curled horns and velvet eyes, were standing close against the women's huts for shelter. It looked as if we shouldn't get away till late. There was no sign of the carriers: it was not until half-past six when the rain had stopped, though the lightning flickered on, that they drifted into the compound, wet and hungry and miserable.

I called Vande, gave him half a crown to buy a goat with whenever he chose, and told them to cook the little rice we had with us and eat it before starting. Then the young chief appeared in the compound; he had an aching head and a dry mouth, and he was embarrassed and ashamed. I pretended not to notice him until he climbed on to my verandah, and then I didn't offer him a chair. I waited until my carriers were close and then I cursed him. I was very Imperialist, very prefectorial as I told him that a chief must be judged by his discipline, that he ought not to allow his headman to disobey him. *He* couldn't tell my satiric self-criticism as the ghost of Arnold of Rugby addressed his head prefect through my lips.

We did not get away from Sakripie till nine-thirty; we had never before been so late in starting, for by ten the heat was always intense. The paths were rougher than any we had encountered since Zigita, and the storm gave us an indication of how impossible the route would be when the rains set in. Already the paths were turning into swamps and the men had sometimes to wade waist-deep in water. We were not taking the quickest route to Tapee, which would have involved two long and scorching days on a path cleared of shade, and the villagers we now passed saw white faces for the first time. They ran screaming beside us, waving sprays of leaves, until we reached the boundary of the village land; there they always stopped at some invisible line across the forest path. Once they tried to seize my cousin's hammock and rush it triumphantly through a village, but Amedoo drew his sword and held them off.

After five hours we reached Baplai. We were by this time among the Gio tribe, who live on the extreme edge of subsistence in the great bush. The steep pointed roofs were falling in, and the inhabitants were quite naked except for loincloths. They were so thin one expected to see the bones through the venereal sores. The presence of a 'civilized man', however, ensured their keeping a rest-house, one musty little hut with two rooms the size of large dog kennels, where, I suppose, Liberian Government agents slept if ever they came up into the Gio tribe.

Mr Nelson appeared from his own hut next door. He wore a pair of torn white trousers, backless slippers on his grey naked feet and a torn pyjama jacket which had lost most of its buttons. On his head was a kind of rough-rider's hat, and his eyeballs were yellow and malarious. All vitality, except a little malice and covetousness, had been drained out of the half-caste, who lived here, year in, year out, squeezing taxes out of the village, with no pay but the percentage he chose to steal. He was officially reckoned civilized because he could speak English and write his name.

When I came in with my carriers he thought I was a Government agent and asked me what my 'privileges' were: how many free labourers I was allowed, how many hampers of rice unpaid for from this starved village. I said I had no privileges but wished to buy food for my men.

'Buy?' Mr Nelson said. 'Buy? That's not so easy.' He said with a faint flicker of hatred. 'These people would rather be forced to give than sell.' Later I photographed him with his wife, an old Gio woman naked to the waist, and he came and sat beside me and talked languidly of politics. I spoke of the coming election. He said that Mr King had no chance of re-election, but all his opinion meant was that he owed his position, if you could call his dreary exile by that name, to Mr Barclay's party. If King succeeded Barclay, even the Nelsons would be ruined. I asked him about Mr Faulkner, who con-

tested the election in 1928 against King and who had started
the League of Nations inquiry into slavery. Mr Faulkner had
won the uneasy respect of everyone in Liberia; he had refused
minor offices of every Government, he had spent all his own
money, earned as an electrical engineer and the owner of Monrovia's only refrigerating plant, in fighting president after president in the course of reform. 'But no,' Mr Nelson said, turning
his yellow malicious eyes over the painted leaking huts, 'we
don't like Faulkner.' After a while he found enough vitality to
explain, 'You see, he has an idea.'

'What idea?' I said.

'Nobody knows,' Mr Nelson said, 'but we don't like it.'

A young man came out of the forest in the evening light followed by a boy with a gun. He was a native, with a round sad
gentle face, dressed in plus-fours with bright little tassels below
the knee and the same rough-rider hat as Mr Nelson wore. He
introduced himself: he was Victor Prosser, a Bassa man, schoolmaster of Toweh-Ta. He had been on a visit to the Catholic
priest at Sanoquelleh, two days' march away, to make his confession and fetch back to school his youngest pupil. He was a
devout young man who had been educated by the Catholic fathers on the Coast, and was now established as the head of a
little mission school. When he heard that I was a Catholic too,
he was overjoyed. He sat there beside Mr Nelson, repeating
over and over again in a soft hesitating English I had to bend
my head to catch, 'That's very good. That's *good*. Very good.
That *is* good.' Mr Nelson eyed him sourly and cynically and
left us.

Victor Prosser said that he would call his youngest pupil to
read me the Catechism, and gave an order to the boy with the
gun. He didn't ask whether I would like to hear the child; he assumed that any Catholic would be pleased to hear the Catechism recited at any time. The piccaninny appeared: a tiny
creature of about three years old, dressed in nothing but a
transparent shirt. The dark settled over Baplai as he began rapidly to read, his pronunciation so odd that I could only recognize occasional words—venial: purgatory: Communion of
Saints. Victor Prosser interrupted him, 'What is purgatory?'

and the small Gio repeated rapidly the definition established by I know not what council of the medieval church, 'Purgatory is that state . . .' He wasn't really reading, I could tell that: he had learnt the whole thing off by heart, but if I were inclined to criticize the value of *that,* there before me was Victor Prosser who had in his time too been a piccaninny with nothing but a retentive memory for words which meant nothing to him at all, and now sat there visibly entranced over 'purgatory' and 'the communion of saints'. The child, too, had an ancient English reader with little steel engravings of ladies in bustles and gentlemen with trousers buckled below their boots. Victor Prosser refused the drink I offered him, and rising to go, said that he would lead us himself next morning on our road as far as Toweh-Ta.

So this bare grimy pool in the deep forest had more goodness in it than we had expected: even the fat chief in his dirty robe and battered bowler, who had greeted us so surlily when we entered, mistaking us, as Mr Nelson had done, for Government agents, proved himself to possess a kindly heart. Amah and Vande were quite drunk with palm wine long before dark, and when we ourselves were sitting at dinner the waving of half a dozen torches announced the chief's approach with the carriers' chop. He stood there swaying in front of us between two tipsy torch-bearers, while Vande whispered in my ear, 'Chief good man. Chief very good man,' and his men brought up between the pointed huts, under the light of the flaming splinters, bowl after bowl of food. The carriers had never seen such a feast. Its stink reeked in the hot flyey night, the stink of fourteen bowls of chop and three bowls of meat scraps.

Later I was a little drunk myself, not this time for fear of rats but from mere good fellowship. I remember wandering round the village listening to the laughter and the music among the little glowing fires and thinking that, after all, the whole journey was worth while: it did reawaken a kind of hope in human nature. If one could get back to this bareness, simplicity, instinctive friendliness, feeling rather than thought, and start again . . .

I was more spellbound, I suppose, than Vande, who clutched my sleeve in the shadow of a hut and begged me to take the

half-crown I had given him that morning into safe keeping: he
was afraid to carry such wealth about him among this low
bush tribe. He took a green leaf out of his pocket and un-
wrapped it: inside the leaf was a match-box: inside the match-
box another leaf, and inside that the silver coin. Then he went
back to his palm wine and later I encountered him again wandering in blissful drunkenness, hand in hand with the headman
of the village, who had reserved for him a special bowl.

'ALL HAIL, LIBERIA, HAIL!'

I woke at five. In my dream someone had been reciting Milton's
Ode on the Morning of Christ's Nativity. The version belonged
entirely to sleep, but it seemed to me more moving than any poetry I had ever heard before. Two lines, 'Angels bright Bathed
in white light', brought tears to my eyes, and for a long while
after I woke I believed them to be beautiful and even to have
been written by Milton. The darkness was thinning behind the
pointed huts. The smell of goats blew in on the damp misty
wind. It was Victor Prosser, I suppose, who was responsible,
who had brought the idea of God and heavenly hierarchies, of
crystal spheres and light insufferable, into the empty pagan
land.

I said good-bye to the chief and Mr Nelson. When I gave the
chief a present of money he was taken aback, he wasn't used to
payment and automatically held it out to the tax-gatherer, and
automatically Mr Nelson's hand moved towards it. Then he remembered he was observed and turned the movement into a
jest, a hollow jest unshared by the drained malarious eyes.

Victor Prosser had gone ahead with my cousin. There were a
lot of things he wanted to learn before he reached Toweh-Ta.
Was it true that Queen Elizabeth was a Protestant, and Mary
Queen of Scots a Catholic like himself? Where did the Thames
rise? Was London on the Tiber as well as the Thames? Were
Sweden and Switzerland the same country? He asked what
London was like, and my cousin chose to tell him of the underground trains, but it wasn't an easy idea to convey to someone who had never seen an ordinary train. 'Very remarkable,'
he said coldly and disbelievingly at the end of it and changed

the subject by humming *God Save the King*. The boy with the gun walked behind and last followed the tiny piccaninny in the transparent vest. Victor Prosser walked very slowly, and with some pain, because he wore backless slippers for the sake of his prestige as head teacher of Toweh-Ta.

He asked my cousin to join him in singing *God Save the King*, which the Catholic missionaries on the Coast had taught him; I can't imagine why, for they were all of them Irish. He said he knew some Protestant hymns and insisted they should sing *Onward Christian Soldiers* together as they picked their way through the Liberian jungle. When I joined them he and two schoolboys were singing the Liberian national anthem:

> All hail, Liberia, hail!
> All hail, Liberia, hail!
> This glorious land of liberty shall long be ours,
> Tho' new her name, green be her fame,
> And mighty be her powers.
> In joy and gladness with our hearts united,
> We'll shout the freedom of a land benighted.
> Long live Liberia, happy land,
> A home of glorious liberty by God's command.
> All hail, Liberia, hail!
> All hail, Liberia, hail!
> In union strong success is sure, we cannot fail
> With God above our rights to prove.
> We will o'er all prevail.
> With heart and hand our country's cause defending,
> We'll meet the foe with valour unpretending.
> Long live Liberia, happy land,
> A home of glorious liberty by God's command.

The patriotic sentiments sounded better as I heard them later bawled by a school of two hundred children in Monrovia; here it was 'the land benighted', the tall trees standing like cliffs of dull green stone on either side, which really prevailed. After a while Victor Prosser ceased to sing and dropped farther and farther behind in his flopping slippers. I could hear him humming

Venite, Adoremus, as we passed the coffin-shaped holes dug by some Dutch prospector, who had been that way alone a year before.

Toweh-Ta was quite a large town; a Paramount Chief had his compound there, and the forest was cleared away from its outskirts. A broad bare road sloped up to it and a big square hut behind a fence at the beginning of the road was Victor Prosser's school. His manner had altered; here he was someone of importance. It was about half-past nine by our time, which agreed roughly with the handsome silver watch Victor Prosser had won on the Coast. School, he said, would have started; his assistant would be controlling the boys till his coming, and he asked us in to see the class at work. But when he opened the door there was no class: only a little room of empty benches, a cane balanced on two nails, a desk which just succeded in standing of four loose crooked legs. And when Victor Prosser angrily demanded why the school bell had not been rung, the young assistant pointed to a rusty kitchen alarm clock on the desk. By *his* time it was only eight-forty-five. Victor Prosser was embarrassed: we all compared watches: then he rang the bell, put the clock to nine and led us up the hill to the Paramount Chief's cookhouse.

This impressive building was too large for me to photograph: I couldn't get far enough from it. A circular building with open sides, it had a huge cone chimney of smoothly plaited reeds. Where it fitted down over us like a fool's cap it must have been about a hundred and fifty feet in diameter, and it narrowed very gradually until through the top, more than the height of Salisbury Cathedral nave, a handkerchief of sky was visible. Here the town chief came and dashed me a chicken and a hamper of rice—embarrassingly, for the hamper was a man's load and my cousin's hammock-men had had to be reduced to three.

It was another five hours' march to Greh, by a track of appalling monotony. I tried to think of my next novel, but I was afraid to think of it for long, for then there might be nothing to think about next day. Greh, at the end of it all, proved an even more primitive village than Baplai. It was impossible for us to sleep in the huts, for their roofs were built so low that we could not stand upright, and there was no room for the poles of the mosquito-nets. So I ordered our beds to be put up in the cook-house in the centre of the village, to Amedoo's distress; he had never travelled before with white people outside Sierra Leone, and we lost caste by exposing ourselves to the stares of the villagers in the wall-less cookhouse.

There was one boy, the chief's son, who could speak English, for he had been educated on the Coast and called himself Samuel Johnson, and there were strange bits and pieces of 'civilization' scattered about the primitive place, which seemed to indicate that at last one was going south. In the cook-house someone had painted little bright child-like pictures of steamships; a boy carrying an umbrella was naked except for a piece of blue cloth strung on beads over the genitals and a European schoolboy's belt with a snake clasp which he wore half-way up his torso, between his breasts and navel; and what seemed another scrap of 'civilization', for sexual inversion is rare among the blacks, a pair of naked homosexuals stood side by side all day with their arms locked and their hair plaited in ringlets staring at me. Vande got drunk again with palm wine and Amah cut off the top of his finger with one of my swords chopping meat for the carriers' meal. I felt irritated with every-one and everything; I could no longer afford to drink much whisky, for my case was nearly exhausted; I went to bed and lay awake all night because the goats came blundering in, trip-ping up over our boxes. I was vexed with them in a personal way, as if they could help their stupidity, their clumsiness. I would have exchanged them happily for rats; rats were almost as noisy, but I told myself that there was something purposeful in their noise; they knew what they were doing, but these goats were stupid. . . . I could have cried with exhaustion and anger and want of sleep.

TAPEE-TA

And then, when he came in the morning to wake me, Amedoo said that Laminah was too sick to walk. He had lain awake all night in pain from his gum where the tooth had been drawn. The aspirin I had given him was useless. Now he was getting a little sleep for the first time. This was far more serious than the sickness of a carrier; I had less responsibility for a carrier; he was in his own country if not in his own tribe; but Laminah I had brought from another country, he couldn't be simply jettisoned. But neither could I bear the thought of another day in Greh. I had promised the carriers a rest in Tapee-Ta because that was a large place with a District Commissioner where I could hope to buy fresh fruit, which we were beginning to need badly. Even limes had given out at Sakripie and we had seen no oranges for two weeks, but in that respect Tapee was to disappoint us.

I suggested to Amedoo that Laminah should stay behind for a day and we would wait for him at Tapee-Ta. But Amedoo said that he was afraid of being left. 'This is Gio country,' Amedoo explained, 'they chop people here.' So my cousin gave up the hammock to Laminah, who looked half dead when he was laid in it; and I wondered what my conscience would say to me if he died, if my curiosity for new experiences led to the death of someone so charming, so simple, capable of such enjoyment. I was afraid of blood poisoning, but I need not have been frightened. I think it was cowardice Laminah was suffering from, for he recovered very quickly at Tapee.

Three hours through the forest brought us out into a rough road as wide as Oxford Street. Here was an example of what the President had told me of the road-building in the interior. Although the road was too rough for any kind of mechanical transport, it was impressive to see the enormous rampart of trees on either side from which it had been cut.

We were coming in range again of Liberian authority. I had already heard tales of the half-caste Commissioner at Tapee-Ta, and I was anxious to meet him. But I had not foreseen the extent of my good fortune. Colonel Elwood Davis, the leader of the campaign on the Kru Coast, the man responsible for the atrocities described in the British Blue Book, was at Tapee-Ta; I heard his name repeated by passing natives all along the great four-mile stretch of road. His name carried weight; his friends in admiration and his enemies in derision, I discovered later, called him 'The Dictator of Grand Bassa'.

The road did not stretch as far as Tapee-Ta. After an hour we reached the end, where a gang of naked men was at work felling an enormous silvery cotton tree in the centre of the road. They had dug a trench about three feet deep and squatted it in singing and hacking at the trunk with ordinary bush cutlasses, the rhythm given them by two men with drums. Then there were several more hours of forest path before, in the hottest part of the day, when the sun was directly overhead, we came out of the forest on to a wide exposed road again. The powdered soil was quite white under the sun: it blinded the eyes, even behind smoked glasses.

Amedoo joined me: he had been talking to Mark and the other carriers, and he was uneasy about the great man at Tapee. He was a wicked man, he said. 'Will he make trouble for massa?' I wasn't at all sure that he mightn't. The Liberians were under the impression that I was travelling only in the Western Province, and here I was, a long way to the east, in the Central Province. I had no proper papers: my Liberian visa only gave me permission to land at accredited ports.

I was a little uneasy. I hadn't met Colonel Davis then and I think I pictured him as something rather ferocious in the manner of Emperor Christophe. I couldn't help remembering the Blue Book phrases: the murdered children, the women in the burning huts, Nimley's pathetic dignity, 'And when I learnt that Colonel Davis had fought with Tiempoh, who are my children . . .' It certainly did seem to me that there might be trouble.

I was more uneasy still when we came in sight of the District Commissioner's compound (the town of Tapee lay beyond). It was an impressive group of verandahed bungalows behind a stockade with an armed sentry at every gate, and the Liberian flag flying from a staff in the middle. Although it was time for siesta, there seemed to be a lot of movement; many things were going on. From the journalist's point of view, I seemed to have come at a favourable moment, but from the Liberian point of view I couldn't help feeling that I must look very like a spy (the moment was too opportune to be accidental) as I led my odd caravan round the stockade to the main gate.

3
The Dictator of Grand Bassa

BLACK MERCENARY

I felt very dirty as I followed the sentry into the wide clean compound and rather absurd, with my stockings over my ankles, my stained shorts, my too, too British Khaki sun helmet. I was very much at a disadvantage, standing beneath a verandah crowded with black gentlemen in the smartest of tropical lounge suits and uniforms. They had just finished lunch and were smoking cigars and drinking coffee: I wondered which was Colonel Davis. There was an air of subdued activity as I stood there in dirty neglect in the sun: clerks kept on delivering messages and running briskly off again, sentries saluted, and the supercilious diplomatic gentlemen leant over the verandah and studied with well-bred curiosity the dusty arrival.

The sentry returned and led me across the compound to another bungalow, a less smart one this time, with a few rickety chairs on the verandah. The District Commissioner appeared in the doorway, a slatternly mulatto woman peered over his shoulder. He was a middle-aged man with a yellow face and Victorian side-whiskers; he hadn't shaved for a long time; his teeth were bad, and he wore a shabby khaki uniform and the dirtiest old peeling white sun helmet I had ever seen. He was like a stern and sadistic papa in a Victorian children's story; his name was Wordsworth, but he was more like Mr Fairchild than the poet. I think his appearance maligned him and that really he was shy and afraid of humiliation; I think quite possibly, like Mr Fairchild, he had a heart of gold under that repressive exterior. Now he stood above me like a little yellow tyrant, and I really believed at first that he would refuse me a house, but instead he called his younger brother, the Quarter-master.

Mr Wordsworth, junior, was quite different. He had a round seal-grey face with soft lips (there seemed to be less white blood in his veins) and he had a passion for friendship. He it was who had raised his hat to me at the crossing of path and road at Ganta. He led me to the next bungalow: a palatial building of four rooms and a cookhouse. In one of the rooms we found the Paramount Chief, squatting on the native bed, eating his lunch with the clan chief; he was very like the ex-King of Spain and wore a soft hat and a native robe. We had arrived at Tapee during a conference of the local chiefs. They had made complaints against the District Commissioners, especially against Mr Wordsworth, and Colonel Davis had arrived as the President's special agent to hear the complaints. There were several DCs now staying in the compound. We had arrived in the lunch interval.

I sat down in a wooden chair and waited for the others to arrive. The Paramount Chief hastily came out of the bedroom and said the chair was his. I could sit in it, but it was his. The palaver-house in the compound began to fill up with chiefs who streamed in at the gates in soft hats under umbrellas, their chairs carried by boys. I began to ask the Paramount Chief to sell me rice for my men. Thin, vital, Bourbon-nosed, he seemed to pay no attention whatever. He strode away to say something to the clan chiefs, then strode back and said I could have rice at four shillings a hamper. I said that was too much, but he was gone again. His mind was full of state affairs, he hardly had time to bring the price down to three shillings, and before I could propose half a crown, he was off to the palaver-house. Then a bugle blew and Colonel Davis, accompanied by the DCs, walked across the compound to the council.

Even at a distance there was something attractive about the dictator of Grand Bassa. He had personality. He carried himself with a straight military swagger, he was very well dressed in a tropical suit with a silk handkerchief stuck in the breast pocket. He had a small pointed beard and one couldn't at that distance see the gold teeth which rather weakened his mouth. He was like a young-black Captain Kettle and reminded me of Conrad's Mr J. K. Blunt who used to declare with proud simplicity in the Marseilles cafés, 'I live by my sword.' He had noted our arrival and presently the seedy Commissioner appeared to say that the President's special agent wished to see our papers.

It was the first time in Liberia that our passports had been examined. The absconding financier whom I have imagined settling in the unpoliced hinterland of Liberia, taking his holidays at will in French Guinea, a good enough substitute for Le Touquet without any tiresome bother about papers, would do well to avoid Tapee-Te. For there is a prison in the compound at Tapee-Ta, and though the dictator of Grand Bassa was satisfied with our passports, which certainly did not include permission to pass through Central Liberia, the financier might have fared worse.

That prison, next door to our own bungalow, combined behind its thatch and whitewashed walls and tiny port-holes the sense of darkness and airlessness, and the kind of mindless brutality which sometimes vents itself in this country in the torture of a cat (the head warder was a moron and a cripple). Each port-hole, the size of a man's head, represented a cell. The prisoners within, men and women, were tied by ropes to a stick which was laid crosswise against the port-hole outside. There were two or three men who were driven out to work each morning, two skinny old women who carried in the food and water, their ropes coiled round their waists, an old man who was allowed to lie outside on a mat tied to one of the posts which supported the thatch. In a dark cavernous entrance, where the whitewash stopped, a few warders used to lounge all through the day shouting and squabbling and sometimes diving, club in hand, into one of the tiny cells. The old prisoner was a half-wit; I saw one of the warders beating him with his club to make him move to the tin basin in which he was to wash, but he didn't seem to feel the blows. Life to him was narrowed into a few very simple, very pale sensations, of warmth on his mat in the sun and cold in his cell, for Tapee-Ta at night was very cold. One of the old women had been in prison a month awaiting trial. She was accused of having made lightning in her village, and there was a pathetic impotence in her daily purgatory under the staggering weight of water from the stream half a mile away. If she could make lightning, why did she not burn the prison down or strike the dilatory Commissioner dead? Very likely she had made lightning (I could not disbelieve these stories; they were too well attested), but per-

haps the natural force had died in her during her imprisonment, or perhaps she simply hadn't the right medicines with her
in that place. I asked the Quartermaster when she would be
tried; he didn't know.

The council in the palaver-house went on till after five: the
place was packed. It must have been appallingly hot. One suspected that the whole inquiry was designed to quiet the chiefs
rather than try the Commissioners, for the judge was a cousin
of the principal accused. But at any rate he showed patience
and endurance.

Later that evening came the ceremony of lowering the Liberian flag, carried out with solemnity; two buglers played a few
bars of the national anthem—

> In joy and gladness with our hearts united,
> We'll shout the freedom of a land benighted . . .

and everyone on the verandahs stood at attention. When it was
over I sent a note across to Colonel Davis asking for an interview and received a reply that he was worn out by nine hours
of council, but would spare me a few minutes.

The 'few minutes' developed into several hours, for the
Colonel was garrulous, and after more than an hour's conversation on his verandah we adjourned to mine for whisky. He
had once been a private in the American army and his career, if
frankly written, would prove one of the most entertaining adventure stories in the world. As a private or a medical orderly
in a black regiment—I forget which—he had served in Pershing's disastrous Mexican expedition when hundreds of men
died in the desert for lack of water; later he had seen service in
the Philippines; and finally, for what reason I do not know, he
had left America and come to Monrovia. He was very soon appointed medical officer of health, though I do not think he had
any kind of medical degree, and from this vantage point he had
worked his way into politics. Under Mr King's presidency he
had been appointed Colonel Commandant of the Frontier Force
and had managed to shift his allegiance to Mr Barclay when
Mr King was forced to resign after the League of Nations

inquiry. No story was undramatic to Colonel Davis, and the whole shabby tale of Mr King's participation in the shipping of forced labour to Fernando Po and his rather cowardly acceptance of the League's condemnation, which threatened Liberian sovereignty, followed by his resignation when the Legislature proposed to impeach him, became an exciting melodrama in which Colonel Davis had played an heroic part.

'They were thirsting for his blood,' Colonel Davis said dramatically, but nothing which I saw later of the coastal Liberians lessened my doubt whether they had the vitality to assault anyone; with cane juice they would work themselves up to a height of oratory, but as for murder . . . He lowered his voice. 'For twenty-four hours,' he said, 'I never left Mr King's side. The mobs were going about the streets, thirsting for blood. But they all said, "We cannot kill King without killing Davis."' The Colonel flashed his gold teeth at me, deprecatingly. 'Of course—'

'Of course,' I said.

I approached the subject of the Kru war by way of the Colonel's other military exploits. I felt that after the British Consul's report he might feel shy of the subject, but I always over-estimated the Colonel's shyness. When I expressed my admiration for the way in which he had disarmed the tribes, the Colonel took up the subject with enthusiasm. As far as I could make out the operation had turned on a cup of Ovaltine rather than on rifles or machine-guns, for he was a sweet-tempered man: butter wouldn't have melted between the gold teeth. One tribe had sent out armed men to ambush him, but he had learnt their plans from his spies, had taken a different path and entered the town while it was quite empty except for women and old men. From the report on the Kru war I should have expected Colonel Davis to have set fire to the town while his men raped the women: but no: he called for the oldest man, made him sit down, gave him a glass of Ovaltine (with the barest glance at the opposite verandah, where my whisky and glasses were laid out, the Colonel remarked, 'I always have a glass of Ovaltine at the end of a day's trek'), made friends with him, and had him send messages out to the warriors to return in peace. 'Of course,' the Colonel said, 'I made him understand that he and the other old men would have to remain as my guests until the arms were handed over . . .'

The character of the Colonel eluded me. Lord Cecil in the House of Lords had called him a 'buccaneer', but that was perhaps pardonable exaggeration. He was obviously a man of great ability; his disarming of the tribes testified to it, and that he had courage as well as brag the whole Kru story showed. I had not only his own word for it: the fact emerged even from the unfriendly report of the British Consul. He had come down into Chief Nimley's district as the President's special agent, under a guard of soldiers, to collect long overdue taxes. He knew well the man he had to deal with and he knew the risk he was running when he agreed to meet him at a palaver in the village. It had been agreed that neither should bring armed men, but when Davis arrived at the palaver-house with his clerk he found Nimley and his leading men sitting there fully armed. Even then, Davis thought, all would have gone well had not the Commander of the Frontier Force, Major Grant, who had taken a stroll round the village, rushed into the hut, interrupted the palaver, and cried out that Nimley had armed men concealed in the banana plantations. Davis commanded him to stay where he was, but Grant, crying out that he was responsible to the President for Davis's safety, ran from the hut to summon his soldiers.

Davis's later opinion was that Grant was in the pay of the Krus, for his action had the immediate effect of endangering Davis's life. Nimley left the hut and his warriors swarmed round the Colonel. Naturally he made the most of the situation to me, as he leant there over the Tapee verandah with one eye on the drinks. ('I said to my clerk, "Take the papers. They won't harm you. Walk slowly up to the camp and stop the soldiers from coming here." I stood with my back to the wall and they flourished their spears in my face. My clerk said, "Colonel, I will not leave you. I will die here with you." I said to him, "There is no point in dying. Obey orders."') But the facts were undisputed. He had been a prisoner and he had escaped. He said that when his clerk had gone, he left the wall and walked very slowly to the door. They made gestures of stabbing, but no one would stab first. Then an old man appeared with a great staff and beat them back and cleared a way for Davis through the village. 'Afterwards Nimley killed the old man.'

His cook appeared on the verandah behind us and said that dinner was served, but the Colonel wouldn't let me go: he had an audience for a story which had probably become rather stale on the Coast.

'That night I was sitting on my verandah, as it might be tonight; it was ten o'clock, and there, just where the sentry is, I saw a big warrior dressed in war paint with little bells tied under his knees. He came up and said, "Who's the big man around here?" I said, "I guess I'm the biggest man here. What do you want?" He said, "Chief Nimley send me to tell you he's coming up here at five o'clock in the morning to collect his tax money." So I said, "You tell Chief Nimley that I'll be waiting for him."

'And at eleven o'clock I looked up and there was another warrior, a small man, all in war paint. He came up to the verandah and said, "Are you the big man here?" "Waal," I said, "I guess you won't find anyone bigger around this place. What do you want?" He said, "Chief Nimley send me to tell you that at five o'clock he come to see if he's a man or you are a man." So I said, "You go back to Chief Nimley and tell him if he comes up here at five o'clock, I'll show him which is the man."

'And at midnight I looked up and there was a little piccaninny in Boy Scout uniform, but all dressed in war paint. He came up to the verandah and he said, "Where's the big man?" So I said, "Are you a Boy Scout?" and he said, "Yes," I said, "Who's your National Director of Boy Scouts?" He said, "Colonel Elwood Davis." I said, "Where's Colonel Davis now?" and he said, "In Monrovia." "No," I said, "I'm Colonel Davis. Now what do you mean by appearing before your National Director of Boy Scouts in war paint?" So he got kind of shy and said, "Chief Nimley told me to come up here." I said, "You go back to Chief Nimley and say I wouldn't let a Boy Scout deliver a message like that."'

That seemed to be the end of the story. I said, 'And did Chief Nimley come?'

'Oh no.' Colonel Davis said, 'he just made lightning. But there were a lot of Buzie men in the camp, members of the Lightning Society, and they laid out their medicines and the lightning hit the trees on the beach and didn't do any harm.'

He brought up the subject of the British Consul's report himself. He said what had gone most to his heart in a very unfair document was the story that six children had been burnt alive. There was no one who loved children more than he did. He had piccaninnies of his own, and I had only to ask his wife, his second wife, whether every night he didn't read them stories before they went to bed. His enemies in Monrovia, who were jealous of his position, had pretended to believe in these atrocities, and even his mother, back in America, had read about them; but she knew him better, she'd dandled him on her knee, and she didn't believe. Colonel Davis said, 'If you want to know the truth of that story—'

Apparently one evening he had heard children crying and had sent soldiers from the camp who found two babies in the swamps. They had been hidden there when Nimley's tribe took to the bush. The next day he sent more soldiers to search the neighbourhood, and they brought in four more children. He was a mother to those children. He had made the soldiers wash them, had given up his own porridge and the last of his own vaseline; then next day he had sent men to capture a few women to look after them. These were the very children he had been accused of having burnt alive.

His cook again appeared and said that chop was getting cold. Davis snapped at him, but he had no control over his servants. He was very smart, very astute, but I think it was this which was wrong with him. He came over to my verandah and drank whisky and told us all about his first marriage to a teetotaller and how he had cured her by guile of her prejudice, and his servant kept on popping up at intervals to remind him of chop, while Davis stubbornly sat on, just to show who was master.

It is the simplest explanation of the facts contained in Blue Book, Cmd. 4614: the woman just delivered of twins shot in her bed and her children burnt; children cut down with cutlasses; the heads and limbs of victims carried on poles; for otherwise Colonel Davis has to be pictured as a monster, and a monster one simply couldn't believe him to be, as he flashed his gold teeth over the whisky, a bit doggish, a bit charmingly and consciously shy and small boy in the manner of the black singer Hutch.

He came across again the next evening for whisky and nearly finished all we had. It was a bitterly cold night, and a heavy storm came up: there could be no doubt that the rains were on us. After an hour or two the Colonel grew sentimental, leaning back in his chair with a wistful misunderstood air, and it became difficult to believe that he had even so much as witnessed the atrocities. 'I was on a liner once,' the Colonel said, 'and I remember the Captain calling me up to the bridge after dinner. He made a remark I have never forgotten. He pointed to a boat that was going by and said it reminded him of three books that were in the library down below: *Ships that Pass in the Night*—can you guess the others?'

We couldn't.

'Well, the Captain pointed down at the deck where the other passengers were and said to me, "There, Davis: *The People We Meet*", and then he turned to me and said, "But more important still, Davis, *The Friends We Love*."'

I filled the dictator's glass. 'It was a beautiful thought,' he said, looking away.

I worked the conversation back to Liberia and politics. Colonel Davis was North American by birth, but he was a Liberian patriot. 'As the poet wrote,' Colonel Davis said, "Is there a man with soul so dead, Who never has said, I love my own, my own country?"' I asked him about Mr Barclay and his chances, and whether Mr Faulkner would be opposing him as well as Mr King. No, he said, Mr Faulkner had retired from politics. He had seen Mr Faulkner in the Post Office just before leaving Monrovia and Faulkner had told him that he was neither supporting nor opposing either candidate. 'So I said to him, "Mr Faulkner, there is a parable in the Bible. A disciple came to Christ and said, 'One in the next village is casting out devils in Beelzebub's name,' and Christ said, 'Who is not with me is against me.'"' My ignorance of Monrovia contributed to the drama of the political scene: I couldn't tell that the Post Office was a loft in a wooden shed to which one climbed by a ladder.

VICTORIAN SUNDAY

I woke next morning with a bad cold after spending the night under two blankets with a sweater over my pyjamas. A letter was waiting for me at breakfast from the Quartermaster:

> Dear Friend Mr Green: Good morning. I'm about to ask a favour of you this morning which I hope you will be able to grant. If you have any Brandy kindly send me a little or anything else if Brandy is out. Some would be very appreciated by me. I'm feeling very, very cold this a.m. you know hope you both well. With best wishes for health. Your friend Wordsworth. Q. M.

> N. B.—I'll bring my sisters to pay a visit to you and cousin this p.m. as they like you for their friends.

I sent him a glass of whisky and asked for a coconut and some palm nuts which the cook needed for lard. Presently back came a coconut and a bottle of palm oil and a note:

> Dear Friend: Too many thanks for such a kind treat this a.m. it was highly appreciated. I shall always regard you as my friend . . .

The place was very still: it was Sunday and a heavy Victorian peace settled over Tapee. Even native dances were forbidden. The prisoners were driven out to wash tied together by ropes, and a gramophone from the bungalow where two DCs were staying played hymn-tunes across the hot empty compound: *Hark, the herald angels sing* and *Nearer, my God, to Thee.* But after a while these gave place to dance music and American hot songs. I went for a walk; I was feeling ill and homesick; the Coast seemed as far away as ever. I felt crazy to be here in the middle of Liberia when everything I knew intimately was European. It was like a bad dream. I couldn't remember why I had come. I wanted to be away at once, but I simply hadn't the

strength, and Dr. Harley's warning against walking any distance in the West African climate weighed on my mind. *I had*
to have these days of rest, and so did the boys. Mark was dead
tired, and even the nerves of Amedoo and Leminah were strained.
I tried to comfort myself with the thought that it was only six
days to Grand Bassa and if Colonel Davis were to be believed
we should not have to wait longer than a week at that miserable little port before a boat passed.

While I was having a bath in preparation for a long siesta the
Quartermaster arrived. He wanted to buy a bottle of whisky
for his brother and his brother had sent five shillings. I said I
had none left, or at any rate only just enough to see me to the
Coast. Then at two-thirty by my watch, when I had just fallen
asleep, he came again with a note from the DC inviting me to
dinner at two o'clock. We had eaten a large lunch already, but
I went, taking with me half a bottle of whisky very diluted.

I was reminded of one of those curious thick crude groups by
Samuel Butler. One had slipped back sixty years in time to a
Victorian Sunday dinner. The only thing lacking was the wife;
she helped to serve the dinner. There at the end of the table
sat Papa, yellow-faced Wordsworth in his heavy side-whiskers
dressed in a thick dark Sunday suit with a gold watch-chain
across his stomach and a gold seal dangling from it. On the walls
were faded Victorian photographs of family groups, whiskers
and bustles and parasols, in Oxford frames. All except myself
and Colonel Davis, who sat at the other end of the table and
carved the goose, were in Sunday clothes: an old negro who
had withered inside his clothes like a dried nut in its shell and
who was one of the Judges of Assize, the native Commissioner
from Grand Bassa and another Commissioner who was very
shy and scared of Colonel Davis and whom I suspected of having played the hymns. The Commissioner of Grand Bassa, I
suppose, was responsible for the hot music.

Conversation was halting: the weather, devils and secret societies, the small talk of Liberia. Colonel Davis was a firm be-
liever in the power of the lightning societies. He had visited
towns where the members had performed in his honour. They
would tell him that lightning would be made at a certain hour,

and at that hour out of a cloudless sky along all the hills for miles around it would begin to play. Mr Justice Page capped the story with a few legal decisions of his own on the subject of lightning-makers, but Colonel Davis was determined to raise the conversation to a high social level: to food. He had toured Europe with Mr King and he remembered very well the caviare.

Colonel Davis explained to the dark blank faces, 'Caviare is the black eggs of little fishes.' He turned to me, 'Of course, in England now, you no longer get the Russian cigarette.' I said I really didn't know: I thought I'd seen them in tobacconists'. 'Not real ones,' Colonel Davis said, 'they are very rare indeed. A season or two ago in Monrovia they formed a course in themselves at dinner parties.'

'Where did the course come?' I asked

'After the fish and before the salad,' Colonel Davis said, while the Commissioner from Grand Bassa leant forward and drank in every syllable describing the gilded life of the capital. 'The lights were lowered,' he paused impressively, 'and one cigarette would be served to each guest.' The judge nodded; he came from Monrovia as well.

I remember saying to Colonel Davis how surprised I was not to have seen a single mosquito. He, too, he said, had not seen one since the last rains; he was suffering a little from prickly heat, but Liberia was really the healthiest place in Africa.

He was always inclined to over-state his case, as when he told me that in the Kru war no women had been killed, only one woman accidentally wounded, while the British Consul's report spoke of seventy-two women and children dead. Now he remarked that there had never been any yellow fever in Liberia; the manager of the British bank who had died of it in Monrovia (his death was one of the reasons why the British Bank of West Africa withdrew altogether from Liberia) had brought the infection with him from Lagos. All the other deaths could be traced to inoculation. There was less malaria, he went on, in Liberia than in any other part of the West Coast: I had seen myself, he said, that there were no mosquitoes. But providence gave Colonel Davis a raw deal in this case because, when evening came and we were waiting for him to join us over our whisky, the Quartermaster brought news that the colonel was down with a bad attack of fever.

So the Quartermaster entertained us our last evening in Tapee-Ta, sitting moonily opposite with his great seal's eyes begging, begging all the time for friendship. He had taken an immediate fancy to me, he said, when he saw me come out of the French path by Ganta; he had felt then that we would be friends. He would write to me and I would write to him. It was lonely in Tapee: he was used to the life of the capital; in Monrovia it was so gay, the dancing and the cafés on the beach. By the time we arrived the Season would be over, but it would still be gay, so much to do and see, dancing by moonlight . . . His great lustrous romantic eyes never left me. He said, because his mind was full of love and friendship, dancing and the moon, 'You come from Buzie country. They have wonderful medicines there. There is a medicine for venereal disease. You tie a rope round your waist. I have never tried it.' He said wistfully, 'I guess you white people aren't troubled with venereal disease.' He brooded a long time on our departure. He wished he was coming too, but he would always be my friend. He would have letters from me. That night when I was making my way out of the compound into the forest he intercepted me. He said he hoped I wouldn't mind his stopping me, but there was a very good closet behind the Colonel's bungalow with a wooden seat. It was more suitable for me than the bush, he said, but I couldn't help remembering that he had not yet tried the Buzie medicine and I went inexorably on into the forest. He got up very early next morning to see us go, and the last I remember of Tapee was his warm damp romantic handshake in the grey deserted compound.

4
The Last Lap

A TOUCH OF FEVER

I had never imagined that Grand Bassa would one day become my ideal of a place to sleep and rest in. But now it seemed like heaven. There would be another white man there; the sea in front instead of bush; there might be beer to drink. I hadn't realized until I began to walk again how down-and-out I was. No amount of Epsom salts had any effect on me; I used to take a handful morning and night in hot tea, but I might have been taking sugar. I felt sick and tired before I had walked a step and now there was no hammock I could use. Six days, they had said at Ganta, would bring us from Tapee to Grand Bassa, but now at Tapee they said that the journey would take a week at the very least, perhaps ten days. I could no longer count time in such long periods: even four days might have been eternity for all my mind was capable of conceiving it. Not until I could say 'tomorrow' would I believe that we were really drawing nearer to the Coast. My brain felt as sick as my body. The responsibility of the journey had been mine, the choice of route, the care of the men, and now my mind had almost ceased to function. I simply couldn't believe that we should ever reach Grand Bassa, that I had ever led a life different from this life.

To reach our next stop, Zigi's Town, I found difficult enough. It was nearly nine hours' solid trek from Tapee, going down all the while into a damper closer heat, and the first few miles of path were flooded waist-high. Our guide, whom the Commissioner of Grand Bassa had lent to lead us to the door of the PZ store on Bassa beach, proved useless from the start. Dressed in a ragged blue uniform, a rifle over his shoulder which wouldn't have fired even if he'd had the rounds, with all his belongings in a little tin pail, he dropped behind at the first village we reached. He was called Tommie and he had a brazen boyish charm. He knew the way, but he had no intention of walking at *our* rate. He started each day well, but after half an hour he would slip aside into the bush and not catch up again until the midday halt. By that time he was usually a little drunk. Because he wore a uniform he could rob any village he passed of palm wine, fruit and vegetables.

I remember nothing of the trek to Zigi's Town and very little of the succeeding days. I was so exhausted that I couldn't write more than a few lines in my diary; I hope never to be so tired again. I retain an impression of continuous forest, occasional hills emerging above the bush so that we could catch a glimpse on either side of the great whalebacked forests driving to the sea. Outside Zigi's Town there was a stream trickling down the slope and a few ducks with a curiously English air about them. I remembered trying to sit down, but immediately having to deal with the town chief over food for the carriers, trying to sit down again and rising to look for threepenny-bits the cook needed for buying a chicken, trying to sit down and being forced up again to dress a carrier's sores. I couldn't stand any more of it; I swallowed two tablespoonfuls of Epsom in a cup of strong tea (we had finished our tinned milk long ago) and left my cousin to deal with anything else that turned up. My temperature was high. I swallowed twenty grains of quinine with a glass of whisky, took off my clothes, wrapped myself in blankets under the mosquito-net and tried to sleep.

A thunderstorm came up. It was the third storm we'd had in a few days; there wasn't any time to lose if we were to reach the Coast, and I lay in the dark as scared as I have ever been. There were no rats, at any rate, but I caught a jigger under my toe when I crawled out to dry myself. I was sweating as if I had in-fluenza; I couldn't keep dry for more than fifteen seconds. The hurricane lamp I left burning low on an up-ended chop box and beside it an old whisky bottle full of warm filtered water. I kept remembering Van Gogh at Bolahun burnt out with fever. He said you had to lie up for at least a week: there wasn't any danger in malaria if you lay up long enough; but I couldn't bear the thought of staying a week here, another seven days from Grand Bassa. Malaria or not, I'd got to go on next day and I was afraid.

The fever would not let me sleep at all, but by the early morning it was sweated out of me. My temperature was a long way below normal, but the worst boredom of the trek for the time being was over. I had made a discovery during the night which interested me. I had discovered in myself a passionate in-terest in living. I had always assumed before, as a matter of course, that death was desirable.

It seemed that night an important discovery. It was like a conversion, and I had never experienced a conversion before. (I had not been converted to a religious faith. I had been convinced by specific arguments in the probability of its creed.) If the experience had not been so new to me, it would have seemed less important, I should have known that conversions don't last, or if they last at all it is only as a little sediment at the bottom of the brain. Perhaps the sediment has value, the memory of a conversion may have some force in an emergency; I may be able to strengthen myself with the intellectual idea that once in Zigi's Town I had been completely convinced of the beauty and desirability of the mere act of living.

THE EDGE OF 'CIVILIZATION'

It was supposed to be a seven-hour trek from Zigi's Town to Bassa Town, the first stop inside Bassa territory. I was doubtful if I could make it without some help from a hammock, so I took on two extra carriers and my men hacked a pole to take the place of the one I had discarded. I was feeling very weak, but I hadn't enough carriers to let myself be carried all the way, so I walked the first two hours and then had ten minutes in the hammock and walked again. I didn't like being carried. A two-man hammock puts a great strain on the carriers and my men were already tired by the long trek. One heard the hammock strings grinding on the pole and saw the shoulder muscles strain under the weight. It was too close to using men as animals for me to be happy.

The villages we passed were all deserted except for a few women. An elephant had been killed somewhere in the bush, I suppose with the poisoned spears the natives in these parts shoot from ancient guns, and all the men for miles around had gathered to strip its flesh. To our surprise we arrived, in less than four hours, at Bassa Town. I was glad, save that it made the Coast seem farther away than ever. We were two days now from Tapee, but the young native sub-Commissioner here still spoke of Grand Bassa as seven days away. He was the only man in the place, a new village built of square low huts; all the others were off after the elephant, so I was a little afraid of what my carriers might do in a town deserted of its menfolk.

But I couldn't be bothered. As soon as I'd eaten some lunch I went to bed and sweated again between the blankets, for the fever had returned. The huts were too low for me to stand up-right, and instead of rats there were huge spiders everywhere. I had just enough energy to note depressingly in my diary: 'Last tin of biscuits, last tin of butter, last piece of bread.' It was as-tonishing how important these luxuries had become; there were ten biscuits each, we separated them in the tin and ra-tioned them each in our own way, but the butter proved to be rancid and had to be used for cooking.

I noted, too, a sign that we were meeting the edge of civiliza-tion pushing up from the Coast. A young girl hung around all day posturing with her thighs and hips, suggestively, like a tart. Naked to the waist, she was conscious of her nakedness; she knew that breasts had a significance to the white men they didn't have to the native. There couldn't be any doubt that she had known whites before. There were other signs too: the scarcity of food and the high price of rice. It would be higher still, the sub-Commissioner said, when we got nearer to Grand Bassa. He wanted me to buy a couple of hampers in Bassa Town and so save perhaps sixpence on each hamper. There are limitations to native mathematics, and Laminah could never understand why I refused, why it would cost more to save a shilling on rice and employ two extra men to carry it.

That day was the last short trek on the way to the coast. There was no longer any talk of 'too far'. The carriers longed as much as I did to escape from the bush and reach the sea, and as for my poor servants, they were dog-tired. Their nerves were on edge and one evening Amedoo and the head carrier came to blows in front of me over a dish of dirty meat scraps. It was February the twenty-seventh when we left Bassa Town, and we had been walking since February the third. An eight-hour march brought us to Gyon, but it did not seem to bring us any closer to Grand Bassa. That remained, according to rumour, a week away. It still seemed impossible to me that we should ever reach it. My fever did not return after Bassa Town, but my tem-perature remained a long way below normal.

The vitality of both of us reached the lowest ebb that day and the next. We had to be very careful all the time not to quar-

rel. We only saw each other for an hour or two at the end of the
day, but even then it was not easy to avoid subjects on which
we might disagree. The range of such subjects, indeed, had become almost as wide as life itself. At first it was enough to
avoid politics of any kind, but now we were capable of quar-
relling over the merits of tea. The only thing was to remain
silent, but there was always danger that silence might strike
one of us as sullenness. My nerves were the worst affected and
it was to my cousin's credit that we never let our irritation with
each other out into words.

Gyon was an empty inhospitable place of square dirty huts
painted on the outside with white splashes on a kind of liver-
brown mud. Some association in a tired brain with the plague-
marked houses in Stuart London made me think the place
unhealthy, and it was one of the curious results of complete
exhaustion that the mind couldn't separate fantasy from re-
ality. The place was only empty because all the men were away
on their farms except the headman, who would do as little for
us as he could, but to this day I find it hard to realize that the
village was not emptied by disease.

We had to sit on our boxes for more than three hours before
the men returned and we could find huts for ourselves. As for
my servants, I could find nothing for them; they had to sleep in
the open cookhouse round their fire, and they got little sleep,
for they were afraid of wild beasts, particularly of elephants
and leopards. We were in leopard country, every road into
Tapee had been guarded by a trap, wooden boxes in which a
kid could be tied with a drop-door weighted with bundles of
shells.

There was no longer enough whisky for sundowners and we
rationed the last half-bottle in teaspoonfuls, which we drank in
our tea. As we ate our supper some kind of trial was being held
by the carriers in front of Amedoo as judge. They sat before
him in two long lines and each witness in turn stated his case
with the gestures and intonations of accomplished orators. It
was still going on when I went to bed at eight, and I learned the
next day from Mark that the trial was not over till midnight.

I never properly knew what it was all about, but early next

morning Kolieva, who had once been my favourite hammock-man with Babu, came to me as I sat in the village kitchen wait-ing for breakfast and wondering whether I could stand another long trek (my shoes had given way, the soles had worn evenly down until they were as thin as tissue-paper, and then they sim-ply disappeared. I had only left a pair of gym shoes with crêpe soles). I couldn't understand what he said to me; the other car-riers clustered round; it was obvious that a Court of Appeal was supposed to be sitting. Amedoo explained, but I'm not sure that I understood him correctly.

One of the carriers who was called Bukkai had left some-thing behind at the spot where we stopped for lunch. It had been taken by Fadai, the thin emaciated boy with lovely eyes and venereal disease who called himself a British subject be-cause he had been born in Sierra Leone. When Bukkai accused Fadai of the theft and threatened to bring the case to trial, Fadai was quite ready to return whatever it was (I think it was a needle and cotton) rather than make trouble, but Kolieva, taking him down to the stream below the village, had extorted money from him by threats and by promising to bear false wit-ness on his behalf. The trial took place, but Kolieva remained silent and Fadai told the whole story. Then Kolieva became the accused, and to bear false witness in their eyes was a more se-rious offence than to steal. He was found guilty and fined four shillings by Amedoo, a very large sum representing nearly ten days' wages. As I was uncertain whether I understood the facts, and as I knew how reliable Amedoo was and the sentence seemed popular, I said, 'I agree,' and because Kolieva would have argued it, the absurd imperial phrase, which never failed to silence them, 'Palaver finished'. At first Kolieva declared that he would come no farther and demanded his pay, but the thought of the long trek alone through strange tribes daunted him.

THE DETECTIVE OF DARNDO

That day was another long trek, nearly eight hours of it. Our guide slipped behind at the first village we reached; and I could feel every root and stone through my gym shoes. The carriers whom we had taken on at Bassa Town and who had asked to come with us failed half-way and I couldn't use my hammock at all. It was typical of the Bassa tribe to promise and then to fail. I developed a bitter dislike of the very appearance of Bassa men, the large well-covered bodies, the round heads, the soft effeminate eyes. The Coast had corrupted them, had made them liars, swindlers, lazy, weak, completely undependable. But it was from the Bassa tribe, and from the Vais, whose territory, too, touched the decadent sea-board, that the governing class recruits new members. To the criticism that the native has no hand in the administration, the American-Liberian will point to Bassa and Vai men in the Government departments, Bassa and Vai Commissioners and clerks.*

I shall call the next village we stayed in Darndo. It sounded like Darndo, and it is marked on no map. I reached it with one or two carriers a long way ahead of the others. In a small square hut with a verandah draped with the Liberian flag, a number of elderly natives were sitting with a half-caste. He was dressed in dirty pyjamas, he had a yellow face, a few decaying teeth, a glass eye; he was one of the ugliest men I met in Liberia, but there is no one there for whom I feel now a greater affection. He gave me a chair, he brought me the first fresh fruit I had seen for weeks, large bitter oranges and limes; he arranged a hut for me, and he expected no return.

He was an absurd and a heroic figure. He said to me, 'You are a missionary, of course?' and when I said 'No,' he fixed me with his one eye, while the other raked the glaring afternoon sky above the dirty huts. He said, 'I believe you to be a member of the Royal Family.' I asked him why he believed that. 'Ah,' he said, 'it is my business. You see I am a detective.' But he had run completely out of paper; there was none to be got nearer than the Coast; and when I gave him a dozen pages out of my notebook, he was embarrassingly grateful. I thought he was going to weep from his single eye, and he disappeared at once into his hut to write a report that a member of the British Royal Family was wandering through the interior of the Republic.

---

*It is the pride of the Vai people that they have the only written language in Africa, but the Bassa are imitating them, and I found a piece of their script stuck, perhaps as a charm in the roof of my hut.

But I have said he was heroic. Like Mr Nelson he was a tax-gatherer. He belonged to the Coast, to the cafés of Mr Wordsworth's dreams, and here he was stuck away in a tiny village of a strange tribe. Like Mr Nelson he was unpaid, he had to live on what the natives gave him, but unlike Mr Nelson he gave something in return. They trusted him and he defended them as far as he could, with what vitality was left in his fever-drained body, from the exactions of the uniformed messengers who streamed back and forth between Tapee and the Coast. It needed courage and it needed tact.

I think his kindness saved us both that day from complete collapse, that and the news he gave us that there was a road for twelve miles out of Grand Bassa to a place called Harlingsville and that a Dutch company in the port possessed a motor lorry, for that might easily shorten the distance by a day. With the dark another storm came up, rumbling over the hills between us and Tapee. A miserable man dragged himself over to my hut across the coffee beans which were lying in the dust to dry. He asked me whether I was a doctor and I said that I had a few medicines, but when he told me it was gonorrhoea he suffered from, I had to admit that nothing I had with me would help him. The information took a long time to penetrate. The sight of a white man had made him hope; he just stood there waiting for the magic pill, the magic ointment then moved dispiritedly away to sit in his own hut and wait for another miracle.

That night I couldn't eat my food, I felt sick as well as exhausted, and a new fear had been put in my mind by Souri, the cook, who, when he had seen me eating the half-caste's oranges, had taken them away from me. He said these bitter oranges were not fit to eat, they would make a white man ill, and I remembered how I had been warned against over-ripe fruit by Dr Harley at Ganta, so that now the fear of dysentery was added to the fear of fever as I lay awake too tired to sleep and the rain came down in a solid wall of water of Darndo.

I didn't believe that I should be able to walk a step next day, and so I asked the detective to get me six extra carriers. By that means I thought I should be able to use the hammock continuously next day without tiring my own men, who had the long trek behind them. But in the morning I felt better and rather than delay while men were fetched from the farm accepted two carriers only, one a typical Bassa, tall, boasting, fleshy, with the usual false boyish sullenness. The detective was very proud of him, calling him Samson and boasting of his strength, but long before King Peter's Town Samson was the last carrier, holding up the whole train, grumbling at the weight of his load.

We were aiming at King Peter's Town and Grand Bassa was still something to be hardly hoped for, in the vague future, when suddenly at lunch-time from a friendly village chief I heard that it was close, that with the help of the lorry from Harlingsville it was only one day's march from King Peter's Town. The news spread to the boys, to the carriers. We sat and grinned at each other, blacks and whites, closer in this happiness than we had been all through the trek; in our relief of spirit there was no longer any need to control the temper, one could curse and quarrel as well as laugh, and to the carriers' joy I broke out at the hated Tommie with a flow of obscenity I hadn't known was at my command. This was the greatest happiness of all: to feel that restraint was no longer necessary. Rashly I told the boys about the lorry that I would get to meet us at Harlingsville and soon every carrier knew of it; they had never seen a car, but they knew what it meant, twelve blessed miles without loads, without effort.

It was a seven-and-a-half-hours' trek to King Peter's Town and a shabby village at the end of it, but we were happier than we had been since we left Bolahun. I scribbled a note in pencil to the manager of the PZ store announcing our arrival and asking him to send the lorry up to the end of the road to meet us, and not even the warnings of the three extra Bassa carriers I hired for the next day that Harlingsville was 'too far, too far', that it was a twelve-hour trek, depressed me. I pretended for the sake of my own men to disbelieve them, but secretly I put my watch back a couple of hours, determined that even if it were a twelve-hour trek, we should yet do it and sleep in Grand Bassa. The messenger stuck the note into a cleft stick and with some of our last oil in his lamp set off to walk to Grand Bassa all night through the forest. I remember a whistle blowing among the shabby huts as Tommie marshalled a few ragged uniformed messengers with rifles as useless as his own before a flagstaff in the centre of the village and the Liberian flag waved up and down again while Tommie tried to make his awkward squad stand at the 'present'. But they laughed at him and someone stole his whistle, and all that evening Tommie went glowering up and down the village looking for it.

GRAND BASSA

We rose at four-fifteen, but the new carriers and Tommie de-layed us and we did not leave King Peter's Town till six. I wasn't quite so cheerful then, the Bassa men persisted that it was twelve hours to Harlingsville, five hours first to a Seventh Day Adventist mission, where they wanted us to spend the night. But the smash-and-grab raid was nearly over; it was only later that I could separate the physical tiredness which was caused by the long fast trek from the actual circumstances of the prim-itive life; I thought then that it was the interior I was weary of, when it was only the march, the forest, the inadequate re-sources of my own brain. I wasn't going to waste another day in the interior if we had to walk the clock round to avoid it. As it might be a very long trek I avoided using the hammock until the very end, though if it hadn't been for the strain on the car-riers, there would have been an almost unalloyed delight in the swinging motion and the long stare upwards, the sight of the blue cracks moving through the great fan of leaves between the tapering grey boles, the sense of being carried south with no more exertion, back to the life I began to think I cared for more than I had known.

To my relief the Bassa men proved, as usual, to be liars. The first of us reached the mission after only three and a half hours. It was a Saturday and a bell was ringing for church in a cluster of white buildings on a hill-top. The missionary came down to the path and brought us in, a German living there with his wife, trying to convert the Bassa tribe to a belief in the millennium and the sacred distinction between the Sabbath and the Sunday. They fed us on real German ginger cake and gave us iced grape juice to drink, and talked about wireless sets in throaty English, and the touch of iced drink on the lips was like the end of everything, so that already I began to look back on Kpangbla-mai and Nicoboozu as something gone out of my life for ever. Grand Bassa, they said, was only eight hours away and Harlingsville six hours, but when I mentioned the lorry that I hoped would meet us there, they had bad news. There was only one car in Grand Bassa and that had broken down some months before, and they doubted whether it had been repaired. I wished then that I had not told my servants and the carriers of the lorry. The thought that when I got them to Harlingsville they would still be faced with another two hours' trek worried me as much as the growing suspicion that another eight hours of walking would be too much for me.

We came out of the forest altogether a few hours later on to a broad grassy path across long rolling downs, which seemed to indicate the sea was near. We had been in the forest now almost uninterruptedly since the day we crossed the border on the other side of Liberia. It was like breathing again to leave it. At every crest now we hoped to see the Atlantic. After lunch Tommie overtook us, tipsy and singing some unintelligible song the carriers took up and handed down their line till it faded over the crests. That encouraged me, for if Harlingsville was far off, our guide would have stayed behind to drink and rob. More and more people came up the path from the direction of the sea, and of each Tommie asked if there was a car in Harlingsville, but they all said there was no car. We passed an unfinished concrete bridge marking where the road had once reached, for *this* road had gone backward. Then a few seedy houses appeared, definitely houses now and not huts, with a first floor and tin roofs but without glass in the windows, with the air of old-fashioned chicken coops magnified to take men. Through a window I saw a group of half-castes playing cards round a bottle of cane juice. It was the familiar Africa of the films, of semi-Parisian revues and Leicester Square. Sometimes there were chickens or a goat or an allotment. This was civilization; we had seen it last in Freetown.

And then at three o'clock unexpectedly we were in Harlingsville, the wooden houses rising to two floors, with outside staircases, a smell of human ordure drawn up by the sun, a Post Office marked in chalk letters, men and women in trousers and shirts leaning over fences, and as the path bent, there at the beginning of a wider road a motor-lorry stood. I wanted to laugh and shout and cry; it was the end, the end of the worst boredom I had ever experienced, the worst fear and the worst exhaustion. If I had not been so tired (it was March the second, we had been walking for exactly four weeks and covered about three hundred and fifty miles), civilization might not have seemed quite so desirable in comparison with what I was leaving: the complete simplicity on the edge of subsistence, the little groves of rice-birds, the graves of the chiefs, the tiny fires at sundown, the torchlight, the devils and the dancing. But civilization, for the moment, I was ready to swallow whole, even the tin roofs, the stinking lurching lorry from which the natives on the way from market in Grand Bassa drew back with the same dread as their fellows had shown on the road to Kailahun, hiding their faces against the banks as the monstrosity ground by. The journey had begun and ended in a lorry in the stink of petrol.

Civilization, of course, even at the Grand Bassa level, offered a little more than that; it offered iced beer in the home of the PZ manager over the store which was just closing down from want of trade, fresh Liberian beef of unbelievable toughness, a straggling row of wooden houses ending on the clean wide beach with the surf breaking beyond, for the surf had saved Grand Bassa, like all other Liberian trading stations, from quays and docks; it offered a selection of hideous churches, one of which woke me early next morning with the sound of what must have been a gramophone record, repeating over and over again, 'Come to church. Come to church. Come to church.'

It offered, too, a wooden police station with a little group of uniformed figures avidly watching my carriers collect in the courtyard of the store to be paid off. In a way I was glad to see the last of them, but as I listened to the manager warning them to be gone as quickly as possible from Grand Bassa, for the police would be after their money, I felt sorry for the end of something which was unlikely ever to happen again. One was never likely to live for long in a company so simple and uncorrupted; they had none of them before seen so many stores, the sea, a motor-lorry; their eyes were full of excitement and wonder at Grand Bassa, and they didn't even know the way back. Nobody here could tell them, and when Vande suggested that they might make their way along the beach to Monrovia and there get in touch again with the Holy Cross Mission, the manager warned them that none of his own men went that way unless they carried guns. The beach is the most dangerous road in all Liberia to travellers, because its people have been touched by civilization, have learnt to steal and lie and kill.

They drifted away out of the courtyard one by one, with nothing to do, conscious of their native clothes among the trousered Bassa. They didn't take the warning to get clear away out of town with their money, for that night I lay in bed listening to the drunken singing and shouts of Vande and Amah under the wall. Cane juice was the only cheap thing in Grand Bassa, and I could tell the difference between their drunkenness now and the happy sleepy mellow state the palm wine had put them in. This was crude spirit and a crude coastal drunkenness.

THE SEEDY LEVEL

One was back, or, if you will, one had advanced again, to the seedy level. This journey, if it had done nothing else, had reinforced a sense of disappointment with what man had made out of the primitive, what he had made out of childhood. Oh, one wanted to protest, one doesn't believe, of course, in 'the visionary gleam', in the trailing glory, but there was something in that early terror and the bareness of one's needs, a harp strumming behind a hut, a witch on the nursery landing, a handful of kola nuts, a masked dancer, the poisoned flowers. The sense of taste was finer, the sense of pleasure keener, the sense of terror deeper and purer. It isn't a gain to have turned the witch or the masked secret dancer, the sense of supernatural evil, into the small human viciousness of the thin distinguished military grey head in Kensington Gardens with the soft lips and the eye which dwelt with dull lustre on girls and boys of a certain age.

He was an old Etonian. He had an estate in the Highlands.

He said, 'Do they cane at your school?' looking out over the wide flat grass, the nursemaids and the children, with furtive alertness. He said, 'You must come up and stay with me in Scotland. Do you know of any girls' school where they still—you know—' He began to make confidences, and then, suddenly taking a grip of the poor sliding brain, he rose and moved away with stiff military back, the Old Etonian tie, the iron-grey hair, a bachelor belonging to the right clubs, over the green plain among the nursemaids and the babies wetting their napkins.

I could hear a policeman talking to Vande under the wall, and suddenly I remembered (though I told myself still that I was dead sick of Africa) the devil's servant at Zigita waving away the lightning and the rain with an elephant-hair fan, the empty silent town after the drums had beaten the devil's warning. There was cruelty enough in the interior, but had we done wisely exchanging the supernatural cruelty for our own?

I was looking out of the window of the day nursery when the aeroplane fell. I could see it crash out of sight on to the playing fields at the top of the hill. The airman had dived, playing the fool before his younger brother and the other boys, he had miscalculated the height and struck the ground and was dead before he reached hospital. His small brother never looked, never waited to hear if he were alive, but walked steadily away down the hill to the school and shut himself tearlessly in a lavatory. Someone went and found him there, there were no locks on any lavatory doors, nowhere where you could be alone.

The lorries drove up and down the day of the General Strike loaded with armed men. The café had been turned into a dressing station and a squad of Garde Mobile moved down the wide boulevard that runs from Combat to Menilmontant searching everyone on the pavement for arms. The whole of Paris was packed with troops; every corner, every high building sheltered a troop, they clustered along the walls in their blue steel helmets like woodlice. The road of the Revolution from Vincennes to the Place de la Concorde was lined with guns and cavalry. No breaking out here, no return to something earlier, something communal, something primitive.

More police were coming up to get their pickings beneath

the wall. Vande and Amah were being persuaded towards the wooden station. I thought of Vande in the dark urging the carriers over the long gaping swaying bridge at Duogobmai; I remembered they had never had the goat to guard them from the elephants. It wouldn't have been any use now. We were all of us back in the hands of adolescence, and I thought rebelliously: I am glad, for here is iced beer and a wireless set which will pick up the Empire programme from Daventry, and after all it is home, in the sense that we have been taught to know home, where we will soon forget the finer taste, the finer pleasure, the finer terror on which we might have built.

5
Postcript in Monrovia

A BOATLOAD OF POLITICIANS

My host woke me early to say that if I cared to catch it a Liberian motor-launch was leaving that morning for Monrovia. If I missed it, I might have to wait a week for a Dutch cargo-boat, but he advised me all the same to stay.

The boat was making its maiden voyage down the coast from Cape Palmas to Monrovia. It cannot have been more than thirty feet long, not that I was able to pace it when we scrambled on board from the surf boat, for it was packed—packed with black politicians. There were a hundred and fifty of them on board, and if the owner of the boat had not been with us we should not have been allowed to embark. They shouted that there was no room, that we should sink the boat, they implored the captain not to let us on board, they were scared, for most of them had never been at sea before and the previous evening they had run on a rock and narrowly escaped off Sinoe. The launch tilted with their fear, first one way, then the other. But the owner got us on board, he even found us enough room to set up chairs and sit down, though we couldn't, once settled there, stir a foot.

The launch, the owner told me, had been bought second-hand for £18 and repaired for £25. It hadn't even got marine

engines. He had installed two second-hand automobile engines, a Dodge and a Studebaker, and except for the rock off Sinoe, it had done well. We slid farther away from the yellow
sandy strip of Africa, from the fringe of dark green forest behind the tin shacks of Grand Bassa. The captain, a great fat Kru
man in a wide-brimmed hat and a singlet, stood in a little glass
shelter and shouted orders down a telephone to the engine-
room just beneath his feet, the sun came blindingly up over the
thin Japanese cotton awning, a black Methodist minister went
to sleep on my shoulder, and the politicians temporarily ceased
arguing about the election and began to argue with the captain.

'Say, captain,' they protested in their formless nasal American negro voices, 'you don't wanta use both engines yet. You
gotta put out farther before you use both engines,' and the captain argued with them and presently gave way. He couldn't is-
sue any order without setting the passengers arguing with him.

It was sixty miles to Monrovia and the launch took seven
and a half hours, lurching with incredible slowness across the
flat scorching African sea with the rocking motion of the hundred and fifty politicians. It was an Opposition boat and the
presence of a white man on board seemed to the politicians to
have deep significance. Before we reached Monrovia every del-
egate was convinced that England was behind them. There was
to be a Convention in Monrovia of the Unit True Whig Party
to elect a Presidential Candidate to oppose President Barclay
and the True Whig Party. All is fair during a Liberian election
and the Government agent at Cape Palmas had tried to arrest
the owner of the boat and hold it up till the Convention was
over. Some of the delegates were supporters of a Mr Cooper,
some of ex-President King, so though they all belonged to the
same party, they had plenty to argue about, and the arguments
got fiercer after midday, after the tin basins of cassava roots
had been handed round (for meals were included in the tariff)
and the bottles of cane juice. The cane juice in the midday heat
worked quickly; almost immediately half the hundred and fifty
politicians were roaring drunk. They couldn't do anything
about it, because if they moved more than a foot the boat
heeled over, and once there was a panic on board at a loud

crash which reminded them of the rock they had hit the night before. Some tried to stand up and others shouted to them to be still as the boat heeled towards the glassy sea and the captain was heard shouting that he would put any man who moved in irons. I couldn't move because the Methodist minister was asleep on my shoulder, and the panic soon subsided. We hadn't hit a rock, somebody had passed out under the cane juice and his head had hit the deck.

The owner of the boat said to me, 'These men: they are quiet and gentle now, but you wait till they get ashore. They are thirsting for blood. They would rather kill Barclay than see him elected.'

An old man without any teeth suddenly said, 'Do you know in Monrovia they have a map of the whole of Liberia? I am going to go and see it. It is in the possession of a family called Anderson. They have had it for years. Everyone who goes to Monrovia goes to see the map. Sinoe is marked on it, and Grand Bassa and Cape Palmas.' Then a lot of people tried to trap me into saying whether I was financing Mr Cooper or Mr King. I might have made history that day, for I am sure if I had said I was financing Mr Cooper, no one would have voted for Mr King. And all the while behind the frieze of black heads, five hundred yards away, the yellow African beach slid unchangingly by without a sign of human occupation. Somebody was fishing from the end of the boat and with tiresome regularity catching a large fish. It might have been the same fish, just as it might have been the same patch of sand, but every time the captain left the wheel, trod over the sprawl of limbs into the bow and presently announced in a loud commanding voice, as if he were ordering somebody to be clamped into irons, 'A fish!' and entered the fact in a log-book. There would be a momentary break in the babble until a voice began again, 'Mishter Cooper ish, ish a young man.' 'Ex—Presh—Pres—Presh, Mishter King has exshper, experish . . .'

The Nonconformist minister hadn't drunk anything. He woke up suddenly and without removing his head from my shoulder said, 'We shall never go straight in Liberia until we let God into our conventions. We must let God choose.'

I said, 'I agree, of course, but how will you know which candidate God wants to choose?'

He said, 'God made pencils, but man made india-rubber.'

The old man without any teeth said, 'That's a true word.'

The minister said, 'They'll give us cards when we go to the Convention and we shall have to put a mark against a name. But pencil can be rubbed out with india-rubber. If we want God to have a chance in this Convention we must take our pencils and push the point right through one of the names, tear it right out, then they won't be able to do anything with india-rubber.'

By the late afternoon nearly everyone was asleep, but they woke when the promontory that shelters Monrovia came in sight: the German consulate and just above the beach the long white front of the British Legation. Everyone began to tidy themselves for the capital, put on waistcoats and ties, and there, after a brief panic as we heeled over the bar, was a little jetty and a reception committee of smart politicians cheering and waving and embracing each other with excitement.

I never got quite away from my fellow-passengers. For every day I spent in Monrovia some seedy individual would pluck at my sleeve among the wooden shacks of the waterside, and drawing me on one side would remind me that we had travelled together, pointing out to me, as the financier of the Opposition party, that he had left his affairs in Cape Palmas or Sinoe in bad order and was finding the capital city very expensive. Most of the Opposition, indeed, had to be sent home at the expense of the President.

MONROVIA

To the casual visitor, at any rate, Monrovia is a more pleasant town than Freetown. Freetown is like an old trading port that has been left to rot along the beach; it is a spectacle of decay. But Monrovia is like a beginning; true, a beginning which has come to little beyond the two wide grassy main streets intersecting each other and lined with broken-paned houses all of wood and of one storey except for the brick churches, one little brick villa belonging to the Secretary of the Treasury, the three-storeyed Executive Mansion where the President lives, the State Department opposite, and the unfinished stone house of ex-President King. An asphalt drive, 'for motor traffic only', goes down to the water-front, but there are very few motors and all pedestrians use it. Along the waterside are the shops, the big wooden stores of the English PZ, of the German and Dutch companies where you can buy gin as cheap as ninepence a bottle, and the small huts of the Syrians, the wooden shed of the Post Office with a ricketty ladder on the outside. There are telephone poles along the main street and out by the one motor road towards Mount Barclay and the Firestone Rubber Planta- tions, but the telephone service no longer exists. The residential street runs gently uphill towards a waste of scorched rock and sand, the road to the English Legation and the lighthouse, and here and there among the rocks are planted the beginnings of stone houses, sometimes only the foundation laid, sometimes several storeys, so that these unfinished buildings have the ap- pearance of houses gutted by fire.

They are the only form of investment Liberia provides, for though prospectuses have been issued for the Bank of Liberia Ltd., with a capital of 1,000,000 dollars divided into 200,000 shares, nobody has subscribed; as early as 1923 the Legislature granted the bank the exclusive right of issuing banknotes and coins, but Liberia still depends for its currency on the British. The only Liberian coins in circulation are heavy copper pen- nies. So from ex-President King downwards anyone with any money to spare not invested in the Firestone Bank (the British Bank has left Liberia) puts it into building, but the buildings are very seldom finished. The foundations and the first storey usually exhaust the owner's capital, though sometimes years later a few more stones are added to the follies dotting the rough slopes near the sea.

It is easy to make fun of this black capital city; of the Secre- tary of State who, when a white man expressed his amazement that he should occupy such a position at so young an age as thirty-four, replied, 'Pitt was a Prime Minister at thirty', of a town where almost every other man is a lawyer and every man a politician. 'There is no body of men,' Thomas Paine wrote, 'more jealous of their privileges than the Commons: because they sell them,' and one cannot doubt that this motive forms a part of Liberian patriotism. The native in the interior, if he comes in close contact with a Government agent, has every reason to deplore 'the mighty calamity of Government'. But there is a pathos about these stunted settlements along the coast, the grassy streets, the follies on the rocky hillside, the pathos of a black people planted down, without money or a home, on a coast of yellow fever and malaria to make what they can of an Africa from which their families had been torn centuries before. No one can pretend they have made much of their country. Colonel Davis's conduct of the Kru campaign is only one example of the horrors of their history, but to me it seems remarkable that they have retained their independence at all: a kind of patriotism has emerged from the graft and the privation.

England and France in the last century robbed them of territory; America has done worse, for she has lent them money. Without any resources of their own, except what they could squeeze out of the unfriendly natives in an undeveloped interior, they have had to borrow again and again. Each fresh loan has only paid off the previous indebtedness and left them with a smaller surplus and an inflated interest. They have tried to build roads before, as they are trying to build them now, and I had seen outside Grand Bassa how previous roads had gone backward, not forward. They once had a telephone system, but now they have only the leaning poles by the roadside. They had bought machines, but they hadn't had the money to work them, and driving out to the rubber plantations one passed the old dredges rusting in the scrub. I couldn't wonder at their ination in the soaking heat. I remember that one day, going out to Mount Barclay, we passed a motor-lorry broken down on the road with one wheel off; there were the remains of a camp fire and the crew were sleeping in the bush. It was only twenty miles from Monrovia, but as I went out next day to visit ex-President King the lorry and the crew were still camping there waiting for something to happen.

Nor can you wonder at their hatred and suspicion of the white man. The last loan and the last concession to the Firestone Company of Ohio all but surrendered their sovereignty to a commercial company with no interests in Liberia but rubber and dividends. The Liberian has quite rightly been condemned for his abuse of power in the interior, but the native can hardly expect a much higher standard of treatment from a commercial company without any responsibility to world opinion. It was a quite unconstitutional concession, in return for a loan, of 1,000,000 acres of Liberian territory on a lease of ninety-nine years. In 1935 only 60,000 acres were under cultivation: 45,000 acres outside Monrovia and 15,000 at Cape Palmas, but the concession remains an impediment to any form of development.

It was imagined, one may charitably suppose, that Firestone's would bring more than money into the country, that they would provide employment and stimulate trade. The year of my visit they were employing 6,000 natives supplied by the chiefs; no one could really tell whether that labour was voluntary or forced, but if the million acres should ever be cultivated and the employment figures rise in proportion, voluntary labour will certainly not supply the demand, and there is a great moral distinction between the usual form of forced labour in Africa, which at least pretends to be for the good of the community, and forced labour for the good of shareholders.

The wages paid, though it must be admitted that they compared favourably with some of the British Government's rates in Sierra Leone, were not likely to bring prosperity to the Liberian tribes. The wages of tappers ran from eightpence to a shilling and a penny a day, of clearers from sevenpence to a shilling. Out of this they had to buy their own food, but not to the benefit of local trade. They must buy at the Firestone stores and Firestone's imported their own rice, so that it had to be sold at a rate one and sixpence in the hundredweight, dearer than it could be bought in Monrovian stores, and the rate in Monrovian stores was already much dearer than anywhere else in Liberia.

Little wonder, then, if in the past the Liberian Legislature had chosen to look on the white man as somebody to be squeezed in return, and nobody can say they have not shown imagination in their methods. At one time a German shipping agent was the chief sufferer. His chauffeur killed a dog and the next day was arrested at the suit of the owner. The German agent was brought into court, and the owner in evidence said that last year her bitch, which she valued at ten dollars, had had five puppies which had fetched ten dollars each: that in a week or two she would have borne five more puppies, which she would have sold for the same figure. The court fined the German sixty dollars.

On another occasion the same agent was fetched out of bed by the police to meet a claim for damages suffered by a Liberian woman who was travelling in an Italian steamer for which the German line acted. She had been scratched by a monkey belonging to another passenger while the steamer was in Spanish territorial waters. The doctor had put iodine on the scratch and no harm was done, but the woman mentioned the incident in a letter to her husband and he brought an action against the only person who could be reached, the German agent. The court awarded him 30,000 dollars. This was going too far and after a protest by the representatives of England, France and Germany, the Supreme Court found that the action lay outside the scope of the Liberian courts.

THE EXILES

A curious international life was led by the few whites in the little shabby capital. Apart from the Firestone employees, who lived outside in European comfort on the plantation, there were not more than three dozen whites in Monrovia; there were Poles, Germans, Dutch, Americans, Italians, a Hungarian, French, and English; two of them were doctors, others were storekeepers, gold smugglers, shipping agents, and consuls. There was some comfort to be found at the legations; and though there was not such a thing as a water-closet in Monrovia, nearly everyone had an ice-box, for in the little dingy town there was little to do but drink, drink and wait for the fortnightly mail-boat which might bring frozen meat but was unlikely to bring a passenger.

These men and women were more exiled than the English in

Freetown; they had less comfort and far less amusement; there was no golf course and the surf was far too dangerous for bathing. Once a week they played a little tennis at the British Legation or had a game of billiards, and once a week, too, the older men of the white colony shot with a pistol at bottles perched above the beach at the edge of the British Legation ground. That custom had been going on for years, every Saturday evening until the light was too bad to see. One advantage their isolation had: it killed snobbery. Chargé d'Affaires and shop assistant, Consul-General's wife and storekeeper's wife were equal in Monrovia. It was the democracy of men and women wrecked together on a deserted coast, and to the casual visitor social life there seemed more human and kindly than in an English colony, in spite of the scandals and the tiny commercial and diplomatic intrigues and the fever, always the fever. I was only in Monrovia for ten days during the most healthy season of the year, but eight of the tiny population of whites went down with fever while I was there.

One couldn't expect them to do anything else but drink, beginning after breakfast with beer at each other's houses and ending with whisky at four in the morning. But what was worst was the iced *crème de menthe*. It was served everywhere automatically after lunch and dinner: it would have been thought eccentric not to like the sweet nauseating stuff, as it would have been thought curious not to enjoy at sundown, in the damp heat of the evening, while the backs of the hands and the armpits sweated all the time, the heavy cloying Tokay the Hungarian doctor kept. They had every reason to drink; you couldn't read much in a climate which rotted your books; you couldn't even deceive yourself that you were there for some good, ruling the natives, for it was the natives in this case who ruled you and presented, so far as the Cabinet Ministers were concerned, a depressing example of sobriety and attention to business; you couldn't womanize, for the range was too embarrassingly limited; there were no games to play, no strangers regularly bringing the gossip of one's own country; there was no ambition, for Liberia, whether to the diplomat or to the storekeeper, was about the deadest of all ends; there was really nothing but drink and the wireless, and of the two the drink was preferable.

But, nevertheless, all the English had wireless: at six o'clock they would turn on the Empire Programme from Daventry, but even that limited and depressing choice of entertainment was inaudible; the West Coast defeated any instrument; and as a background to every drink and to all conversation the powerful instruments would wheeze and groan and whistle until eleven o'clock. This was the nearest they got to Home, this piercing din over the Atlantic. By eleven o'clock one was too drunk to mind, anyway.

As for the intrigues which brought a little liveliness into the hot damp day, a little activity, a small sense of importance, there were two while I was there. A gentleman with a great financial reputation had arrived in Monrovia to try to obtain for a big British trust the concession for all gold and precious minerals that might be found in the interior and to drive out such small lonely prospectors as Van Gogh. It was a confirmation of the story I had heard in Bo. He had arrived at the right moment, within two months of the Presidential election, when money was urgently needed, and he was prepared to spend £30,000 on easing the concession through. The only danger was that he might be backing the wrong horse, but in a Liberian election this risk is small; no one really doubted that Mr Barclay would be re-elected. Unfortunately within a few days of his arrival the financial expert was taken ill before he had been able to interview the President, and nothing would persuade the Liberia Ministers but that this was an astute move to lower the price. They were the soul of stiff politeness, but it was obvious that they intended to show that they could bargain too.

The other intrigue was diplomatic and concerned the Royal Jubilee. The Secretary of State had been for a very long while trying to persuade the British Chargé d'Affaires to go to church and hear the sermons of the Minister for Education. There was nothing political in *his* motives, he was an earnest humourless young man, he just thought that it would do anyone good to go to church, and the services at this church were almost identical

with those of the Church of England. But his reforming zeal
gave the British representative a chance to perform a diplomatic *coup*. He told the Secretary of State that not only would
he come to church, but he would guarantee the presence of
every British subject and probably of the other foreign representatives as well if on the particular Sunday the Minister of
Education included in the prayers some reference to the Royal
Jubilee. The Secretary of State, I think, was a little taken aback:
he asked for time to consult the Minister of Education, but
alas! I did not stay long enough at Monrovia to hear whether
the bargain was struck.

One could hardly wonder that the more excitable representatives in the international colony craved for a faster life. They
were living on the barren edge of the country; not one of them
had been more than a few days' trek into the interior, they had
the most meagre and mistaken ideas of the native tribes; nor
would any longer journeys or a more profound knowledge of
Liberian conditions have been welcome to the Government,
who had seen what damage a roving foreigner could do them
in the British Blue Book based on a Vice-Consul's journey down
the Kru Coast. There was an occasion, many years ago, when
the British residents raised the English flag in Monrovia, trying
to re-enact on a miniature scale the Outlander revolt in Johannesburg, but the result failed as ignominiously as the Jameson
Raid. I do not think there was any imperial ambition among
the storekeepers of Monrovia, or among the foreign representatives, nor had they much to complain about from the Government. There was less discrimination against the white than
there was against the black in most white colonies, and I think
a fair observer would have been astonished at the moderation
of the black rulers. What the whites suffered, they suffered
with the whole population, from the lack of drainage, medical
services, communications, and the desire to intervene was an
expression of boredom rather than of imperialism. The man,
perhaps, most to be pitied was the American financial adviser,
an elderly man who had seen successful service in Arabia and
the Philippines, but whom Liberia had defeated. For since the
President had declared a moratorium, he had been without any

work. Two Poles were the active unofficial advisers, and the American lived on in Monrovia at a reduced salary with nothing to do but shoot at bottles and hit billiard balls.

A flare-up of nervous irritation occurred a short while before my visit. The chauffeur of the French Consul had committed some offences, and an ignorant policeman who knew nothing about diplomatic immunities followed the servant into the Consulate and tried to arrest him. The Consul threw the man out, put on his diplomatic uniform and went down to the State building to demand from the Secretary of State an official apology from the Government. The Minister, young earnest Mr Simpson, was quite prepared to apologize himself, but he refused to apologize on behalf of the Government. The whole affair would have been comic if it had not been a little tragic, for it showed to what absurdity, to what frayed nerves, the scorching damp, the bare exile, the shooting of bottles on Saturday evenings, the whistling loudspeaker lead. The French Consul went up the hill to the wireless station, which is run by a French company, and sent a message to a French gunboat he knew was passing down the coast. The gunboat anchored off Monrovia, the captain came ashore in a surf boat and the two solemn uniformed Frenchmen returned to Mr Simpson's office. The captain laid his sword on Mr Simpson's desk and said it would remain there until the Consul received an apology from the Government. The apology was given, the gunboat steamed away. I don't know what happened to the policeman.

Quite outside this strained, dreary and yet kindly life, at the end of several hours' rough driving from the capital, live the Firestone men in houses containing shower baths and running water and electric light, with a wireless station, tennis courts and a bathing pool, and a new neat hospital in the middle of plantations which smell all the day through of latex, as it drips into little cups tied beneath incisions in the trunks. They, more than the English or the French, are the official Enemy, and no story of whipping post, smuggled arms or burnt villages is too wild to be circulated and believed among Liberians of both parties.

POLITICS

We arrived in Monrovia when the political campaign was getting under way; those politicians embracing each other on the jetty were only a foretaste of the excitement. For the curious thing about a Liberian election campaign, which goes on for more than two months if there's enough money in hand, is that, although the result is always a foregone conclusion, everyone behaves as if the votes and the speeches and the pamphlets matter. The Government prints the ballot papers, the Government owns both the newspapers, the Government polices the polling booths, but no one assumes beforehand that the Government will win, or if it is the turn of the Opposition, the Opposition. A curious fiction is kept up even among the foreign representatives. There are excited conversations at dinner parties; bets are always on the point of being laid. But the fiction, of course, stops short of losing money. Perhaps to an American, who is used to his state elections, the conditions seem less odd.

At this election, though, there may have been a very slight uncertainty just because the President was taking it so seriously and instead of surrendering his office was ensuring, by his plebiscite, that he would hold it for more than the length of three terms. There were rumours that the Cabinet was split, that Mr Gabriel Dennis, the Secretary of the Treasury, who had distinguished himself by the sharp eye he kept on the funds of the Republic, was going to be jettisoned by his colleagues, and there was the unusual factor, too, that the President in power had as his opponent a former President who had shown his astuteness in manipulating the political machine. For years the Presidential opponent had been Mr Faulkner, the head of the People's Party and of the Monrovian ice factory, who had no experience in the finer shades of political manipulation. Indeed, ex-President King won the first round. When Mr Faulkner finally retired from the contest and his supporters joined the Unit True Whig Party, otherwise known as the Dissident Whigs, half a dozen members of the People's Party kept together long enough to hold a convention to nominate Mr King. As Mr

King was also nominated by the Unit True Whig Party, by Liberian law he would be able to have a representative of each party at every polling booth, while the Government would only have one, a very important point.

It will be seen that Liberian politics are complicated. Corruption does not make for simplicity as might be supposed. It may be all a question of cash and printing presses and armed police, but things have to be done with an air. Crudity as far as possible is avoided. For example, Mr King could not be the only candidate at the convention of the Unit True Whig Party; at some expense supporters for Mr Cooper had to be brought to the convention, even though it was known beforehand that Mr King would be nominated. I received on the morning of the convention a programme issued by the organizers, signed by Mr Doughba Carmo Caranda, the General Secretary, and attested by Mr Abayomi Karnga, the national chairman (the names indicated the policy of the party, Liberia for the Liberians, everyone had been busy finding themselves native names to contrast with the Dunbars, Barclays, Simpsons, Dennises of the Government). The proceedings, I read, were to end with a procession to the house of the nominated candidate, but rather ingenuously the route of the procession was given, by the Masonic Hall, up Broad Street, on to Front Street, 'to the residence of the candidate'. It was Mr King who had a house in Front Street, not Mr Cooper, so that the programme took some of the edge off of the excitement. Rather damping, too, was the non-arrival of most of the delegates, for the second launch was not so successful as the one in which we travelled and stuck on a sandbank outside Monrovia. The convention was to open with prayer at two-thirty, but when we arrived at three-thirty they were still waiting for the marooned delegates. Afterwards things got rather rushed, for when we arrived back at five the convention was over. The brass band was trying to get out of the ground and head the procession, but the mob was too great, and our Legation car helped to block the road. Several delegates hissed feebly at the little flag on the hood and a fat perspiring black pushed his head in at the window and asked furiously whether we did not know that this was a national oc-

casion. There was a reek of cane juice and a few people looked
nearly drunk enough to throw stones.

Meanwhile the President had staged another demonstration
in front of his house: native dancers from the water-side slum
of Kru Town rushed up and down before the Executive Mansion waving knives. They looked like Red Indians in their
feathered head-dresses, and their spirited performance robbed
the convention of a great many spectators. Later, when the
blare of brass warned Monrovia that the procession was on its
way, a rival procession was formed hastily outside the offices of
state with large banners inscribed 'Barclay the Hero of Liberia'
and a rather enigmatic statement: 'We want no King. We want
no car. We want no money for our vote. Barclay is the Man.'
For some time I thought it was inevitable that the processions
would meet in tiny Monrovia, but I had under-estimated the in-
genuity of their leaders. Drunk as everyone was by this time,
they were not drunk enough to risk a fight. The Kru dancers
and their friends swarmed into the Executive Mansion and
were given free drinks, to the disgust of the President's True
Whig supporters, who had received nothing but the dictator's
thanks from a balcony at his formal nomination.

The Opposition procession meanwhile trampled into the
front garden of Mr King's house, his wooden house in Front
Street, not the large uncompleted stone palace in Broad Street.
It was quite dark by that time, but a few paraffin lamps indoors
cast a pale light on the eyeballs of the crowd. Mr King, who
had been ill, spoke a few words from a balcony, but there was
too much cheering and drinking going on all over the town for
one to hear more than a few phrases: 'national independence',
'hand of friendship', 'foremost part among the nations'. The
voice was tired and mechanical: it occurred to me that the fiction might be a sad one to the principal, who must go through
all the right posturings without any hope at all. No one knew
better than Mr King that a President is never defeated by votes.

I visited Mr King a few days later at his farmhouse outside
Monrovia. With an old blue bargee's cap on the back of his
head and a cigar in his mouth, he put up an excellent imitation
of the old simple statesman in retirement. There was no doubt

that he was a sick man. We both drank a good deal of gin while he went over and over the events of his downfall. From his obscure corner of West Africa he had managed to attract quite a lot of notice with the shipping of forced labour to Fernando Po and the pawning of children. He had feathered his nest nicely: he had his own little plantation of rubber trees he was waiting for Firestone to buy; he had his two and a half houses. But he hadn't really any hope of a return; he was quite ready, he said, if he was elected to accept the League of Nations plan of assistance, tie his finances to European advisers, put white Commissioners in charge of the interior, give away Liberian sovereignty altogether, but he knew quite well he wasn't going to be elected. All the rumours of Firestone money, all the speeches meant nothing at all. He was complying with a custom; one could see that he would be glad to go back to bed. He had had a finer fling than most Liberian Presidents: banquets in Sierra Leone, royal salutes from the gun-boat in the harbour, a reception at Buckingham Palace, a turn at the tables at Monte Carlo. He stood with his arm round his pretty wife's shoulders on his stoop while I photographed him, a black Cincinnatus back on his farm.

A CABINET MINISTER

The Secretary of the Treasury belonged to a newer, more scrupulous Liberia just coming into existence. He, too, had travelled to Geneva and the United States. Plump, well-dressed, with soft sad spectacled eyes, he had a dignity unknown to the Creole of an English colony. There were no prefects to laugh at him, he laughed at himself, softly, without emphasis, for being honest, for caring for other things than politics, for letting slip so many of the crap-game chances. Mr King had built himself houses and brought himself a rubber plantation; all the Secretary had bought was a little speed-boat in which to play about in the Monrovian delta among the mangrove swamps.

He lived in a little brick villa on grassy Broad Street; he was a bachelor; and when he gave us tea it was served by young clerks from the Treasury Department. He had dressed himself for the occasion (there was to be a little music) in an open-necked shirt and a large artistic tie. He was like a black Mr Pickwick with a touch of Shelley. After tea we went into the music room, a little cramped mid-Victorian parlour with family groups on the walls, the Venus of Milo, hideous coloured plaster casts of Tyrolean boys in sentimental attitudes, and paraffin lamps on high occasional tables. He played some songs the President had composed; the piano, of course, in that climate was out of tune. They were rather noisy, breathless songs, of which the President had written the words as well as the music; romantic love and piety: 'Ave Maria' and 'I sent my love a red, red rose, and she returned me a white.' Then he played the President's setting of 'I arise from dreams of thee'. His friend the President, he said sadly, twirling on his stool, had once written much music and poetry: now—the Secretary of the Treasury sighed at the way in which politics encroached. He said, 'Perhaps you know this song,' and while the clerks from the Treasury went round lighting the paraffin lamps and turning the shades so that the glow fell in a friendly way on the Tyrolean children caressing their dogs or listening to stories at their mothers' knees, he began to sing: 'Whate'er befall I still recall that sun-lit mountain side.' It was aestheticism at the lowest level if you will, but it was genuine aestheticism, the pathos of it was that this was the best material coastal Liberia could offer to a sensitive gentle mind: the music of Mr Edwin Barclay, the plaster casts, *The Maid of the Mountains,* the paraffin lamps, a sentimental song called *Trees,* and the President's patriotic verses which he now beat out upon the piano: *The Lone Star Forever.*

> When Freedom raised her glowing form on
>   Montserrado's verdant height,
> She set within the dome of Night
> 'Midst lowering skies and thunderstorm
> The star of Liberty!
> And seizing from the waking Morn
> Its burnished shield of golden flame
> She lifted it in her proud name
> And roused a people long forlorn
> To nobler destiny.

It was no worse than most patriotic songs from older countries. To a stranger, I think, coming from a European colony, Monrovia and coastal Liberia would be genuinely impressive. He would find a simplicity, a pathos about the place which would redeem it from the complete seediness of a colony like Sierra Leone: planted without resources on this unhealthy strip of land they have held out; if they have brought with them the corruption of American politics, they have nurtured at the same time a sentiment, a patriotism, even a starveling culture. It is something, after all, to have a President who writes verses, however bad, and music, however banal, I could not be quite fair to them, coming as I did from an interior where there was a greater simplicity, an older more natural culture, and traditions of honesty and hospitality. After a trek of more than three hundred miles through dense deserted forest, after the little villages and the communal ember, the great silver anklets, the masked devil swaying between the huts, it was less easy to appreciate this civilization of the coast. It seemed to me that they, almost as much as oneself, had lost touch with the true primitive source. It was not their fault. Two hundred years of American servitude separated them from Africa; gave them their politics: their education at Liberia College: their Press: gave them this:

The Press

WORDS BUILDING
MOTHER

First Prize : Four Shillings
Second Prize : Two Shillings
First Entry Sixpence : Additional Entry 3d
Closes March 2 : Results March 9

Use the letters in Mother to spell as many words as you can. The competitor who sends in the largest number of words entitles to the First Prize and the Second Prize goes to the Competitor who sends in the next largest number of words.

Address all Communications to the Editor.

'The Unit True Whig Party now comes forward claiming to have the financial backing of Firestone to defeat the Administration. This claim is wild enough, base enough and false enough to form a suitable crown for its four years of strenuous efforts to fool the people and overthrow the Republic. But it has reckoned without its host. This is the time too many when the pitcher goes to the well and is broken. The last straw that breaks the camel's back. Or more appropriately the closing of the stable door after the horse has escaped.'

'My appeal is directed to the young people of Liberia, and particularly to the young people of the Kru tribe, and it is an appeal for us to prepare ourselves for world leadership.'

'Coming home to ourselves, we ask the question, what has Liberia contributed, and is contributing towards world advancement and improvement? What are we doing individually to make the world better, and Liberia safe for democracy?

'With such a situation confronting the patriotic citizens of the country, and as loyal True Whigs, the question remains, what shall we do to be saved? It is highly gratifying to tell you boldly from genuine personal and otherwise reports received from Cape Palmas to Cape Mount we have the day for King. Watch out and see us victoriously rise.'

'The Congo Progressive Association met in semi-annual conclave at the residence of Hon. Abayomi Karnga last week, and while there feasted and talked liberally. The feast ended in a clean sweep, and the talk in a muddle. Thus in this first coup nothing was added to the Unit. But if it keeps on springing such surprises upon unsuspecting guests, even that which it seemeth to have will be taken away from it, and itself cast out as being unprofitable.'

FLOREAT COLLEGIUM LIBERIA
BY R.T.D.

When Church was o'er, the line was formed as before,
In caps, gowns, hoods, black and white, we did implore
The sympathy of the noblest and all the poor
Who made us feel like still,
Floreat Collegium Liberia.

On Thursday noon, the Commencement was begun,
Methought I heard the sound of thundering gun,
Telling us the day is come, the night is gone —
The day was calm, serene and fine,
Floreat Collegium Liberia.

I heard the Band to sound, the Clay-Ashland Band,
And busy though I was, I could no later stand,
For the sound was mighty and did peal through the land.
It made me sing this sweet refrain,
Floreat Collegium Liberia.

The College sang a song and prayer was said,
Then the 'Sal' rose, greeted us and nobly pled,
And he roused the silence of the heroic dead.
My heart did throb within and say:
Floreat Collegium Liberia.

Then followed the 'Val', the leader of the Class.
and with word transparent as a shining glass,
He gave us true mental food, yet not in brass.
He made us feel and wish within:
Floreat Collegium Liberia.

A song was sung; then rose the Speaker of the Day,
This humorous man did make us laugh and play;
His speech was fine; full of humour and delay.
He made us feel and wish within:
Floreat Collegium Liberia.

Unlike the Commencements of the previous days,
A thing was done that true credit wrought and praise —
It was worthy prizes offered for the plays,
By the first Lady of the land:
Floreat Collegium Liberia.

Unlike the Commencements preceded this,
The degrees were conferred in ceremonious ways,
And all who saw this would truly praise for days
The efforts of the Acting Sage,
Floreat Collegium Liberia.

All hail! all hail!! hail the closing day of mirth,
That to us this day doth give a joyous birth
And make us prone heavenward and not to earth,
Lux in Tenebris, from thee is heard.
Floreat Collegium Liberia.

Farewell, farewell, to thee thou dying year of toil
Now is ease as then was labour for our soil,
In thee our time we nonetheless did spoil;
But laboured hard and wishing still,
Floreat Collegium Liberia.

Welcome, welcome, thou season of rest and ease,
The year has brought thee from across the seas;
O bid fair, bid fair to us to make us please,
To sing this longing strain for aye,
Flo-re-at Col-le-gi-um Li-be-ria!

RETURN

But though it was this impression that followed me on board
the cargo steamer which had been wirelessed to call off Monrovia
for passengers, the memory, too, of hundreds of children in the
Catholic school bellowing out the National Anthem:

With heart and hand our country's cause defending,
We'll meet the foe with valour unpretending.

Long live Liberia, happy land,
A home of glorious liberty by God's command

—one realized, going out by surf boat towards the bar, that thin line of white which divided this world from the other, the world of the smokestack, the siren that called us impatiently on board, the officer on the captain's bridge who watched us through glasses, how much less separated they really were from the true primitive than we. It was at their back, it wasn't centuries away. If they had taken the wrong road, they had only to retrace their steps a very little distance in space and not in time. The little jetty moved jerkily backwards, the river came into sight, the silver mangrove branches straddling like the ribs of old umbrellas on either side. Two hundred and fifty miles up that stream still existed the exact spot, the broken tree-trunk, the swarm of red ants where I had waited for my lost companions. The half-built Customs house, the waterside squalor of Kru Town, the asphalt road up to grassy Broad Street, they slipped behind with the sweep of the oars, but they belonged to the same world as the huddled huts at Duogobmai, the devil's servant fanning away the storm, the old woman who had made lightning trailing back to her prison with the rope round her waist. They were all gathered together behind the white line of the bar no European steamer ever crossed.

How happy I had thought I should be, while I was struggling down to Grand Bassa, back in *my* world. The bar took the prow and lifted it out of the water, one wave curled beneath us and broke along the beach of Kru Town, the second line broke above us, stinging the face, washing along the boards of the wide shallow boat, and there we were beyond, looking back at the bar and behind it Africa. A mammy chair came rattling down from the tarred English side. Of course I was happy, I told myself, opening the bathroom door, examining again a real water-closet, studying the menu at lunch, while out of the port-hole Cape Mount slid away, Liberia slid away, with Abyssinia the only part of Africa where white men do not rule. One had been scared and sick and one was well again, in the world to which one belonged.

But what had astonished me about Africa was that it had never been really strange. Gibraltar and Tangier—those extended just parted hands—seemed more than ever to represent an unnatural breach. The 'heart of darkness' was common to us both. Freud has made us conscious as we have never been before of those ancestral threads which still exist in our unconscious minds to lead us back. The need, of course, has always been felt, to go back and begin again. Mungo Park, Livingstone, Stanley, Rimbaud, Conrad represented only another method to Freud's, a more costly, less easy method, calling for physical as well as mental strength. The writers, Rimbaud and Conrad, were conscious of this purpose, but one is not certain how far the explorers knew the nature of the fascination which worked on them in the dirt, the disease, the barbarity and the familiarity of Africa.

The captain leant over the rail, old and dissatisfied, complaining of his men: 'Boil the whole bloody lot of the men in the ship together and you wouldn't make an ordinary seaman'; he was looking back—to the age of sail. At Freetown guests came on board and we drank ourselves free from Africa. An officer came and eyed me like an enemy across the table in the smoking-room. 'I'd send my ticket to the Board of Trade, my dear friend, and tell them to—I tell you, my dear friend . . .' The captain stuck his fingers down his throat, brought up his drink and was dead sober again, and the ship went out of the harbour, out of Africa. But their dissatisfaction was like a navel-string that tied them to its coast.

For there are times when the nearest the European has ever got to the interior, to the communal life with its terror and its gentleness, seems to be the Coast; Major Grant ringing up the brothel in Savile Row, the Old Etonian in Kensington Gardens, the Nottingham 'tart' and the droshky-drivers of Riga dwell on that rim of land which is known all the world over as the Coast, the one and only coast. They are not, after all, so far from the central darkness: Miss Kilvane listening to the ghost of Joanna just as the circle of blacks in Tailahun listened to the enigmatic speech of Landow; the Catholic priest saying, 'And now the Immaculate Conception' as the bus drove through the market, the tangle of stalls and overhead wires, the neo-Gothic hotels under the black overhead Midland fog. This may explain the deep appeal of the seedy. It *is* nearer the beginning; like Monrovia its building has begun wrong, but at least it has only begun; it hasn't reached so far away as the smart, the new, the chic, the cerebral.

It isn't that one wants to stay in Africa: I have no yearning for a mindless sensuality, even if it were to be found there: it is only that when one has appreciated such a beginning, its terrors as well as its placidity, the power as well as the gentleness, the pity for what we have done with ourselves is driven more forcibly home.

> While I was fishing in the dull canal
> On a winter evening round behind the gashouse
> Musing upon the king my brother's wreck
> And on the king my father's death before him.

After the blinding sunlight on the sand beyond the bar, after the long push of the Atlantic sea, the lights of Dover burning at four in the morning, a cold April mist coming out from shore with the tender. A child was crying in a tenement not far from the Lord Warden, the wail of a child too young to speak, too young to have learnt what the dark may conceal in the way of lust and murder, crying for no intelligible reason but because it still possessed the ancestral fear, the devil was dancing in its sleep. There, I thought, standing in the cold empty Customs shed with a couple of suitcases, a few pieces of silver jewellery, a piece of script found in a Bassa hut, an old sword or two, the only loot I had brought with me, was as far back as one needed to go, was Africa: the innocence, the virginity, the graves not opened yet for gold, the mine not broken with sledges.

> "No serious writer of [the twentieth century] has
> more thoroughly invaded and shaped the public
> imagination as did Graham Greene."
> —*Time*

A Burnt-Out Case
A world famous architect anonymously begins working at a leper colony in order to cure his "disease of the mind." *ISBN 0-14-018539-9*

The Captain and the Enemy
Introduction by John Auchard
Greene's final novel is a fascinating tale of adventure and intrigue that follows an Englishman from his childhood to gun-smuggling in Panama.
ISBN 0-14-303929-6

The Comedians
Introduction by Paul Theroux
Three men meet on a ship bound for Haiti, a world in the grip of the corrupt "Papa Doc" and his sinister secret police. *ISBN 0-14-303919-9*

Complete Short Stories
Introduction by Pico Iyer
Affairs, obsessions, fantasy, fear, pity, and violence—this magnificent new collection of stories illuminates all corners of the human experience. Including four previously uncollected stories, this edition reveals a range of contrasting moods, sometimes cynical and witty, sometimes searching and philosophical.
ISBN 0-14-303910-5

England Made Me
A tour de force of moral suspense, this is the story of a confirmed liar and cheat whose untimely discovery of decency may cost him his job—and his life.
ISBN 0-14-018551-8

A Gun for Sale
Introduction by Samuel Hynes
Raven's cold-blooded killing of the Minister of War is an act of violence with chilling repercussions, not just for Raven himself but for England as a whole.
ISBN 0-14-303930-X

Journey Without Maps
Introduction by Paul Theroux
This chronicle of Greene's journey through Liberia in the 1930s is at once vivid reportage and a powerful document of spiritual hunger and renewal.
ISBN 0-14-303972-5

"Greene had wit and grace and character and story and a transcendent universal compassion that places him for all time in the ranks of world literature." —John le Carré

The Lawless Roads
Introduction by David Rieff
This story of Greene's visit to Mexico emerged after he was commissioned to find out how ordinary people had reacted to the brutal anticlerical purges of President Calles. *ISBN 0-14-303973-3*

Loser Takes All
Greene offers up a tale of an unsuccessful accountant's second try at luck and love. *ISBN 0-14-018542-9*

The Man Within
Introduction by Jonathan Yardley
Themes of betrayal, pursuit, and the search for peace run through Greene's first published novel about a smuggler who takes refuge from his avengers. *ISBN 0-14-303921-0*

The Ministry of Fear
Introduction by Alan Furst
This is a complex portrait of the shadowy inner landscape of Arthur Rowe, a man torn apart with guilt over mercifully murdering his sick wife. *ISBN 0-14-303911-3*

Our Man in Havana
In this comic novel, Wormwold tries to keep his job as a secret agent in Havana by filing bogus reports and dreaming up military installations from vacuum-cleaner designs. *ISBN 0-14-018493-7*

The Portable Graham Greene
Introduction by Philip Stratford
Includes short stories, selections from Greene's memoirs and travel writings, essays on English and American Literature, and public statements on issues that range from repression in the Soviet Union to torture in Northern Ireland to the paradoxical virtue of disloyalty. *ISBN 0-14-303918-0*

The Power and the Glory
Introduction by John Updike
Greene's masterpiece is a compelling depiction of a "whiskey priest" struggling to overcome physical and moral cowardice and find redemption. *ISBN 0-14-243730-1*

The Third Man and *The Fallen Idol*
This edition pairs Greene's legendary thriller *The Third Man* with *The Fallen Idol*, in which a small boy discovers the deadly truths of the adult world. *ISBN 0-14-018533-X*

CLICK ON A CLASSIC
www.penguinclassics.com

The world's greatest literature at your fingertips

Constantly updated information on more than a thousand titles, from Icelandic sagas to ancient Indian epics, Russian drama to Italian romance, American greats to African masterpieces

•

The latest news on recent additions to the list, updated editions, and specially commissioned translations

•

Original essays by leading writers

•

A wealth of background material, including biographies of every classic author from Aristotle to Zamyatin, plot synopses, readers' and teachers' guides, useful web links

•

Online desk and examination copy assistance for academics

•

Trivia quizzes, competitions, giveaways, news on forthcoming screen adaptations